BULGARIAN F.

Bulgarian Harmony
In Village, Wedding, and Choral Music of the
Last Century

KALIN S. KIRILOV
Towson University, USA

LONDON AND NEW YORK

First published 2015 by Ashgate Publishing

2 Park Square, Milton Park, Abingdon, Oxfordshire OX14 4RN
52 Vanderbilt Avenue, New York, NY 10017

Routledge is an imprint of the Taylor & Francis Group, an informa business

First issued in paperback 2020

British Library Cataloguing in Publication Data
A catalogue record for this book is available from the British Library.

The Library of Congress has cataloged the printed edition as follows:
Kirilov, Kalin, 1975-
 Bulgarian harmony : in village, wedding, and choral music of the last century / by Kalin S. Kirilov.
     pages cm. -- (SOAS musicology series)
 Includes bibliographical references and index.
 ISBN 978-1-4724-3748-8 (hardcover) 1. Folk music--Bulgaria--History and criticism. 2. Folk music--Bulgaria--Analysis, appreciation. I. Title.
 ML3602.K57 2015
 781.2'509499--dc23

                                                                  2015016393

ISBN 13: 978-1-4724-3748-8 (hbk)
ISBN 13: 978-0-367-59785-6 (pbk)

Bach musicological font developed by © Yo Tomita.

Contents

Supplementary Resources Disclaimer

Additional resources were previously made available for this title on CD. However, as CD has become a less accessible format, all resources have been moved to a more convenient online download option.

You can find these resources available here: https://www.routledge.com/9781472437488

Please note: Where this title mentions the associated disc, please use the downloadable resources instead.

List of Maps and Music Examples

Maps

Music Examples

Preface

In the fall of 2005, I was touring the United States as the guitar player for Ivo Papazov, a renowned performer of Bulgarian wedding music. After a concert in Detroit, Michigan, I was approached by a jazz bass player. He asked, "Could you teach me Bulgarian harmony?" To his surprise, I replied, "I do not know exactly what I am doing. I apply chords by ear. After many years of practice a musician develops a feeling of how to harmonize Bulgarian music." Obviously disappointed by my response, the bass player asked if there were any published books or articles on the topic of Bulgarian harmony. When I replied that there were none, he added, "Then, you have to write something. You grew up in the culture and you are also a music theorist who knows Western terminology. There are many musicians like me who want to know how this amazing music works!"

As I continued touring with Papazov, more professional musicians approached me with similar questions and my embarrassment kept growing. I came to the unsettling realization that I could provide multiple analyses of pieces written by Western composers, but knew nothing about the Bulgarian harmonic progressions I played every day. Moreover, I began to question whether my Western music theory training had provided me with the proper analytical tools to codify the harmonic practice of a non-Western musical tradition that blends Middle Eastern makams, diatonic modes, microtonal scales, pentatonics, and major/minor collections.

In the summer of 2006, I was asked to teach a class on Bulgarian harmony during a Balkan music and dance workshop in Mendocino, California. As a teacher, I intended to provide multiple harmonizations of Bulgarian melodies and leave it up to my students to choose which progressions they liked best. To my surprise, while demonstrating various harmonizations, I began to notice harmonic patterns, standard cadential gestures, vertical harmonic displacements, typical tonicizations, and modulation formulas. My observations quickly formed an answer to my main pending question: indeed, there *is* a Bulgarian harmonic system in existence, and I have all the necessary analytical tools to map it out on paper.

In this book of Bulgarian harmony, I retrace my own path of learning the Bulgarian harmonic tradition. In the mid-1980s, I became increasingly interested in the harmony of the music and the process of accompanying. In 1982, I joined a folk orchestra at the Dobri Hristov Music School in Vidin, Bulgaria, and later, in 1987, I became a soloist in the Dunav (Danube) ensemble in Vidin. As a high school student, I became interested in arranging music for folk orchestras, folk choirs, and vocal quartets. Despite the official restrictions on wedding music during the socialist period in Bulgaria, I performed and mastered the wedding style. Decades later, I toured the United States as a guitar player with the most influential

Bulgarian wedding band, Ivo Papazov's wedding orchestra. My conclusions about typical cadences, standard harmonizations, and tonicizations are derived from 20 years of experience studying and performing Bulgarian music. This experience includes memorizing hundreds of songs and instrumental tunes, and analyzing a wide variety of recordings.

Growing up during a communist regime, I was influenced by a nationalist agenda promoting the uniqueness and exceptionality of Bulgarian music folklore. Moreover, I came to the United States (in 2001) thinking that the complexity and richness of Bulgarian folk music surpassed the musical traditions of any other Balkan culture. What was my surprise to hear the same asymmetrical meters appear in Greek music; similar harmonic progressions in Serbian music; similarly complex ornamentation in Romanian music; identical songs sung by Macedonians; and microtonal versions of Bulgarian songs performed by Turks. In my further studies of Balkan music I began to notice that Balkan musical traditions floated freely across all political borders, and that it was difficult, from a scholarly perspective, to trace or map any cultural and musical influences. If modes and scales in Bulgaria are labeled with Greek, Turkish, or Western names, would there be anything in the Bulgarian musical culture that could be labeled as distinctly Bulgarian, other than the use of the Bulgarian language? My further studies illustrated that, due to Bulgaria's geographical location as a crossroads between the East and the West, its territory became the place where several mighty musical systems collided: the Middle Eastern microtonal system (makams), the Greek modal system, and the Western major-minor system. This "clash of titans" resulted in a unique amalgamation of scales and modes mapped onto equal temperament. The harmonic practice that emerged from these hybrid scales and modes is a unique phenomenon that I refer to as Bulgarian harmony.

I consider this text suitable for graduate-level seminars in Music Theory and Ethnomusicology. The book could also be adopted in an undergraduate World Music Analysis course (completion of the Music Theory sequence should be a prerequisite). This study could serve as a reference guide for composers employing World Music repertoires and modal harmony. It could also be used as a practical manual for harmonization by both professional and amateur performers of Bulgarian music. For scholars, this book provides a model of inquiry that can be applied to the music of other East European countries.

I wish to express sincere appreciation to Professors Jack Boss, Tim Pack, Mark Levy, and Carol Silverman for their assistance in the preparation of this book. In addition, special thanks are due to my parents, Stancho and Tsvetanka Georgievi; my wife, Mina Kirkova; and my colleagues, Caitlin Snyder and Rob Schultz for their support. I received invaluable advice from the renowned Bulgarian musicians Tzvetanka Varimezova, Stoyan Kostov, and Vasil Bebelekov. Additionally, I would like to express my appreciation to: Vanya Moneva, Dimitŭr Hristov, Ethel Raim, Lauren Brody, Timothy Rice, Carl Schmitt, Yves Moreau, Larry Weiner, Milen Ivanov, Plamen Bŭrziiski, and Ivaylo Kraychovski. I would like to express my gratitude to Ronald Caltabiano who allowed me to use his Sicilian Numerals font in this book. This publication would not have been possible without the kind assistance of Anna Levy from Vox Bulgarica Music Publishing who gave me permission to use a number of choral scores for my music examples and harmonic analysis. I would also like to thank the anonymous reader from Ashgate Publishing for their detailed comments. Finally, I wish to thank my unknown colleague from Detroit who made me start this project. It is my sincere hope that this book will answer his questions about how Bulgarian harmony works.

Kalin Kirilov
December 11, 2014

Chapter 1

Introduction

Overview

This study traces the development of harmonic vocabulary in Bulgarian music. It analyzes the incorporation of harmony[1] into village music from the 1930s to the 1990s, "wedding music" from the 1970s to 1990s, and choral arrangements (*obrabotki*),[2] which were creations of the socialist period (1944–1989).[3] This study also explains how terms frequently applied to Bulgarian music, such as "westernization," "socialist-style arrangements," or "Middle Eastern influence," depict sophisticated networks of non-codified rules for harmonization which to date have not been studied. The book classifies different approaches to harmony in the above-mentioned styles and situates them in historical and cultural contexts; examines existing principles for harmonizing and arranging Bulgarian music; and establishes new systems for analysis. It suggests that the harmonic language found in Bulgarian music is based upon systems of rules which can be approached and analyzed using Western music theory. My analysis of harmony in Bulgarian music focuses on representative examples of each style discussed. These selections are taken from the most popular and well-received compositions available in the repertoire.

As a study written in the twenty-first century, this book aims to investigate a music phenomenon by looking beyond the conventional borders of the Balkans defended by nationalism-influenced scholarship. The remarkable cultural cross-pollination found in the Balkans was observed by Bartók nearly a century ago. According to him, "[c]omparison of the folk music of these peoples [Eastern Europeans] made it clear that there was a continuing give and take of melodies, a constant crossing and recrossing which had persisted through centuries" (1976: 30).

Research Issues

This study discusses a number of issues related to the study of Bulgarian music, such as the formation of the Bulgarian harmonic practice, comparisons between

---

[1] When I use the word harmony in this book I mean Western-influenced harmony; when I use the word polyphony I mean a drone-based polyphonic texture.

[2] Later in this book, I use the term *obrabotka*, which is the singular of *obrabotki*.

[3] These three categories are collectively labeled "folk music" for the purpose of this book.

Bulgarian and Western harmony, and existing analytical models. The main research issues confronted in this book are systematized in four categories below:

Problems of Current Scholarship and Limitations of Existing Musical Vocabulary

1. The relevance of existing scale and meter classification systems to the analysis of harmonized repertoire and the need for the establishment of a new system that reflects changes in Bulgarian music under the influence of harmony.
2. Problems in Bulgarian scholarship which prevent a thorough study of Bulgarian harmony, such as nationalism, "authenticity," and the use of the Bulgarian system for functional harmonic analysis.[4]

Harmony in Historical Context

1. The formation, development, and gradual expansion of the Bulgarian harmonic practice and the impact of monophony and drone-based polyphony on the development of Bulgarian harmony.
2. Precursors in older layers of the Bulgarian musical tradition for tonicizations and modulations in the harmonized repertoire.
3. Western influences on harmony in Bulgarian music.
4. Trendsetting composers, performers, and arrangers of harmonized Bulgarian music as well as influential repertoire.

Analysis of Bulgarian Harmony

1. The adaptation of Western analytical methods (Roman numerals,[5] pitch-class set analysis, motivic analysis, Schenkerian analysis, and formal analysis) to examine representative examples of Bulgarian music.
2. The importance of interrelated aspects of Bulgarian music (meters, rhythm, form, and ornamentation) in understanding harmony.

Bulgarian and Western Harmonic Traditions

1. Similarities and differences between Western chordal vocabularies and those applied to Bulgarian scales.
2. The structure of cadences in Bulgarian harmonized repertoire without the presence of leading tones and major-minor seventh chords.
3. Tonicizations and modulations in modal contexts.

---

[4] Functional harmonic analysis, as used by Bulgarian music theorists, is described later in Chapter 1.

[5] Roman numerals and figured bass created with the Sicilian Numerals font by Ronald Caltabiano and available at www.caltabiano.net.

4. Chord qualities and functions.
5. Relationships between Bulgarian polymodality[6] and harmony.

An Interdisciplinary Study of Bulgarian Harmony

The folk music of Bulgaria is an excellent example of a complex musical tradition which has increasingly gained the appreciation of audiences worldwide in recent decades. This book is part of a growing trend of modifying Western analytical tools to examine new repertoires currently outside the scope of Western Art Music.[7] Currently defined as the Analysis of World Music, this academic subfield bridges the fields of ethnomusicology and music theory. As a music theorist, an ethnomusicologist, and most importantly a performer of Bulgarian music who grew up in the culture, I find myself in a unique position to fill the gaps in the scholarship regarding analysis of harmonized Bulgarian repertoires.

The melodic foundation of Bulgarian music is formed by a complex amalgam of Middle Eastern makams, regional microtonal structures, pentatonic scales, diatonic modes, and major and minor collections. This study compares these melodic structures using a scale classification system established by Bulgarian ethnomusicologists such as Stoyan Dzhudzhev (1970: 258–349). In order to provide an appropriate analysis of pieces based on the scales listed above, in this book each scale is analyzed systematically, focusing on the derived vertical harmonies and resulting chordal functions. Additional interrelated aspects of the Bulgarian musical tradition, such as ornamentation and asymmetrical meters, are explained in detail as well.

This book combines several methodologies from the fields of music theory and ethnomusicology. On the one hand, it employs standard Western methods of music analysis adapted to the specifics of Bulgarian music. On the other hand, it applies ethnomusicological methods (participant observation and consultations with Bulgarian musicians) which situate the musical analysis in cultural and historical contexts.

The analysis of chordal verticals by Roman numerals is a standard Western theoretical approach to indicating harmony which to date has not been applied to Bulgarian music. Other than Abrashev's study *Obrabotka i Orkestratsia na Bŭlgarskata Narodna Muzika* (1990 and 1995), there are no other published

---

[6] The term was used by Bartók in his 1943 Harvard lectures. Bartók provides an example of a polymode resulting from the superposing of Lydian and Phrygian pentachord with a common fundamental tone (1976: 367). Polymodality, as found in Bulgarian music, is discussed in chapters 3 and 4.

[7] The growing trend for analyzing non-Western music was inspired and supported by the international conferences on Analytical Approaches to World Music (AAWM). The first AAWM conference took place the US in 2010, followed by a conference in Canada in 2012 and a joint conference with the British Forum for Ethnomusicology in the UK in 2014.

analyses of Bulgarian harmony. In the first volume of his book, Abrashev provides analysis through functional Roman numerals for his own examples of harmonization.[8] Functional harmonic analysis, as applied by Abrashev, is related to Roman numeral analysis, with a stronger emphasis on labeling harmonic functions: tonic, subdominant, and dominant. This system, initially developed by the German theorist Hugo Riemann in the nineteenth century, is currently used in Russia, Bulgaria, and most of the East European countries of the former Soviet bloc. This type of harmonic analysis is less appropriate than the Roman numeral approach for analyzing Bulgarian music, as functional harmonic theory is rooted in the Western major/minor system, which is not the predominant system in Bulgarian music. Roman numeral analysis, as applied in the present study, is also rooted in the Western system, but it does not emphasize harmonic functions. Functional harmonic analysis, as used by Abrashev, applies only to a limited portion of the Bulgarian repertoire and creates major difficulties in analyzing pieces which are modal or based on makams.

To a limited extent, I have incorporated two modern Western theoretical tools: pitch-class set theory and Schenkerian analysis. Pitch-class set analysis, a theoretical approach typically associated with atonal music, is applicable for the examination of certain avant-garde choral arrangements which are not based on triadic harmony.[9] A Schenkerian reduction illustrates the existence of a background fundamental structure (*Ursatz*). As will become evident in Chapter 7, a reductive graph adapted to the specifics of the Bulgarian scales and harmony can illustrate remarkable parallels between the complex harmony of a choral obrabotka and traditional, drone-based polyphony.[10]

For this study, I use recordings that I collected during the 1980s and early 1990s to illustrate the styles that I discuss. My field recordings primarily feature performers in wedding bands who learn and transmit their repertoire orally. My experience as an active Bulgarian musician has offered the advantage of having professional interactions with musicians and composers from all styles discussed in this book. My personal contacts with professional and amateur musicians, composers, and arrangers from Bulgaria have provided me opportunities to gather a variety of perspectives about the changes in Bulgarian harmonic style and the processes which have influenced those changes. Regarding the selections of repertoire analyzed in this study, for which I did not have first-hand performance experience, I consulted Tsvetanka Varimezova, Bulgarian singer and a music instructor at University of California, Los Angeles; Stoyan Kostov, a *tambura*[11]

---

[8]   See Chapter 2, Example 2.1b and Example 2.2.
[9]   See Chapter 7, Example 7.45.
[10]   See Chapter 7, Example 7.31.
[11]   The Bulgarian tambura is a long-necked, fretted, stringed instrument that comes in three styles: four-string (two pairs), six-strings (three pairs), and eight-string (four pairs) played with a plectrum. The eight-string tambura is known as the modern Bulgarian tambura. It was developed in the 1950s for the purposes of playing chordal accompaniment

player currently residing in Pittsburgh, Pennsylvania; and Vassil Bebelekov, a *gaida*[12] player currently residing in San Jose, California.

Book Structure

The first two chapters of the book include introductory material and a historical overview of the three musical styles at the core of this inquiry. Chapter 3 provides the foundation for analysis through the establishment of a musical vocabulary appropriate to Bulgarian folk music. This chapter summarizes structure and phrasing in the three styles analyzed, existing systems of scale classification, aspects of metric organization, and primary ornamentation vocabulary. Chapter 3 also discusses traditional Bulgarian polyphony as a precursor of harmony. The core chapter of this book, Chapter 4, provides essential information for the understanding of Bulgarian harmonic repertoires. This chapter introduces a new system of scale categorization, explains chord derivation, and discusses chordal vocabularies in scales found in the harmonized repertoire. The content of Chapter 4 serves as primary reference for the subsequent analytical chapters, as it provides summaries of standard chord progressions and typical cadences for each mode and scale found in the harmonized Bulgarian repertoires analyzed in this book. Chapters 5–7 analyze repertoires that illustrate the formation and expansion of a unique harmonic practice. In each of the chapters devoted to a particular style, I trace the incorporation of harmony, beginning with less harmonically complex pieces and proceeding with more harmonically intricate repertoire.

This book includes several appendices and a compilation CD which provides the source recordings for my music transcriptions.[13] Appendix A includes a complete track list of the compilation CD. Appendix B contains biographies of Bulgarian composers. In Appendix C, I provide a pronunciation guide to the sounds in the Bulgarian alphabet as used for transliteration in this book. Appendix D contains a glossary of Bulgarian terms.

---

in the state folk ensembles. In the 1950s the tambura was tuned E-A-F-C. The modern tambura is tuned E-B-G-D. Prior to the socialist period the tambura provided melody and drone rather than chordal accompaniment.

[12]   A gaida is a traditional goat-skin bagpipe.

[13]   For a full citation of the source recordings, refer to Appendix A and the Discography.

Chapter 2
Mapping the Cultural Terrain

Bulgarian folk music was shaped and reshaped by a number of political events that suppressed particular music styles while serving as catalysts for the development of others. Prior to explaining the characteristics of Bulgarian music and proceeding with analysis of repertoire, I find it necessary to contextualize the musical tradition historically, politically, and culturally.

Historical and Political Influences on the Development of Bulgarian Music

Bulgarians adopted harmony as part of their musical vocabulary rather late in comparison to other Western European countries. From 1396 to 1878, the Ottoman Empire ruled the Bulgarian territories (Rice 2004). During this period of Ottoman political and cultural domination, Bulgarians had limited exposure to Western European music, where harmony reigned supreme. According to Rice, "this period isolated them from the modernizing trends in Western Europe and seems to have had the effect of preserving some of the ancient ways of music making" (2004: 23). Although there were no official prohibitions of Western music during the Ottoman period, it is highly likely that the majority of Bulgarians had very limited "harmonic influence" resulting from exposure to Western-European, and especially Austro-German, music. In the mid-nineteenth century, Western cultural influences emerged in urban areas such as the cities of Plovdiv, Shumen, and Ruse, where the Bulgarian elite began performing Western music repertoires and patriotic songs based on Western melodies. It is also possible that some harmonic practices might have been introduced to the Bulgarian lands by migrating Vlachs and Wallachian Roma during the first half of the nineteenth century, who settled along the Bulgarian bank of the Danube River (Kirilov 2003).

After the liberation of Bulgaria in 1878, Bulgarian music became influenced by the West, which resulted in the blossoming of different styles of music throughout the twentieth century. Timothy Rice elaborates on the changes in Bulgarian music traditions after 1978 (2004: 25):

> Composers and instrument makers came from central Europe to teach Bulgarians European classical music …. European harmony and musical instruments such as the clarinet, violin, and accordion began to filter into village music, in some cases replacing traditional village instruments such as the *gaida* and adding chordal accompaniment to traditional solo and unison performance styles.

The socialist period (1944–1989) also had a tremendous impact on musical traditions (Rice 2004). Following the nationalist models of the Nazi and Soviet regimes, the Bulgarian communist party considered "authentic" traditional music[1] a principal tool for uniting the nation, a source of ancient "Bulgarian-ness," and a national cultural treasure (Kirilov 2011). Enormous efforts and funds were directed toward collecting and preserving old folk melodies and organizing state-sponsored festivals featuring "authentic" folklore (Silverman 1983). As a result, the ruling communist party favored certain styles and marginalized others. The favored styles were "authentic" village music and obrabotki (arrangements for choirs, folk orchestras,[2] and brass orchestras). Communist censorship suppressed wedding music, music of all ethnic minorities (Vlachs,[3] Roma,[4] and Bulgarian Turks),[5] and other types of Bulgarian music that featured foreign influences (Kirilov 2011). According to Rice (2004: 61):

> One new idea was that rural music, as an expression of the common man (the proletariat), could be a useful symbol of the new society. As a consequence of this belief, party functionaries invented new institutions to support traditional rural music and place it at the center of national attention and consciousness.

Hiding behind Marxism, an ethnic nationalism was driving the agenda. Similar music purification processes took places in neighboring socialist countries such as Romania (Radulescu 1997).

---

[1] From the viewpoint of contemporary ethnomusicology, the concept of "authentic" music is highly problematic as it attempts to divide folk music into "pure" (authentic) and "impure" (non-authentic) with the help of biased political criteria serving nationalistic agendas.

[2] The primary Bulgarian folk instruments used in folk orchestras are the gaida (goat-skin bagpipe); *kaval* (an end-blown flute that is similar to the Turkish kaval and the Arabic *ney*); *gŭdulka* (a bowed string instrument held vertically); *tŭpan* (a large cylindrical drum worn over the shoulder and hit with a beater on one side and a thin stick on the other); tambura (a long-necked plucked lute); and *tarambuka* (an hourglass-shaped hand-drum similar to the Turkish and North African *darbooka* and the Greek *doumbeleki*). State-sponsored ensembles also included artificially created instruments on the basis of gŭdulka such as viola gŭdulka, cello gŭdulka, and bass gŭdulka. Due to its poor sound quality, the bass gŭdulka was replaced by a double bass in the 1970s.

[3] Bulgarian Vlachs can be considered part of a large group of people speaking languages based on Latin who live all over the Balkans. For more information about Bulgarian Vlachs, see Kirilov (2003).

[4] Roma (also known as Gypsies) are an ethnic minority originally from Northern India who arrived in the Balkans in the fourteenth century. For more information about Roma, see Silverman (1996).

[5] Bulgarian Turks are descendants of Ottoman Turks who settled in Bulgaria during the period of Ottoman rule (fourteenth–nineteenth centuries).

The post-socialist transition period also influenced Bulgarian music. After 1989, Bulgaria experienced a decade of political instability, hyperinflation, and a crisis of values. Wedding music began to decline in the early 1990s due to the impoverishment of its patrons. State-sponsored ensembles and composers, who wrote obrabotki, also lost the support of the state. During post-socialism, all prior layers declined in performance contexts as well (Kirilov 2011).

Layers of Folk Music

In this study, the term "folk" is used in its more restricted, post-Bartókian academic sense, versus the popular sense of the word. In my discussion of Bulgarian music traditions, I deliberately chose the term "layers" versus "styles" due to a merging of folk music styles that occurred in the 1980s. In this period, a number of musicians performed in multiple styles—village, wedding, and obrabotki specifically. This performance overlap led to a fusion of approaches to harmony that progressively blurred the boundaries between each style. Perhaps this can explain why Bulgarians refer to all of these various styles by the general term "folk music." Regardless, distinctions can still be made on the basis of music-making processes, musical education of the performers, instrumentation, performance contexts, and accompaniment styles. In terms of harmony, however, all the layers merged in the 1980s and 1990s, creating a broader palette of timbres and music.

In Bulgaria, the term "folk music" (*narodna muzika*) is often politicized and contested. Scholars use it to mean "authentic" or traditional village music. However, as indicated above, Bulgarians increasingly use the term folk music to embrace wedding music, obrabotki, and village music. In this book, I use it in this latter sense. In the context of globalization, modern Bulgarians view anything that is Bulgarian but not "classical" or "pop" as "folk" by default without considering any further folk music subcategorization.

Village Music

The village style,[6] as referred to by American scholars (Rice 1994, Silverman 1989, and Buchanan 1995), is what Bulgarian folklorists and ethnomusicologists primarily consider "authentic" music folklore. The concept of authenticity has been critiqued in Western scholarship since the 1980s.[7] In Bulgaria, however, this concept still prevails due to nationalism (Kirilov 2011). According to Bartók (1976: 25):

---

[6]   In this book, I use village and traditional interchangeably while recognizing that there are various layers within these terms.

[7]   For more information about "authenticity" refer to Bendix (1997) and Buchanan (2006).

The discovery of the values of folklore and folk music excited the national pride, and as there were no means whatever for comparison at the outset, the members of each nation were convinced that the possession of such treasures was their only and particular privilege. Small nations, especially the politically oppressed ones, found a certain consolidation in these treasures, their self-consciousness grew stronger and consolidated ...

The oldest existing layer of traditional Bulgarian music is monophonic or diaphonic (melody and drone). This layer continued to exist throughout the twentieth century, and is the basis of subsequent styles traditionally categorized as folk music. Regardless of media influences, urbanization, and globalization processes, a number of villages in Bulgarian rural areas preserved older layers of their music, often assisted by government cultural agencies. In the early 1950s, a movement called *Hudozhestvena Samodeinost* (Amateur Art) was institutionalized by the socialist government. The major purpose of that movement was the creation and establishment of amateur performing ensembles in every settlement within the borders of the Bulgarian state (Kirilov 2011). Following the socialist agenda, these ensembles had the task of preserving and presenting "the beauty of the local folklore" on stage. According to Silverman (1989: 146):

On the village level, government sponsored *kolektivi*, or collectives for folk music, were formed in the 1950s in nearly all Bulgarian villages. These amateur groups rehearse the folk music, dances, and rituals of the recent past, the pre 1950s. The result is a staged presentation of preserved folklore. Kolektivi are most visible at folk festivals, where participation is carefully screened with an eye to 'authenticity.'

Parallel to the older layers, starting as early as the beginning of the twentieth century, a newer layer of music began to form as a result of the exposure of Bulgarian musicians to Western classical music and other contemporary musical genres. Attracted by the harmony and polyphony heard on recordings, musicians began experimenting by adding bass lines and simple chordal progressions to preexisting music. This process of building and establishing new harmonic languages developed gradually, starting from integrating primary triads (at the beginning of the twentieth century), through vertical chord displacements and chord substitutions (in the 1970s and 1980s), to borrowing harmony from modern jazz (late 1980s and 1990s). All innovations which occurred within the oral tradition (including the expansion of harmonic languages) remained unrecognized by Bulgarian scholars, who focused on past monophonic and diaphonic styles rather than emerging multi-voice structures.

In the 1920s and 1930s, the Bulgarian National Radio (BNR) broadcast the first recordings of authentic village music with the new addition of chordal harmony. Most frequently, the accompaniment was provided by a tuba (bass line) and an accordion. In the 1950s, after the modernization of the traditional

Bulgarian tambura, ensembles were created with tambura as the primary accompanying chordal instrument. Tambura players adapted chords by ear and gradually created an accompaniment style specific to the instrument. Despite the increasing popularity of the tambura in ensemble settings, the accordion still dominated as the primary harmony-generating instrument in rural and urban performing contexts.

After the formation of the first professional folk music and dance ensembles in the 1950s, the tambura players, who participated both in the state ensembles and village-type bands, began adapting chordal progressions from composed instrumental obrabotki to village repertoire. In Chapter 5, I reflect on this correlation by referring to particular examples of village music as ensemble influenced.

Bulgarian Wedding Music

During the late 1970s, in the middle of the socialist period in Bulgaria, a new layer of folk music developed. It shared many melodic and rhythmic characteristics with village music, but it introduced a new emphasis on improvisation, harmony, ornamentation, and influences from American and European rock, jazz, and Indian film music (Kirilov 2011). Wedding music, performed by amplified bands,[8] gradually developed into a new style and became an alternative to the socialist, censorship-regulated folk music dominating this same period. In this context, Timothy Rice compares the wedding style to the "official" state-sponsored and regulated folk music (1994: 242):

> The important differences between wedding music and the state's version of 'narodna muzika' included (1) new musical instruments, (2) new recording technology, (3) expanded repertoire, (4) growth in technique and virtuosity, (5) more modern techniques from jazz and popular music, and (6) more freedom to improvise.

Wedding orchestras performed in various contexts, including calendrical holidays[9] and family celebrations. At weddings, these orchestras performed in restaurants and *palatki* (large tents temporarily erected on the streets). During the 1970s, weddings—which are the central life-cycle celebrations of Bulgarians—were festive events involving hundreds of guests. Such weddings lasted up to three days and included processions, indoor activities, and dance events in the village or town squares (Kirilov 2011). Because of the performing context, musicians and

---

[8] Typical instrumentation in wedding bands includes: clarinet, saxophone, accordion(s), rhythm guitar, and a drum set. Wedding bands may also include a trumpet, bass guitar, and synthesizer(s), as well as traditional Bulgarian instruments such as kaval, gŭdulka, and gaida.

[9] Calendrical holidays follow the calendar of the Eastern Orthodox Church.

scholars, both in Bulgaria and abroad, began to refer to the music as "wedding music" or "wedding style."

During socialism, the ruling communist party prohibited any kind of ethnic expression other than Bulgarian. Officially, wedding orchestras were prohibited from performing Serbian, Greek, Turkish, Romanian, or any kind of "ethnic" music—particularly the music of the Roma. Commissions from *Direktsiya Muzika* (a government agency that controlled music activities) organized competitions in order to determine the performing level (*kategoriya*) of every wedding orchestra. These competitions were a form of government control of the growing phenomenon of wedding music during the 1980s. The incorporation of Western rock and jazz elements, which typify wedding music of this period, was considered a particularly dangerous trend since they promoted styles popular in the capitalist West.

Due to political ideology and nationalistic sensibilities, Bulgarian scholars completely disregarded wedding music during socialism and throughout the first decade of the post-socialist transition. To Bulgarian scholars, performers of wedding music were a class of non-professionally trained musicians playing a poorly organized, semi-improvisatory music that endangered the old, "authentic" Bulgarian culture. In contrast, Western ethnomusicologists and folklorists, such as Carol Silverman and Timothy Rice,[10] studied in depth the performance and cultural aspects of the wedding style, and particularly the tension between wedding musicians and the socialist state.

During the late 1970s and 1980s, performers of folk instruments increasingly adopted features of wedding music (played on "Western" instruments). Many village bands adopted some characteristics of wedding style. However, wedding bands relied heavily on amplification, while village bands performed acoustically. Although village music increasingly took on stylistic elements from wedding music, some significant differences remained. Wedding bands often aim for large, varied repertoires, the fusion of styles from different regions of Bulgaria, and influences from neighboring countries. The repertoire of village groups, on the other hand, remains predominantly local. Another significant difference is found in the nature of improvisatory techniques. Village-style improvisations and soloing techniques are comprised of pre-composed motives that are varied (melodic variations) in short groups of 2–4 measures long. The improvisation in wedding style is accomplished on a larger scale. Wedding musicians improvise in structures of 8–16 measures, and the repetition of motives is displaced by rapid scales, syncopations, register transfers, and metric dissonances,[11] as well as compound melodies.[12]

---

[10]   For more information, refer to Rice (1994) and Silverman (1989).

[11]   Metric dissonance occurs when various musical factors combine to create a metrically ambiguous passage. These ambiguities are then "resolved," analogous to the harmonic resolution of dissonances.

[12]   Compound melody is a melody that implies two or more voices.

Obrabotki

During the socialist period, with the approval and encouragement of the communist party, composers and arrangers began harmonizing "authentic" folk songs and tunes, gradually creating a new harmonic practice based on Western harmony. This new genre was named obrabotka, a term that had multiple interpretations. In addition to its literal translation—which is arranging, modeling, or editing—obrabotka can also mean the actual arrangement made by a composer during the socialist period, a folk song transformed through added harmonic accompaniment, or the state-regulated approach to harmony. The term was applied to arrangements considered to be archetypal of national music. Abrashev writes (1990: 8):

> Today obrabotka is defined as a stand-alone musical genre. Many of the works of well-arranged folklore became classics. Being closer in their expressive meaning to folk music, they are not identical with it. Their purpose is not to literally repeat the folk forms and methods of musical thinking, but to shrink the distance between folk and professional art, between the modern listener and the ancient creator of folk music tradition.

From the viewpoint of repertoire, most obrabotki featured piano accompaniments of traditional songs, arrangements for folk orchestras, and arrangements for female choirs (referred to as folk choirs). According to Silverman (2004: 215):

> In the socialist period, ensemble music became a significant ideological marker of the elevation of 'folk' (or 'peasant') to the realm of 'nation': it was hailed as the 'national music' of Bulgaria, as opposed to competing regional and ethnic musics and to popular/folk fusions played at weddings. Composers, ethnomusicologists, and Party ideologues boasted that they were raising the level of folk music to that of Western art music. This was part of a state-sponsored initiative to 'modernize' peasant culture in diverse realms. Folklore had to be 'cleaned up' and reworked to make it 'art.'

Although Western harmonies were featured, avant-garde and jazz harmonies were deliberately excluded due to their perceived association with contemporary Western music deemed "decadent" by the socialist censors.

In 1951, Filip Kutev[13] founded the first state ensemble, paving the road not only for the development of choral obrabotki, but also for instrumental arrangements, ensemble music, and staged ensemble dance performances. In her article "Metaphors of Power, Metaphors of Truth: The Politics of Music Professionalism in Bulgarian Folk Orchestras," Buchanan provides valuable

---

[13]   For more information about Filip Kutev, refer to Appendix B.

information regarding the models followed by Kutev and his goals as a modernizer of both vocal and instrumental Bulgarian folk music (1995: 388).

> In 1951 Filip Kutev, inspired by the Soviet folk ensemble 'Pyatnitski,' created the first professional, state-supported Bulgarian folk ensemble. Eventually the leading exponent in a larger system of fourteen such organizations established in urban centers throughout Bulgaria, Kutev's ensemble performed arrangements of traditional music and song characterized by harmonies, contrapuntal techniques, and formal structures associated with Western classical music on many of the world's concert stages. The goal of such ensembles was to popularize the musical traditions of Bulgaria's six primary ethnographic regions (the Shope area, the Rhodopes, Thrace, Pirin-Macedonia, Northern Bulgaria, and Dobrudzha) in a new, sophisticated theatrical venue.

From all types of obrabotki created during socialism, this study focuses solely on the choral obrabotki genre that was popularized worldwide by the Bulgarian female choir Le Mystère des Voix Bulgares. The current conductor of the choir, Dora Hristova, describes Le Mystère des Voix Bulgares as a threefold phenomenon that encompasses the talent of the performers, the role of the composer, and the feedback from the audience as an active participant (2007: 13). Hristova highlights three main compositional trends in choral obrabotki. The first trend comes from Filip Kutev, who emphasizes "less functionally determined harmonies based on imitation, heterophony, and polyphony combined with a new, in depth knowledge of the stylistic characteristics of the [Bulgarian] folklore regions." The second trend is represented by the works of Krasimir Kyurkchiiski,[14] whose arrangements are "homophonic, derived from the sharp-dissonant vertical structures of the Shope diaphony."[15] The third trend, characteristic of the 1980s–1990s, interweaves various modern compositional techniques (Hristova 2007: 16). For my analyses, I have chosen primarily homophonic obrabotki, which represent the second trend as described by Hristova.

Choral obrabotki gained increasing popularity in Bulgaria in the 1950s and 1960s through the broadcasts of state-regulated radio and TV as a new, "enriched" form of vocal folk art. Obrabotki remained a local phenomenon until they were "discovered" by Marcel Cellier[16] (Hristova 2004: 14). According to Hristova, Cellier followed the development of the State Radio Choir for a period of 20 years, and in 1975 he released his first album, which included recordings of choral

---

[14]   For more information about Krasimir Kyurkchiiski, refer to Appendix B.

[15]   Shope diaphony is based on melody and drone. I discuss Bulgarian traditional polyphony in Chapter 3.

[16]   Marcel Cellier is a Swiss music producer who produced several albums under the title *Le Mystère des Voix Bulgares*.

obrabotki, under the title *Le Mystère des Voix Bulgares* (2004: 14). As a result of various marketing strategies, the State Radio and Television Choir itself became known as Le Mystère des Voix Bulgares and its music sold to Western audiences as "mysterious," "cosmic," or "angel-like."

The processes of promoting and marketing a "mystery" and the exploitation of women singers have been discussed in great detail by Buchanan (1997) and Silverman (2004). This study, however, takes a different angle to the phenomenon of choral obrabotki by analyzing the harmonic progressions that captivated audiences worldwide. It also proposes to demystify and normalize music that has been marketed for decades as "magical and exotic." This study also suggests possible reasons for the exotic aura surrounding choral obrabotki, including a lack of information, analysis, and scholarship regarding the repertoire of Le Mystère des Voix Bulgares.

Bulgarian and Western Scholarship on Bulgarian Folk Music

As previously stated, the concept of "authenticity" completely dominated Bulgarian scholarship in the twentieth century. Authentic folk music is defined in Bulgaria as the traditional music of the villagers from the pre-socialist and early socialist periods. According to Carol Silverman, during socialism (1944–1989) "the centralized Bulgarian socialist regime has developed far-ranging cultural polices to preserve a selected 'authenticity' of the peasant past while simultaneously developing a new unified socialist culture" (1989: 143). Bulgarian scholarship considers music containing older layers of the tradition more worthy of study than newer styles because it is assumed these older layers represent the core of national identity. Even today, Bulgarian scholarship is highly sensitive regarding the origins of Bulgarian music and comparative studies involving the music of other neighboring Balkan countries. In an essay written in 1937, Bartók foresaw this sensitivity (1976: 27):

> One type, for instance, is the question of the so-called 'Bulgarian' rhythm [$\frac{7}{8}$ grouped as 2+2+3]. Up till now it seemed that this kind of rhythm is a Bulgarian peculiarity. But the most recent researches disclose that it is known also among the Rumanians and the Turkish peoples. Should further researchers verify that that one could really find its origins in Bulgaria, it might very well happen that the poor discoverer would be stoned—only in effigy, of course—by the opposite side; on the other hand, if the researcher arrives to the contrary result the Bulgarians would stone him.

Throughout the twentieth century, Bulgarian folklorists focused their research primarily on monophonic examples of "authentic folklore" and diaphonic songs (melody and drone).[17] Bulgarian scholars also collected polyphonic or heterophonic village songs that are not based on triadic verticals.[18] However, harmonic accompaniment and arrangements (twentieth-century phenomena), along with the emergence of newer layers of music after World War II, had no perceived value for Bulgarian scholars, and remained outside their areas of study.

Western scholars such as Timothy Rice[19] and Martha Forsyth[20] studied older layers of polyphony and heterophony. In the late 1970s and early 1980s, however, most American scholars became more interested in cultural contexts (Silverman 1989), transmission of musical traditions (Rice 1994), socialist censorship policy toward musical folklore (Buchanan 1995 and 2006; Rice 1994; Silverman 1983), and styles of music suppressed by the socialist regime (Silverman 1989). Finding a rich field for research in the tension between the "official," state-sponsored styles of music and the "unofficial" wedding and Romani (Gypsy) music, these American scholars shifted their focus to politics rather than the sound aspects of the music. This was due to general trends in American ethnomusicology and cultural anthropology, which gave priority to cultural contexts rather than the music itself.

Bozhidar Abrashev's *Obrabotka i Orkestratsia na Bŭlgarskata Narodna Muzika* (Arrangement and Orchestration of Bulgarian Folk Music), published in 1990 and 1995, is the only comprehensive study that suggests a systematic approach to harmony in arrangements of Bulgarian folk music. Although the title implies the existence of an already-defined system for harmonization, Abrashev discusses only obrabotki. Some of the drawbacks of Abrashev's book are its narrow view of harmony, its focus on a small portion of repertoire, and the fact that Bulgarian music is viewed through the lens of a classically trained composer influenced by socialist and Western aesthetics. While there are similarities between Abrashev's approach to chord derivation and that of the method used in Chapter 4 of this book, there are significant differences. Abrashev lists primary triads in all scales found in Bulgarian music.[21] However, many of these scales are either not present in the harmonized repertoire (examples 2.1a and 2.1b) or extremely rare.

Example 2.1a   Primary triads in Locrian according to Abrashev

---

[17]   For more information, refer to Kaufman (1958).

[18]   For more information, refer to Kaufman (1958 and 1968), Kaufman and Todorov (1967), and Kuteva (1976).

[19]   For more information, refer to Rice (1977).

[20]   For more information, refer to Forsyth (1996).

[21]   For more information regarding scales used in Bulgarian music, refer to chapters 3 and 4 of this book.

Example 2.1b   Chordal vocabulary in makam Huzzam[22] according to Abrashev

An additional level of complexity is created by Abrashev's use of functional Roman numerals in chord derivation and analysis, as well as examples in a four-part chordal texture typical for Western classical music (Example 2.2).

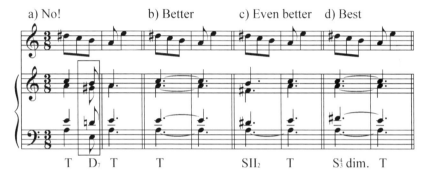

Example 2.2   Recommended cadences in makam Mustear[23] according to Abrashev

As seen in Example 2.2, Abrashev organizes his makam Mustear cadences in a continuum from forbidden ("No!") to the most appropriate ("Best"). In his examples illustrating models of harmonization in each scale, Abrashev follows the rules of Western four-part writing (Example 2.3), which contradict my analyses of the repertoire in this book.

---

[22] Bulgarian makam Huzzam is a non-microtonal mode. A detailed explanation of Bulgarian makams is provided in Chapter 3 of this book.

[23] Bulgarian makam Mustear is a non-microtonal mode. A detailed explanation of Bulgarian makams is provided in Chapter 3 of this book.

Example 2.3   Harmonization in makam Hicaz[24]

Abrashev's harmonic theory is based on neither performance practice nor a wide selection of repertoire, but rather on his own arrangements of Bulgarian folk music. My analyses of the repertoire do not reveal the existence of a defined system of rules regarding dissonance treatment, voice-leading, doubling, or prohibited parallel interval successions. Abrashev is providing a prescriptive theory of one type of music, where it is necessary to give a semblance of a complete "system," while the present study analyses live music of several repertoires, searching for rather than imposing harmonic commonalities.

Harmonic Vocabulary and Music Terminology

While the harmonization practice described in this book evolved and developed, Bulgarian musicians had no formal way of discussing harmony. The lack of vocabulary made the discussions of chords and progressions extremely difficult. Even musicians who had formal training in Western music could communicate about Bulgarian music only in Western terms, which did not apply to a great extent.

While touring the United States with Ivo Papazov's band in 2003 and 2005, I frequently had to guess about the harmonic thinking of Papazov's usual accompanist, Vasil Denev, who I was replacing and to whose chordal progressions the soloists were accustomed. On the rare occasions when my personal accompaniment style prevailed, Papazov would criticize these chords as incorrect. I was left with no other choice but to play various versions of harmonization for particular phrases until I received the positive feedback that they matched Denev's progressions. It is remarkable that Ivo Papazov and his colleagues, recipients of the BBC's audience award in the category "World Music" for 2004, have no vocabulary with which to talk about chords. My experiences playing with many professionally trained folk musicians have

---

[24] Bulgarian makam Hicaz is a non-microtonal mode. A detailed explanation of Bulgarian makams is provided in Chapter 3 of this book.

been similar; the theory described in this book is transmitted orally, without an existing spoken vocabulary.

Most of the arrangers and composers with whom I have interacted prefer to communicate through the music itself rather than using non-established or non-standardized terminology. When arrangers want to discuss ideas, they suggest particular chords with chord labels or simply play progressions on the piano or other accompanying instruments. An example of such communication would be "Try F minor here," which provides no information about mode, function, or the placement of the chord within a longer progression.

In my opinion, the lack of terminology and written theory had a positive, rather than negative effect on Bulgarian musical traditions. Musicians and composers had to devote years to learn the music by memorizing patterns, transcribing melodies, and sharpening their listening skills. With no clear criteria for correct or incorrect harmony in existence, the audience became the primary determining factor. Pieces that were highly praised by both musicians and audiences alike are analyzed in the chapters devoted to the analysis of repertoire (chapters 5–7).

Despite the lack of proper terminology and the fact that no existing publications discuss in detail Bulgarian harmonic practice, this book will provide an explanation of how this practice gradually formed and developed. In this chapter, I situated the music in historical, political, and cultural contexts. In the following chapter, I will examine the musical context, discuss terminology pertaining to Bulgarian music, and establish a proper theoretical foundation.

Chapter 3
Mapping the Musical Terrain

In this chapter, I will discuss the musical fundamentals of Bulgarian music as a preparatory step to analysis. Many of the characteristics of Bulgarian music are unique, and the establishment of a proper music vocabulary is essential for the understanding of this non-Western tradition. I will focus on structure, scales, meters, rhythm, and ornamentation in Bulgarian music.

Structure and Phrasing

Structure and phrasing impact harmony and harmonic rhythm to a great extent as they determine the place of cadences, set boundaries for a harmonic variety, and assist interactive accompanists in predicting what would happen next in melody and harmony.

General Structures and Forms in Instrumental Dance Music

In village and wedding music, the most frequently observed formal pattern found in instrumental music is:

Opening theme[1] →   Solos   →   Shortened repetition of the opening theme

The middle section involves a series of pre-composed or improvised solos performed by different instruments. Thematically, the solos are not related to the opening and ending sections. From the recordings available, it is difficult to determine whether solos prior to the 1960s were pre-composed or improvised. However, after the 1970s, both in village and wedding music, improvised solos became not only the norm but also the criteria for advanced musicianship. Regardless of the strong emphasis on improvisations, the overall framework remained the same. The basic structure above may be preceded by a slow, free-rhythm melodic introduction in the mode of the opening theme. Wedding music from the 1980s and 1990s further extended the basic structural pattern by

---

[1]   A theme is a group of motivically related periods (parallel or contrasting) which explore a common idea. Bulgarian musicians refer to a period as *kolyano*. Motivic relationships between kolyanos are discussed later in this chapter.

combining themes into medleys,[2] inserting improvisations and solos between pre-composed sections, and incorporating songs in the same meters.[3]

General Structures in Concert Music

In concert music[4] the traditional model above is frequently used; however, the repetition of the opening theme at the end is not required. Rather, pieces adopt a model that builds in intensity:

Opening theme   →   Solos   →   Shortened repetition of the opening theme
(moderate tempo)   (fast tempo)   (fastest tempo)

The above structure of form originates from "traditional" dance music, which often follows a similar pattern to gradually increase intensity.

Structures called suites are also typical for the concert repertoire. The term "suite" in Bulgarian music does not imply the same structure of standard Western suites. Rather, suite is used in its broad meaning as a combination of contrasting dances.

Phrasing and Structure of Dance Music

The phrasing and structure of Bulgarian dance music is strongly restricted by dance steps. A primary building block of music organization is the *kolyano* (lit. "knee" or "generation"). Buchanan defines kolyano in the following way: "in nonmusical contexts, kolyano denotes several things: (1) the knee, (2) lineage or parentage, (3) family or genus, and (4) a plant's node" (2006: 127). From a musical perspective, kolyano is a periodic structure with antecedent and consequent phrases. The phrasing is predominately symmetrical, 4+4 or 8+8 measures. Thracian[5] and Rhodope[6] music also commonly includes examples of symmetrical phrasing with uneven numbers of measures of the type 5+5 or 7+7. A performance can be perceived as a chain of kolyanos in different modes which subordinate to the overall structural plans discussed above. According to Peter Manuel: "This type of additive formal structure is particularly common in dance tunes (or genres derived from them), in which the musicians can spontaneously extend pieces *ad libitum*, in accordance with the dancers' mood"

---

[2] *Trakiiski temi* (Thracian themes), a medley of four themes, is analyzed in detail in Chapter 6.

[3] The structure of wedding music is further explained in Chapter 6.

[4] The phenomenon of concert music that emerged during the socialist period is discussed in Chapter 6.

[5] A map of the region of Thrace is provided in Chapter 4 (Map 4.3).

[6] A map of the Rhodope region is provided in Chapter 4 (Map 4.6).

(1989: 75). Kolyanos can be motivically related or not. Buchanan explains that (2006: 128):

> the motivic substance of a horo's [instrumental danceable piece] first kolyano was developed in the second, that of the second in the third, and so forth, such that the piece grew organically. In this respect every kolyano in a horo functioned like a knee joint; it was the hinge or pivot connecting preceding phrases with those that followed, the node in a musical line of descent that could be traced from the beginning of a piece to its conclusion.

While I agree with Buchanan's description of kolyano chains, I can add that the formula above is accurate only for older layers of Bulgarian music. In the newer layers, contrasts become more important than the chain-type kolyano organization. Buchanan's model is particularly applicable to dance repertoire and the head-in themes in wedding music.

Symmetrical phrasing and motivic repetition assist the dance experience. This is why musicians avoid phrase manipulations, such as elision, cadential extension, truncation, and internal expansion. However, musicians and composers use phrase manipulation techniques in free-rhythm, non-dance melodies and songs, as well as in the concert repertoire.

In summary, the relationship between music and dance governs phrasing in Bulgarian folk music. Even in the freest improvisation, hidden structures exist that maintain symmetrical structures on a larger scale. While analyzing repertoire of the twentieth century, I observed a gradual shift toward more symmetrical structures of the 4+4 measures type.

Phrasing and Structure in Instrumental Concert Repertoire

In concert music, the relationship between music and dance is less important to phrase structure and overall compositional form. However, in order to accommodate the listening expectations of the audience, musicians often subordinate their concert music to the symmetrical phrasing typical for dance music.

Folk Songs

Folk songs are an important basis for traditional music. In village music, folk songs often serve as the foundation of instrumental tunes. Wedding-style musicians and composers of obrabotki also draw on folk songs as source material. In terms of structure, folk songs can be classified into strophic songs and songs with a refrain. The phrase structure of "slow songs" (non-metric songs in free rhythm) varies for each individual example.

Songs with accompaniment include instrumental breaks between verses. The instrumental breaks prior to the 1950s were often melodic repetitions of the song or the refrain. Instrumental breaks after the 1960s typically had motivic relationships with the song, but were also melodically independent. In the 1980s, musicians and composers began using two independent instrumental breaks, achieving melodic variety in the song structure. The length of the songs (number of verses) also progressively decreased over time. While prior to the 1960s the story told by the song text was the primary element of interest, in the 1980s song length was reduced to 2–3 verses. The above process was influenced by the recording industry and stage performances.

Structure of Choral Obrabotki

The majority of choral obrabotki[7] preserve the phrasing and verse structure of the original song. A great portion of the choral arrangements are in ternary form, where the middle section involves transposition and developmental techniques often found in Western classical compositions.

Scales: The Established Scholarly Approach

Bulgarian ethnomusicologists classify the scales of Bulgarian music into four primary categories: pentatonic, diatonic, chromatic, and enharmonic (Dzhudzhev 1975: 266).

Pentatonic Collections

The pentatonic group categorizes five-note collections into major/minor, complete/incomplete,[8] and transitional. Transitional pentatonic scales involve minor seconds as structural intervals (Abrashev 1990: 22) and can be viewed as a hybrid between pentatonics and diatonic scales. This explains why Dzhudzhev refers to the transitional pentatonics as "diatonic pentatonics" (1975: 268). Example 3.1 illustrates all complete pentatonics according to descriptions found in current Bulgarian scholarship. Stoyan Dzhudzhev refers to these pentatonics as *anhemitonics*, five-tone scales within the boundaries of an octave which do not involve half-steps (1970: 268).[9]

---

[7] For more information regarding the structure of choral obrabotki, refer to Chapter 7.
[8] Complete pentatonics (anhemitonics) include all five notes of the pentatonic scale. Incomplete pentatonics have fewer than five notes.
[9] Dzhudzhev probably follows Bartók as the same definition of anhemitonics and an example identical to 3.1 appear in Bartók's Harvard Lectures from 1943 (1976: 363–4).

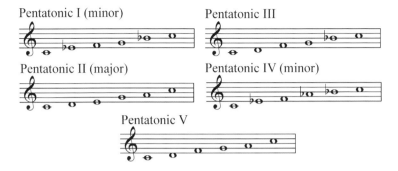

Example 3.1   Anhemitonics (complete pentatonic scales)

According to Bulgarian scholarship, pentatonic songs represent the oldest examples of "authentic" Bulgarian folk music. The idea of pentatonic melodies being the most ancient dates back to pre-scientific studies of folk music from the eighteenth and nineteenth centuries and was particularly emphasized in studies by Bartók and Kodály.[10] Bartók states that "our [Hungarian] peasants have preserved an extremely ancient style, a style over a thousand years old. Characteristic of the melodies of this style is a pentatonic scale without semitones" (1976: 176). According to my observations of Bulgarian music, transitional pentatonics are preferred in more recent harmonized repertoire (Example 3.2).

Pu-sto-no lu - do   i   mla -do,   ish-ti mi, mai-cho, ar- ma- gan,
Ish- ti mi, mai-cho, ar -ma - gan,   cher-ni si o - chi   da mu dam.

Da-li da gi dam   chi kak da gi dam ga ma   mai- ka glio-da ot tam.

Example 3.2   Folk song from the Rhodope region based on a transitional
               minor pentatonic from D

As seen in the popular Rhodope song Pustono Ludo i Mlado, the D minor pentatonic predominates, with the exception of m. 10, where a single pitch (E) is added to the pentatonic collection. The insertion of E transforms the anhemitonic pentatonic into a transitional pentatonic (Example 3.3).

---

[10]   For historical perspectives on pentatonic scales and "ancient" modality, refer to Gelbart (2007).

Example 3.3   D minor transitional pentatonic

Diatonic Collections

The diatonic category includes seven-note scales built on 16 authentic and plagal modes. As a system of modes, it contains similarities to both the ancient Greek system[11] and that established by Glarean[12] in the sixteenth century. The present study uses the Western mode classification system (after Glarean); however, I consider it important to explain which mode names Bulgarian scholars and musicians use.

In the most comprehensive study of the structure of Bulgarian folk music, Stoyan Dzhudzhev's two-volume *Bŭlgarskata Narodna Muzika* (Bulgarian Folk Music), diatonic modes are referred to as *glasove* (voices). Dzhudzhev prefers to organize the modal system using the ancient Greek labels and order of the octave species as follows (modern names are provided on the right):

Lydian	Ionian
Phrygian	Dorian
Dorian	Phrygian
Hypolydian	Lydian
Ionian, Hypophrygian, or Hyperlydian	Mixolydian
Aeolian, Hypodorian, Hyperphrygian, or Locrian	Aeolian
Mixolydian or Hyperdorian	Locrian

Unlike Dzhudzhev, later publications by Bulgarian scholars that describe scales and modes in Bulgarian traditional music incorporate either the diatonic modes of the Greek system and the Western system based on Glarean in tandem (Litova-Nikolova 1982), or only the system according to Glarean (Abrashev 1990: 22). The conflicting mode names found in Bulgarian scholarship confuses not only scholars, but also Bulgarian musicians themselves. For example, a folk musician trained in the 1970s would refer to the collection E-F-G-A-B-C-D-E as Dorian, while a folk musician trained a decade later would label the same collection as Phrygian. The preferences of some Bulgarian scholars towards the Greek mode

---

[11]   Studies of Bulgarian music from the 1960s and 1970s classify diatonic modes according to the ancient Greek system, which is not used in modern music practice. This led to confusion in Bulgarian scholarship regarding mode names and their labeling in collected material.

[12]   Glarean's system of twelve modes is the presently accepted Western classification of modes. As a classification system, it was defined by Glarean in his treatise *Dodecachordon*, published in 1547.

names could be explained as an attempt to emphasize the ancientness of these modes in a quasi-mythic way. It could also be interpreted as an implied suggestion of a Byzantine inheritance, or as a result of the direct translation of treatises from ancient Greek into Bulgarian. In order to avoid confusion in the present study, I will be consistent with the names and structure of the diatonic modes as used in Western music theory after Glarean (Example 3.4).

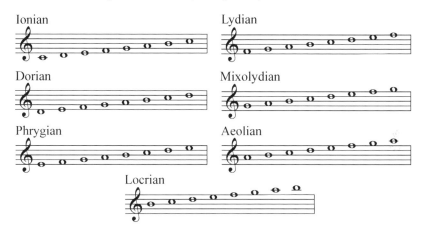

Example 3.4   Diatonic modes as used in the present study

From a non-nationalistic perspective, the wide geographical distribution of diatonic modes in Bulgarian traditional music can be explained by geographical and historical facts. First, Bulgaria shares a common border with Greece (in the south) and, second, Bulgaria accepted Eastern Orthodox Christianity as its official religion in the ninth century. With that came the adoption of the Byzantine chant system. According to Manuel, "the entire Mediterranean area shares, in varying degrees, the musical heritage of the Byzantine Church, although the extent to which this tradition influenced secular music remains unclear" (1989: 75).

In harmonized Bulgarian music, modes do not include some of the characteristic gestures found in Western modal music. For example, in Western modal practice, Aeolian mode frequently uses G♯ as part of a cadential gesture. With the exception of Ionian and major polymodes based on Ionian, the diatonic modes found in the repertoire analyzed in this book do not have a leading tone.[13]

---

[13]   In Chapter 4, I discuss in detail modes and modal chordal vocabularies. The Lydian mode is not present in harmonized repertoire.

Bulgarian scholars define the modes of songs and instrumental pieces according to their *finalis*[14] determined by the final descent.[15] Later in this study (Chapter 4) I will challenge this mode-defining theory, since the results it produces in the context of polymodality and modes whose finalis is not scale degree $\hat{1}$ are questionable.

Chromatic Collections

The third category, chromatic, organizes scales based on the presence of a characteristic interval: the augmented second. Bulgarian scholarship refers to these collections as makams, and borrows their names from similar Turkish makams (Example 3.5).

Example 3.5   Makams (chromatic collections) in Bulgarian music

The earliest study of scales and harmony in Bulgarian music, *Melodichni i Harmonichni Osnovi na Bŭlgarskata Narodna Pesen* (Melodic and Harmonic Foundations of Bulgarian Folk Song) by Asen Karastoyanov, refers to the makams as "exotic scales" (1950: 81), reflecting a narrow, biased attitude. The category designation of "chromatic" was first given by Dzhudzhev in his book *Bŭlgarskata Narodna Muzika*; later it became the standard term to describe these collections.

---

[14]   According to Bulgarian scholarship, the finalis is the last note of a final descent which is considered scale degree $\hat{1}$.

[15]   Typically, these are scale degrees $\hat{3}$-$\hat{2}$-$\hat{1}$ (finalis). According to this classification, minor polymodes with a variable 2nd scale degree are classified as Phrygian due to their final descent ($\hat{3}$-$_\flat\hat{2}$-$\hat{1}$). Major modes with scale degree $\hat{3}$ as finalis are also classified as Phrygian for the same reasons.

Historically, Bulgaria was under the strong political and cultural influence of the Ottoman Empire for almost five centuries (1396–1878). There is a high probability that the Bulgarians adopted the makam system from Turkish culture while under the domination of the Ottoman Empire. Further dissemination of the makams could have occurred through the Romany musicians, who were professional musicians for both the Bulgarian population and the ruling Turks during the period of Ottoman domination.

In order to compare Bulgarian to Turkish makams, I consulted Karl Signell's book *Makam Modal Practice in Turkish Art Music*, published in 1977. Such a comparison was impossible during the socialist period due to political and nationalistic reasons. Bulgarian scholars during socialism were required to document the "purity" of folk music and erase any Turkish influences. In Stoyan Dzhuzhdev's book *Bŭlgarskata Narodna Muzika*, the Turkish-Arabic origins of the makams are mentioned (1970), yet in the studies that follow (Litova-Nikolova 1982 and Abrashev 1990), chromatic scales are referred to as Bulgarian makams, and the words Turkish or Turkey are not present at all. The beginning of the removal of the "Turkish influence" in Bulgarian ethnomusicological writings can be dated to Kaufman and Todorov's book *Narodni Pesni ot Yugozapadna Bŭlgaria: Pirinski Krai* (Folk Songs from Southwestern Bulgaria: Pirin Region), where the authors mention that Turkish music "left hardly a trace among the local Bulgarian populace" (1967: 9).

Examples 3.6a and 3.6b explore the construction of Turkish makams that share scale names with Bulgarian makams falling in the chromatic category. In Turkish music, makams are constructed by combining tetrachords (Example 3.6a) and pentachords (Example 3.6b).

Example 3.6a   Tetrachords used for constructing Turkish makams

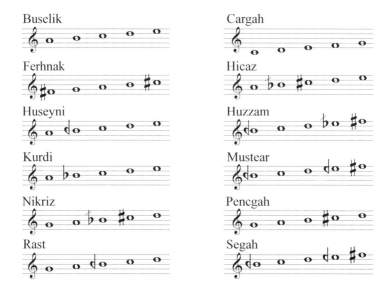

Example 3.6b   Pentachords used for constructing Turkish makams

As seen in the examples, the Turkish tetrachords and pentachords involve microtones, which are not present in Bulgarian makams. The smallest interval in Turkish music is a comma equaling 23 cents, or less than a fourth of an equal-tempered semitone (a semitone equals 100 cents). The Ezgi-Arel notation adopted for the Turkish microtonal makam system uses six accidentals (Signell 1977: 24; Example 3.7).

raises one comma	lowers one comma
raises four commas	lowers four commas
raises five commas	lowers five commas

Example 3.7   Accidentals in Turkish makams

Makam Hicaz, as described in Turkish classical theory (examples 3.8a and 3.8b), has a variable 6th scale degree, which is not noted in the studies of Bulgarian Hicaz (Example 3.5). As we will see further in this book, variable scale degrees, such as the 6th scale degree seen in Turkish Hicaz, play a crucial role in Bulgarian harmony and temporary tonicizations.[16]

---

[16]   Temporary tonicizations are secondary key areas established through cadences.

Example 3.8a   Turkish makam Hicaz

Example 3.8b   Turkish makam Hicaz descending scale

The Turkish version of makam Karcigar differs from its Bulgarian equivalent only in terms of microtones (Example 3.9).

Example 3.9   Turkish makam Karcigar

The absence of microtones is true for all Bulgarian makams. Example 3.10 is a complete chart of Turkish makams that correspond to non-microtonal makams found in Bulgarian music (Example 3.5).

The similarities between Turkish and Bulgarian makams suggest that Bulgarians probably adopted the Turkish makams, but modified them based on European temperament. It is also possible that Bulgarian scholars, who collected and notated thousands of songs at the end of the nineteenth century and continued throughout the twentieth century, "normalized" the collected material by adjusting it to Western notation. On the other hand, Bulgarian performers themselves could have excluded the microtones under the influence of the diatonic system. Bulgarian scholars admit the existence of microtones in Bulgarian music, although these examples are not considered makams but enharmonic collections.[17]

Bulgarian musicians today employ a limited vocabulary while referring to makams. Among all Europeanized makams, Bulgarian musicians recognize and label only Hicaz.

Through observations and my own performance practice, I have noticed that most Bulgarian chromatic scales are related by transposition, i.e. they include a partial or entire Hicaz scale starting from different scale degrees. I define this concept as "movable Hicaz" and suggest it as an easier approach to understanding and constructing non-microtonal Bulgarian makams (Example 3.11).

---

[17]   Enharmonic collections are discussed later in this chapter.

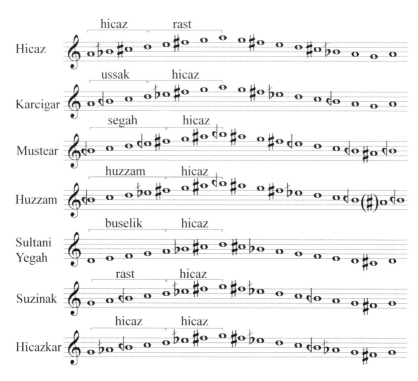

Example 3.10   Turkish makams sharing names with Bulgarian makams

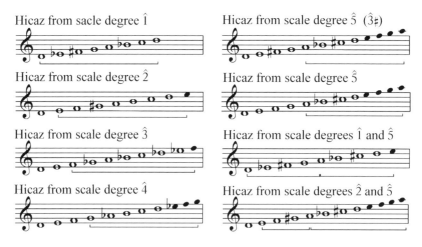

Example 3.11   The concept of "movable Hicaz"

All makams constructed through the "movable Hicaz" approach have equivalents in the chromatic scales described by Bulgarian scholars. The names correspond as follows:

Hicaz from scale degree $\hat{1}$	Makam Hicaz
Hicaz from scale degree $\hat{2}$	Makam Mustear
Hicaz from scale degree $\hat{3}$	Makam Huzzam
Hicaz from scale degree $\hat{4}$	Makam Karcigar
Hicaz from scale degree $\hat{5}$ (in major)	Makam Suzinak
Hicaz from scale degree $\hat{5}$ (in minor)	Makam Sultani Yegah
Hicaz from scale degrees $\hat{1}$ and $\hat{5}$	Makam Hicazkar

Since the order of makams seen above parallels the order of makams in the Bulgarian classification of chromatic collections, it is possible that Bulgarian scholars also observed the transpositional relationship between the makams. This relationship, however, is not mentioned in the Bulgarian literature.

Enharmonic Collections

Bulgarian scholars refer to the final category of scales as enharmonic, including pitch collections that incorporate microtones (Dzhudzhev 1970). The primary reason Bulgarian scholars did not study the microtones in depth is probably a combination of nationalism and anti-Turkism. According to Dzhudzhev, Bulgarians could have adopted microtones from the ancient Greeks or Byzantine chants. Later studies do not mention the Turkish origins of the microtonal pitch collections, regardless of the fact that they are more widely distributed in the Southern regions of Bulgaria, which share a border with Turkey and Greece, versus Northern Bulgaria, which shares a border with Romania.

Many aspects of the Turkish makam system are completely preserved in the traditional music of the Bulgarian Turks and the Roma. Due to the similarities of their music to the makam traditions of Turkey, the music of the Bulgarian Turks and the Roma was marginalized during the socialist period; it was never mentioned, collected, or studied by Bulgarian scholars (Silverman 1989 and 2012).

Scales beyond the Standard Categorization

Although extensive, the categorization of scales adopted by Bulgarian scholars does not cover the wide variety actually present in the music of Bulgaria. During the twentieth century, under the influence of Western harmony, Lydian, Locrian, and some of the chromatic scales disappeared from performance practices. In order to more accurately represent the melodic structure of contemporary Bulgarian music, some of these categories must be clarified, revised, and, in some instances, new categories such as polymodes and a major-minor system must be added.

Polymodality

Polymodality[18] is a widespread characteristic in Bulgarian traditional music that plays a crucial role in the development of harmonic languages. Variable scale degrees produced as a result of polymodality assist temporary tonicizations and modulations, and serve as clues for accompanists to apply particular secondary dominants. Bulgarian scholars disregard variable scale degrees as secondary features of mode, and omit them completely in analyses and discussions of "authentic" songs. I suggest that variable scale degrees must be acknowledged, as they predetermine changes in harmony and allow for greater melodic variety. I also suggest that polymodality could be a result of a gradual shift from microtonal collections to Western European temperament. This is supported by the fact that many variable scale degrees can be found in the place of microtones.[19] Unfortunately, there is not enough analytical data to prove or disprove a claim that an Aeolian/Phrygian polymode (with a variable 2nd scale degree), for example, is merely a byproduct of a makam mapped onto equal temperament. The vast variety of polymodes in Bulgarian music and their relation to harmony will be discussed in detail in Chapter 4.

Major-Minor System

Bulgarian music from the second half of the twentieth century includes other scales commonly found in Western European music. Major (Ionian) appears in the music of all regions of Bulgaria. Natural minor (Aeolian) is frequently set aside in favor of a polymode, incorporating a variable (raised/lowered) 2nd scale degree (Aeolian/Phrygian). Harmonic and melodic minor are typical in the repertoire from Northern Bulgaria, the region most removed from Turkey and Greece. Although harmonic minor exists in the makam system under the name Sultani Yegah (see Example 3.5), this scale is very rarely present in Southern Bulgarian folk music, which implies a Western, rather than Eastern, influence.

All categories of scales discussed to this point suggest that the scales in Bulgarian traditional music form a complex mixture of makams, diatonic modes, microtonal scales, and pentatonic collections, as well as a major/minor system. In Chapter 4, I will suggest a simpler system of organizing the scales of Bulgarian

---

[18]   In one of his Harvard lectures, Bartók explains the essential difference between atonality, polytonality, and polymodality. According to him, "atonal music offers no fundamental tone at all, polytonality offers—or is supposed to offer—several of them, and polymodality offers a single one" (1976: 370).

[19]   For example, the microtonal collection D-E half-flat-F maps onto equal temperament as D-E♭-E♮-F, i.e. the two half-steps (E♭ and E♮) "unfold" a microtone that is no longer found in the middle. In the present study, the scale with variable 2nd scale degree is classified as an Aeolian/Phrygian polymode (see Chapter 4, Example 4.13).

music, which combines similar and interchangeable scales. The suggested system is derived from the harmonic analysis of a large body of repertoire and contemporary performance practice.

Meters

Meters, rhythm, and harmony are closely linked in many tonal and modal styles of music. A thorough explanation of Bulgarian meters and rhythms is necessary to understanding metric placement of chords and progressions, as well as the overall harmonic motion found in Bulgarian village music, wedding music, and choral obrabotki.

Asymmetrical meters[20] represent one of the most essential characteristics of Bulgarian traditional music. They exist in immense variety, from $\frac{5}{8}$ to $\frac{15}{8}$, and occur in different combinations with simple and compound meters. Over the centuries, Bulgarians have explored a massive variety of uneven groupings of twos and threes, combined metric groups (several meters recurring periodically), and heterometric rows (meters which do not follow a particular pattern) (Dzhudzhev 1970: 222). Most asymmetrical meters have corresponding dances.

Simple and Compound Meters

The majority of simple and compound meters found in Western classical music are present in Bulgarian musical traditions. The most widely used are $\frac{2}{4}$ and $\frac{6}{8}$, although asymmetrical meters prevail. Simple or compound meters are often replaced by asymmetrical ones. For example, Bulgarians prefer the asymmetrical $\frac{7}{8}$ (2+2+3 or 3+2+2) or $\frac{8}{8}$ (3+2+3) over $\frac{4}{4}$. Compound meters such as $\frac{9}{8}$ and $\frac{12}{8}$ are found primarily in asymmetrical versions (uneven groupings).

Asymmetrical Meters

Bulgarian ethnomusicologists have developed a precise system for classifying the most common asymmetrical metric structures. Meters are classified by the number of beats in a measure and how those beats are grouped in combinations of twos and threes. For example, $\frac{7}{8}$ of the type 2+2+3 is classified as unevenly grouped (asymmetrical), consisting of 7 beats and 3 groupings where the group of three is placed last. Example 3.12 lists some of the most common asymmetrical meters found in Bulgaria, organized vertically by increasing numbers of beats and horizontally by their prevalence in the repertoire.

---

[20] In this book, asymmetrical meters include all meters with uneven groupings. For example, $\frac{8}{8}$ of the types 3+2+3 or 3+3+2 are classified as asymmetrical.

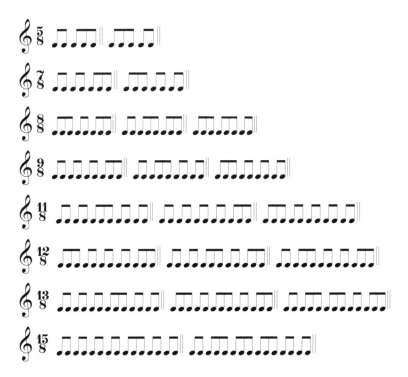

Example 3.12   Asymmetrical meters in Bulgarian music

I suggest a different metric classification system, which merges the system used by Bulgarian scholars with the system currently used in Western music theory. In my classification, $\frac{7}{8}$ of the type 2+2+3 (Example 3.12) has three beats that correspond to the Bulgarian definition of groupings. In contrast to Western classical music, hyperbeats within asymmetrical meters do not occur only on a downbeat at the beginning of a measure. Rather, hyperbeats emphasize changes of grouping.[21] While at a beat level groups of twos are perceived as "short" and groups of threes as "long," at a hypermetrical level, groups of threes are perceived as "short" with a following hyperbeat indicating exactly how "short" they are. The asymmetrical $\frac{15}{8}$ (2+2+2+2+3+2+2) on a hypermetrical level is grouped as 4+4+3+4, and has four hyperbeats.

Not all asymmetrical meters found in Bulgarian music involve a group of three on a hypermeter level. For example, *Elenino Horo* (Elena's Dance), notated in $\frac{14}{16}$, contains four hyperbeats grouped as 4+4+2+4. In fast tempos, the hyperbeats combine, forming a second hypermetrical level of 8+6. This new hypermetrical

---

[21]   On a hypermeter level in $\frac{7}{8}$ (2+2+3), the first two beats (2+2) combine and form a hyperbeat (4). As a result, on a first hypermetric level $\frac{7}{8}$ changes its grouping from 2+2+3 to 4+3. The two groupings (4+3) become hyperbeats.

level involves a grouping of three (the second hyperbeat) and becomes identical to the first hypermetrical level of $\frac{7}{8}$ (4+3) discussed above.

Combined Metric Groups and Heterometric Rows

A number of Bulgarian folk songs and dances contain more than one meter. When meters repeat in a particular pattern, for example $\frac{7}{8}$ and $\frac{11}{8}$, scholars refer to the resulting combinatorial meter ($\frac{7}{8}+\frac{11}{8}$) as a "combined metric group" (Dzhudzhev 1970: 222 and Litova-Nikolova 1982: 118). Example 3.13 contains an excerpt from a transcription of *Yovino Horo* (Yova's Dance), a line dance from Pirin, which is based on a combined metric group $\frac{7}{8}+\frac{7}{8}+\frac{11}{8}$, where the $\frac{7}{8}$ is of the type 3+2+2 and $\frac{11}{8}$ of type 2+2+3+2+2.

Example 3.13   Yovino Horo

Unlike combined metric groups, heterometric rows involve different meters which do not occur in a particular pattern (Example 3.14a).

Example 3.14a   Heterometric row

The antecedent phrase in Example 3.14a contains 14 beats ($\frac{7}{8}+\frac{11}{8}+\frac{5}{8}+\frac{10}{8}$) while the consequent contains 13 beats ($\frac{8}{8}+\frac{5}{8}+\frac{5}{8}+\frac{5}{8}+\frac{11}{8}$).

Heterometric rows are not limited only to asymmetrical meters. Rather, Bulgarian musicians often draw on all available meters when creating metrically sophisticated pieces, as shown in the excerpt from Petür Ralchev's Bulgarian

Suite (Example 3.14b). Ralchev uses a heterometric row, making the meter barely perceivable even for Bulgarian musicians trained in the tradition.[22]

Example 3.14b   Excerpt from Petŭr Ralchev's Bulgarian Suite illustrating
                 heterometric structure

The antecedent phrase, mm. 1–8, observes the metric structure $\frac{2}{4}+\frac{2}{4}+\frac{2}{4}+\frac{2}{4}+\frac{7}{8}+\frac{7}{8}+\frac{7}{8}+\frac{7}{8}+\frac{15}{8}$, while the consequent phrase, mm. 9–15, is organized metrically as $\frac{2}{4}+\frac{2}{4}+\frac{2}{4}+\frac{7}{8}+\frac{7}{8}+\frac{7}{8}+\frac{7}{8}+\frac{15}{8}$. The subtracted measure of $\frac{2}{4}$ in the consequent phrase makes the excerpt an example of a heterometric row, as opposed to a combined metric group.

---

[22]   Transcriptions of heterometric rows are arbitrary. My choices of determining meters within heterometric rows are based on phrasing and chordal accompaniment.

Rhythm

Bulgarian rhythms have fascinated Western audiences, composers, and musicians for decades. The immense variety of asymmetrical meters in Bulgarian music implies the existence of intricate rhythmic organization that needs to be examined in detail.

Rhythm in Dance Music

Due to the relationship between musical and dance traditions, rhythmic patterns are frequently dependent on the skills of the dancers. More experienced dancers allow performers to use syncopations and to group measures, thereby producing more intricate patterns on a larger scale, whereas less experienced dancers often prefer accompanists to emphasize only the strong beats.

Syncopations and Razdrobyavane (Subdivision)

It is difficult to speculate when Bulgarian accompanists and drummers began experimenting with syncopations and accents. However, my observations show an increased desire to experiment with accents and syncopations in the last decades of the twentieth century. Accents are accomplished by drawing the offbeats to the foreground. Example 3.15 illustrates some of the most popular accented groupings in the asymmetrical ⅞ (2+2+3) found in wedding music from the 1980s.

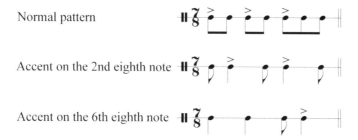

Example 3.15   Accents in ⅞

Accents and syncopations may involve several measures, creating rhythmic patterns on a larger scale. Example 3.16 illustrates three common patterns for ⅞ that combine pairs of measures.

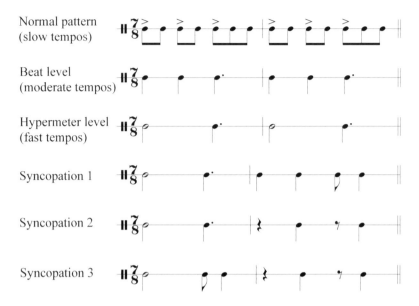

Example 3.16   Accents and syncopations in $\frac{7}{8}$

The first three levels refer to the normal subdivision of $\frac{7}{8}$ in relation to tempo. In slow tempos, the perception of rhythm is at the level of eighth notes. As the tempo increases, the perception changes to a beat level of three quarter notes, the last of which is dotted (quick-quick-slow).[23] In such a context, the second beat is perceived as the weakest and can be omitted or played as an offbeat. Frequently the last eighth note, the 7th, is played as an offbeat, indicating the end of the third beat. The pattern produced is 1–3–5–7, where the underlined eighth notes are played as downbeats.

Syncopations and accents typically are accomplished on a particular level of pulse. Razdrobyavane,[24] however, introduces note durations from sublevels of the beat division (sixteenth notes or smaller) as well as grouping dissonance (duplets for the groupings of three and triplets for the groupings of two). This type of subdivision, if combined with accents on offbeats, produces some of the most rhythmically challenging patterns found in Bulgarian music (Example 3.17).

---

[23]   The hyperbeat levels directly correlate to dance movements, where steps are placed on hyperbeats.

[24]   Razdrobyavane translates as "breaking down into smaller pieces."

Example 3.17   Razdrobyavane in $\frac{7}{8}$

The elaborated rhythmic pattern in Example 3.17 involves sixteenth notes, eighths, and quarters, as well as a triplet. While razdrobyavane introduces smaller note values and alternative beat division within a measure, a different phenomenon that groups multiple measures allows for the creation of larger metric structures.

Megameters and Megameasures

I suggest the terms megameasures and megameters to describe the grouping of measures of the same meter which produce rhythmic patterns conceived across a bar line. I propose a different terminology from the established Schenkerian concepts of hypermeter and hypermeasure due to the fact that, although similar, they are not truly analogous. In Schenkerian terms, hypermeasure is defined as a group of measures in which the measure itself serves as a beat. In Bulgarian music, megameasure is defined as a combined group of measures whose cumulative beats allow for different internal metric and rhythmic organization. This forms a larger metric structure ultimately perceived as a unit due to accents and grouping. In Schenkerian terms, hypermeter is defined as meter above the notated measure. In Bulgarian music, megameter is the cumulative meter within a megameasure. For example, a megameter of two measures of $\frac{15}{16}$ produces a megameasure involving a rhythmic pattern within 30 sixteenth notes or 14 beats (Example 3.18).

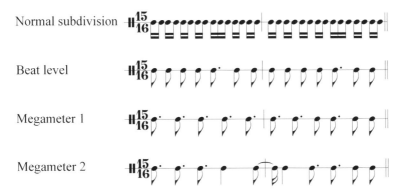

Example 3.18   Megameasure produced by $\frac{15}{16}$

Due to the length of the megameasures and the produced megameters, rhythms such as the one illustrated in Example 3.18 are avoided in dance music. The concept of megameters, however, does exist in dance music repertoire, but usually with fewer beats. In these examples, the downbeats on the second measures are preserved as a reference point for the dancers. The concept of megameters can be traced only in the styles stemming from oral tradition.[25] Styles sponsored by the socialist state never adopted this concept since it was not present in the "authentic" repertoire used as the foundation for obrabotki.

The most basic example of megameter/megameasure in dance music is a typical rhythmic figure for the Bulgarian dance *Pravo Horo* (Straight Dance) as performed in the wedding style.

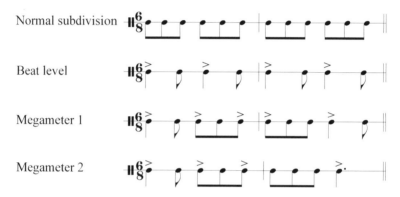

Example 3.19   Megameasures in Pravo Horo

The rhythmic figures shown in Example 3.19 combine two measures of $\frac{6}{8}$. Both megameter versions place an accent on the last eighth note of the first measure, followed by a measure with a standard accent placement.

Wedding-style musicians from the 1980s also explored megameasures combining four measures (Example 3.20).

Example 3.20   A megameasure of $\frac{24}{8}$

This rhythm is heard frequently in recordings of Ivo Papazov's *Trakiya* (Thrace) orchestra from the 1980s and 1990s.

___

[25] Megameters are typical for wedding music from the 1980s–1990s. The practical application of megametrical structures will be discussed further in Chapter 6, as they are primary distinguishers between village and wedding improvisation and accompaniment styles.

In asymmetrical meters, the concept of megameters may be taken to more advanced levels. Example 3.21 shows three rhythmic patterns. The first (megameter 1) is typical of dance music, whereas the second (megameter 2) and third (megameter 3) are typical of the concert style of Ivo Papazov's orchestra.[26]

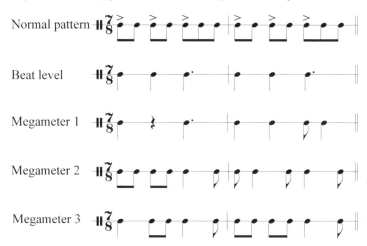

Example 3.21   Megameters of $\frac{14}{8}$

In performance settings, drummers and accompanists frequently experiment with megametrical structures. Performers use visual clues in determining whose megametrical idea has the potential to be further explored and established as a megameter. In its initial stage of development, a megametrical idea combines syncopations, looping rhythmic elements, and accented patterns. The cyclic repetition of a megametrical idea leads to the creation and perception of a megameter. The starting and ending loop points of a megametrical structure mark the bar lines of the produced megameasure.

From a performer's perspective, megameters are a learned technique that allows a musician to simultaneously follow two or more different meters. Megameasure-long accompaniment patterns provide stable frameworks and supply rhythmic cues serving as referential points for soloists. Such rhythmic cues (boxed in Example 3.22) typically anticipate the arrival of the mid-point and the end of a megameasure.

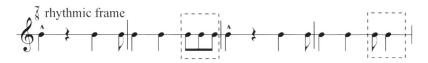

Example 3.22 $\frac{7}{8}$ rhythmic frame forming a megameasure

---

[26] For more information, refer to Chapter 6.

Intentionally sought rhythmic differences between middle and final cues assist performers in differentiating between the two types of cue. Moreover, these rhythmic reminders directly precede downbeats, the most suitable points for reentering the primary meter.

The following examples provide a potential explanation of how a wedding musician acquires the skills to think in more than one meter at a given time. The examples demonstrate the superimposing of two different meters, primary and secondary, followed by a metric alignment necessary for the proper completion of a megameasure.

Example 3.23 illustrates the superimposing of $\frac{6}{8}$ and $\frac{7}{8}$. A performer needs to insert four extra eighth notes at the very end of the cycle in order to complete the megameasure properly.

Example 3.23 Megameter formed by $\frac{6}{8}$ over $\frac{7}{8}$

Example 3.24 illustrates the superimposing of two asymmetrical meters, $\frac{5}{8}$ and $\frac{7}{8}$. An extra measure of $\frac{6}{8}$ enables a successful vertical alignment for the completion of the megameasure.

Example 3.24 Megameter formed by $\frac{5}{8}$ over $\frac{7}{8}$

One particular meter combination intrigues both performers and audience. A megameasure, which is produced by four measures of $\frac{7}{8}$, groups 28 eighth notes: 28 divides into 7 and 4; therefore, a combination of $\frac{7}{8}$ and $\frac{8}{8}$ (or $\frac{2}{4}$) eliminates the need to insert extra notes to align the melodic phrases at the end of a megameasure (Example 3.25).

Example 3.25   Megameter formed by $\frac{8}{8}$ over $\frac{7}{8}$

Soloists are not the only wedding-style performers experimenting with megameters. Accompanists and drummers also utilize any opportunities to demonstrate advanced musicianship. On certain occasions, both accompanists and soloists abandon the primary meter simultaneously. For example, if a soloist explores the rhythmic pattern illustrated in Example 3.23 ($\frac{8}{8}$ over $\frac{7}{8}$) and the accompanists begin experimenting with $\frac{8}{8}$ over $\frac{7}{8}$ (Example 3.25), none of the performers supply stable referential points for reentering the pulse of $\frac{7}{8}$. Such moments of metric ambiguity are typically well masked by skillful arpeggios, chromatic sequences, or chains of syncopations until the pulse of the primary meter is reestablished.

Megameters are typical for wedding concert repertoire. Dancers, both in Bulgaria and abroad, do not appreciate the lack of downbeats or the inertia created by looping rhythmic elements across a bar line (Example 3.26).

Example 3.26   Rhythmic elements creating a looping effect

For a listener who does not have a strong sense of the downbeat in asymmetrical meters, megameasures and their resulting rhythmic variety sound disorganized. According to Stoyan Kostov, a renowned Bulgarian tambura player, only listeners who can imagine the proper downbeats truly appreciate their omission in the music.

Ornamentation

Embellishments are foreground elements that have limited impact on chordal verticals or harmonic rhythm. In certain types of slow songs and non-metered melodies, however, harmony and embellishments are more closely interrelated. As will become evident from the analysis of choral obrabotki (Chapter 7), in a slow, non-metered song, a chord change may not occur before a long embellishment has completed its cycle. Although less structurally significant, ornamentation is an essential component of Bulgarian folk melodies. Therefore, I find it necessary to provide a brief overview of the main types of embellishment found in the three styles of music discussed in this book.

Primary embellishments consist of upper (⁓) and lower mordents (⁓), *vorschlags*[27] and *nachschlags*[28] (♪), and turns (∞), as well as connecting grace notes.[29] Bulgarian scholars Alexander Motsev and Stoyan Dzhudzhev have studied and classified all embellishments present in published collections of "authentic" folk music (Motsev 1961 and Dzhudzhev 1954). These studies are primarily descriptive and focus on regional characteristics. Unfortunately, they provide little insight as to why certain ornaments are used versus others, or how embellishments are applied in general in different styles.

Examples 3.27a and 3.27b illustrate two different styles of embellishment of the same excerpt: village-music embellishment style from the 1960s (Example 3.27a) and wedding-music embellishment style from the 1980s (Example 3.27b). In both examples, I have provided graphic symbols for mordents and auxiliary notes showing how mordents are executed in performance.

Example 3.27a   Excerpt from Rŭchenitsa, dance tune embellished in village
                 style from the 1960s

---

[27]   Vorschlag is a one note grace note (♪) which takes from the value of the note that follows.

[28]   Nachschlag is a one note grace note (♪) which takes from the value of the preceding note.

[29]   For more information, refer to Dzhudzhev (1954).

Example 3.27b   Excerpt from Rǔchenitsa, dance tune embellished in wedding
                 style from the 1980s

As seen in Example 3.27b, in the wedding style the number of auxiliary
(embellishment) notes is almost equal to the number of primary notes in this
melodic excerpt, and triple the number of embellishments seen in Example
3.27a. When occurring between repeated primary notes, the auxiliary notes are
considered mordents: upper (⤳) when involving an upper neighbor or lower
(⤳) when involving a lower neighbor. Due to their placement and duration, the
remaining auxiliary notes should be classified as connecting grace notes rather
than vorschlags and nachschlags. Not all styles of Bulgarian folk music contain
the level of embellishment illustrated in Example 3.27b. Earlier styles from the
village tradition (Example 3.27a) and styles sponsored by the socialist state lack
most of the connecting grace notes, and involve upper and lower mordents only.[30]

Vocal and Instrumental Polyphony

Traditional Bulgarian polyphony generally involves melody and drone. Although
most scholars have focused on the variety of styles and regional differences, my
intention is to group the general patterns of polyphonic traditions into working
formulas. I supplement these scholars' observations with my own personal
knowledge as a performer of Bulgarian music derived from practice and analysis
of recordings.

Drones may be steady in pitch or variable. Map 3.1 marks the regions of
Bulgaria where traditional vocal polyphony continues to exist. In instrumental folk
music, melody and drone polyphony exists in wider areas due to the distribution

---

[30]   In the transcriptions analyzed in this book, I have indicated only the placement
of lower mordents. All repeated notes, which do not have the sign placed above, imply
upper mordents. I have not transcribed grace notes due to the redundant appearance of the
resulting scores.

of bagpipes,[31] gŭdulkas, *dvoyankas*,[32] fiddles,[33] and tamburas,[34] instruments that produce steady or variable drones.

Map 3.1   The consistency distribution of traditional vocal polyphony[35]

The drone tradition played a crucial role in the development of harmonic languages. Reductive analyses of even the most challenging examples of harmonized Bulgarian folk music reveal as a final level of reduction one of the drone types listed below.[36] The two primary categories of drone found in Bulgarian music are steady and variable.[37]

---

[31]   There are two common types of gaida, Thracian gaida and Rhodope gaida (*kaba gaida*) which have steady drones.

[32]   A dvoyanka is a double-pipe flute with one of the pipes producing a steady drone.

[33]   Fiddles are popular among the Vlach population from Northwestern Bulgaria.

[34]   The traditional tambura is tuned in fifths. The top string is used for melody and the lower strings for steady or variable drones.

[35]   This map is based on information taken from Kaufman's book *Bŭlgarska Narodna Muzika* (1977: 56). For a complete citation, refer to the Bibliography.

[36]   A reductive graph illustrating a variable drone at a deeper level of structure is provided in Chapter 7 (Example 7.31).

[37]   The types of drone listed in this chapter have been derived from the following studies by Nikolai Kaufman: *Bŭlgarskata Mnogoglasna Narodna Pesen,* "Dvuglasnoto Narodno Peene v Bulgaria," "Triglasnite Narodni Pesni ot Kostursko," and *Narodni Pesni ot Yugozapadna Bŭlgaria: Pirinski Krai* (for full citations, refer to the Bibliography).

Steady Drones

The category of steady drones subdivides into five main types:

1. drone on the same pitch as the finalis;
2. drone a fourth below the finalis;
3. drones on the same pitch as the finalis and a fourth below;
4. drone a fifth below the finalis;
5. drones on the same pitch as the finalis and a fifth below.

The first type of drone tonicizes scale degree $\hat{1}$ (CD, Track 1). Drones a fourth below the finalis are a variation of the previous category, since the final vertical sonorities imply the tonic fifth (CD, Track 2). A third type of drone combines the first two types (CD, Track 3). While the fourth type of drone tonicizes scale degree $\hat{1}$, it can also be perceived as a drone on scale degree $\hat{4}$ (CD, Track 4). This drone type suggests two different tonics. The fifth type of drone is typical for music played on traditional tamburas (tuned in fifths).

Variable Drones

Three main types of variable drone emerge from observations of older layers of Bulgarian folk music:

1. Drone on scale degree $\hat{1}$ (finalis) interchanged with the subtonic $\hat{7}$.
2. Variable drone in minor between scale degrees $\hat{3}$ and $\hat{1}$, where $\hat{1}$ is the finalis.
3. Variable drone $\hat{4}$—$\hat{1}$, which implies two possible tonics.

The variable drone of the first type implies a dominant-tonic relationship (cadence) at the end of a phrase (CD, Track 5). The second type of variable drone is typical for songs using minor scales. According to Kaufman, this type of drone is characteristic of the Velingrad region (Eastern Rhodope) and the Pazardzhik-Ihtiman region (Eastern Thrace) (1977: 59–61). Kaufman also provides examples of variable drone of the type $\hat{3}$-$\hat{7}$-$\hat{1}$ which combines two types of variable drone (1977: 63). The variable $\hat{3}$-$\hat{1}$ drone type became the foundation for juxtaposing two tonal centers in minor, i.e. tonicizing the relative major and cadencing in the main minor key (CD, Track 6). A few examples involve a variable drone on scale degree $\hat{4}$ (a fifth below) and scale degree $\hat{1}$ (finalis). Examples of this type imply two tonics, creating a harmonic dilemma that can result in various solutions. As will be discussed in Chapter 4, examples of this type illustrate the possibility of two completely different harmonizations: one in major and one in minor.

 In his dissertation *Polyphony in Bulgarian Music*, Rice discusses two additional types of drone, $\hat{3}$-$\hat{2}$-$\hat{1}$ and $\hat{4}$-$\hat{3}$-$\hat{2}$-$\hat{1}$ (1977: 33), which are considered subtypes in the present classification system. In the first of the two, $\hat{2}$ can be viewed as passing tone within the $\hat{3}$-$\hat{1}$ drone type framework discussed above; the second is simply a variation of the $\hat{4}$-$\hat{1}$ drone type transformed into a stepwise descent of the drone part.

Three-Part Singing

According to Kaufman, there is no three-part singing in Bulgaria. He suggests that an Albanian style of three-part singing exists in the Kostur region (Kostursko) of Macedonia (1968: 127). The style of Kostursko three-part singing can be summarized as a diaphony over a steady drone. However, according to Rice, three-part singing can be found in the Shope region of Bulgaria (1977: 58). An example of this type of singing is provided on the CD, Track 7. Although in three parts, the polyphonic examples found by Rice are not based on triadic verticals. Dora Hristova states that three- and four-voice textures are atypical in Bulgarian traditional polyphony, and if encountered in folk song collections, they should be viewed as exceptions (2007: 49).

   Traditional polyphony played a crucial role in the development of contemporary Bulgarian harmony. Drones became the invisible background structure of most complex harmonic progressions. This is why I repeatedly reference the drone types in the following chapters devoted to the harmony and analysis of different repertoires.

Chapter 4
Chordal Vocabulary and Primary Characteristics of the Bulgarian Harmonic Style

In order to explain the different stages of development of Bulgarian harmony, I will discuss in detail the foundational harmonic framework for each scale. From the viewpoint of harmony in the post-World War II repertoire, a different system of scale organization is required to accurately describe the expanding harmonic practice. I propose an alternative system for scale categorization that groups all scales into two primary categories, major and minor, based on the foundational tonic triads. For each of the scales in the primary categories, I will list the basic chordal vocabulary, common cadences, and preferred tonal areas for tonicization and modulation. Although the idea of a classification system based on foundational tonic triads is a novel approach to understanding harmonized Bulgarian folk music, similar systems of scale categorization have already been applied to repertoires from other musical cultures.[1] In harmonized Bulgarian folk music, certain scales or modes, such as Aeolian and Phrygian, frequently mix together, producing polymodes. Other scales often interchange, such as Ionian and makam Hicaz, resulting in different levels of melodic and harmonic intensity. In all observed cases of polymodality or interchange, all scales or modes involved share the same quality of their foundational tonic triads, major or minor.

The classification below focuses on the most commonly used scales found in the repertoire analyzed in this study.[2] This classification system should not be considered an attempt to explain all multi-voice Bulgarian repertoires. Rather, the present system highlights the standard harmonic patterns commonly observed in the three styles analyzed. This chapter provides the reader with essential information to understand Bulgarian harmony as a preparation for the subsequent analysis of repertoire.

---

[1] For more information, refer to Bárdos (1978).
[2] Although extremely rare, some of the historically obsolete scales and modes might surface in the middle of performances, often taking accompanists by surprise.

The Major Scale Category

I group all scale collections (diatonic modes, makams, and polymodes) that generate a major triad from scale degrees $\hat{1}$, $\hat{3}$, and $\hat{5}$ into a category labeled "the major scale category." In practice, Bulgarian instrumental melodies and songs frequently involve combinations of scales where the common denominator is the foundational tonic triad. For example, Ionian and Hicaz are often used interchangeably in wedding-style improvisations; therefore, the two scales should be grouped together. The major scale category also includes scales whose finalis is not scale degree $\hat{1}$. Despite that, I will list these scales as major scales, since their tonic triads are major.

Ionian (Natural Major)

Ionian mode in Bulgarian music is the same as natural major in the Western tradition (Example 4.1) and is a common collection for songs and instrumental melodies throughout Bulgaria.

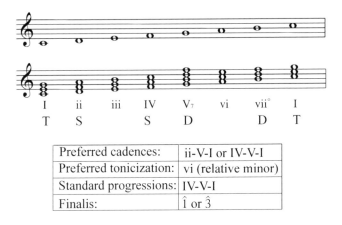

Preferred cadences:	ii-V-I or IV-V-I
Preferred tonicization:	vi (relative minor)
Standard progressions:	IV-V-I
Finalis:	$\hat{1}$ or $\hat{3}$

Example 4.1   Ionian mode

Example 4.1 illustrates that the harmonic vocabulary in Ionian is completely parallel to standard Western practice, with the exception of preferring the tonicization of vi.

A number of examples in Ionian use scale degree $\hat{3}$ as finalis due to the perception of the top line (i.e. parallel thirds above the lower melody) as the primary melody. The scale classification system established by Bulgarian scholarship would define a major scale with finalis $\hat{3}$ as Phrygian due to its finalis and its final melodic descent $\hat{3}$-$\hat{2}$-$\hat{1}$ (Example 4.2, final three measures).

Example 4.2   Padnala e Tŭmna Mŭgla, excerpt from a Thracian wedding song from the repertoire of Dimitŭr Bogdanov

However, the harmonic accompaniment of this particular song is in C Ionian and the tonic triad is located a major third below its finalis. If a parallel voice is added to Bogdanov's song, it would be a third below, following the pitch collection of C Ionian. Harmonizations of Phrygian songs with Ionian chordal vocabulary are typical for the region of Pirin[3] and the neighboring country of Macedonia.

Mixolydian

While used throughout the country, Mixolydian is a typical scale for the folk music of Northeastern Bulgaria and especially the region of Dobrudzha (Map 4.1).

---

3   See Map 4.7.

Map 4.1   The region of Dobrudzha

Example 4.3 lists the basic chordal vocabulary in Mixolydian, which is easily distinguished from Ionian by its minor dominant and major VII.

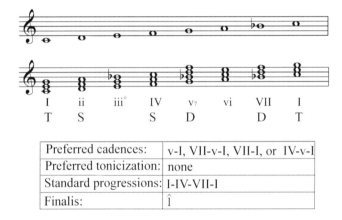

Preferred cadences:	v-I, VII-v-I, VII-I, or IV-v-I
Preferred tonicization:	none
Standard progressions:	I-IV-VII-I
Finalis:	$\hat{1}$

Example 4.3   Mixolydian mode

Rare examples in Mixolydian mode could have scale degree $\hat{3}$ as finalis. Similar to Ionian, as described above, this may result from the perception of the top line as the primary melody. While the top line of Ionian would be in Phrygian, the top line of Mixolydian would be in Locrian, a mode that was not used in musical practice according to Western music theory. As previously stated, in Bulgarian folk music, some of the "obsolete" modes have found unusual paths into modern harmonized repertoires. In the rare cases of songs in Locrian, these examples have subordinated themselves to Mixolydian chordal progressions in order to survive.

Major Polymode #1

Bulgarian musicians have developed scales which fall in the major scale category and have no equivalent in existing Turkish, Western, or modal musical systems. These scales can be described as polymodes comprised of diatonic modes, and they incorporate variable scale degrees. The first of these collections involves the characteristic intervals of Mixolydian (flat 7th), Lydian (raised 4th), and permanently raised scale degree $\hat{2}$. There are two main species of this scale. The first species, which does not involve variable scale degrees, is one of the most common collections found in pre-composed solos and improvisations in wedding music. This scale and its two species are excluded from current studies by Bulgarian scholars (Example 4.4).

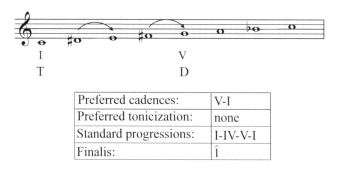

Preferred cadences:	V-I
Preferred tonicization:	none
Standard progressions:	I-IV-V-I
Finalis:	$\hat{1}$

Example 4.4   Improvisatory major polymode #1

The scale in Example 4.4 is accompanied by a limited chordal vocabulary usually reduced to I-♯IV– V₇. The raised 4th scale degree is taken into consideration only in the progression I-I₆-♯IV-vii°/V-V-V⁶₅-i.

Major Polymode #2

Polymode #2 is the second species of the scale discussed above (polymode #1). Polymode #2 is extremely popular in the music of the ethnic Vlachs from Northwestern Bulgaria (Map 4.2).

Map 4.2   The region of Bulgaria with Vlach population

This scale includes a variable 7th scale degree (Mixolydian/Ionian). In ascending motion, the raised 7th scale degree acts as a leading tone, while in descending motion musicians prefer the flat 7th scale degree.

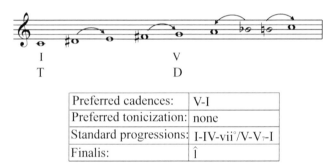

Preferred cadences:	V-I
Preferred tonicization:	none
Standard progressions:	I-IV-vii°/V-V₇-I
Finalis:	$\hat{1}$

Example 4.5   Major polymode #2 (Vlach)

The scale seen in Example 4.5 is also present in wedding-style kolyanos and improvisations.

Major Polymode #3

This scale is typical in music from Thrace (Map 4.3). It can be considered the most preferred major scale for improvisation in wedding and village music, as it allows circular motivic motion around stable scale degrees. In this major polymode, all but scale degrees $\hat{1}$, $\hat{3}$, and $\hat{5}$ are variable.

Map 4.3   The region of Thrace

The variable scale degrees in this collection are used similarly to microtones in the Turkish makam system (Chapter 3). For example, raised scale degrees are preferred for ascents, and flat or natural for descending motion (Example 4.6).

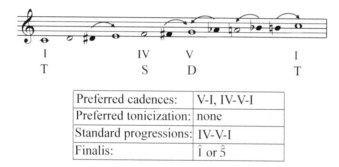

Preferred cadences:	V-I, IV-V-I
Preferred tonicization:	none
Standard progressions:	IV-V-I
Finalis:	$\hat{1}$ or $\hat{5}$

Example 4.6   Major polymode #3 as found in wedding music

In ascending melodic motion, raised scale degrees act as leading tones to stable scale degrees, contributing to the momentum of the musical line. According to Steve Larson's studies of musical forces, half-steps create musical magnetism and pull towards a stable scale degree (2004: 461). At the same time, from the viewpoint of an improviser, this scale is a combination of several scales, allowing a soloist to modulate melodically between E minor, F major, G major, or G minor while the tonic remains centered on C. With respect to harmony, however, all major scales and polymodes described up to this point except Mixolydian are harmonized with the primary triads of Ionian. Another interesting conclusion emerges from analysis of wedding-style improvisations where major polymodes are the norm: the more complex the major polymode, the less complex the supporting chord progressions.

Shope Major

In the region of Western Bulgaria known as the Shope region (Map 4.4), a different major scale is widely used.

Map 4.4   The Shope region

Because of the highly localized use of this collection, this scale is not present in the classification of Bulgarian scholars and, therefore, a new name and classification is suggested as part of this study. Once again, this is due to the fact that Bulgarian scholarship classifies scales on the basis of their finalis and does not take harmony into consideration. Example 4.7 illustrates the Shope major scale, which, according to its finalis and final descent, should be classified as Dorian or Aeolian under the traditional approach.

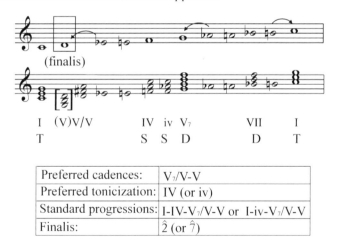

Preferred cadences:	V_7/V-V
Preferred tonicization:	IV (or iv)
Standard progressions:	I-IV-V_7/V-V or I-iv-V_7/V-V
Finalis:	$\hat{2}$ (or $\hat{7}$)

Example 4.7   Shope major scale

This scale is one of the most difficult to classify. It stems from the inclusion of a drone a fifth below the finalis. Because the finalis is scale degree $\hat{2}$, the drone a fifth below the finalis can be considered a permanent dominant pedal. The most intricate characteristic of this type of drone, and the harmony based on it, is that the dominant (major triad) never resolves to tonic. Most of the harmonizations in this scale have a looping effect of the type I-iv-V₇/V-V due to repeating half cadences.[4]

Similar to the Ionian and Hicaz collections, the Shope major scale allows for an added voice a third away from the main melodic line. While in Ionian and Hicaz the parallel voice is a third above (with scale degree $\hat{3}$ as the finalis), in Shope major the parallel voice is a third below the main melody (with scale degree $\hat{7}$ as the finalis).

Even though Bulgarian musicians do not have terminology for discussing harmonic progressions, they have developed a term for harmonizations in this particular scale. The commonly used term is *Shopska harmoniya* (Shope harmony), and it implies that the final triad is constructed downwards. This approach to chord building is opposite to any other scale found in Bulgarian music, which is perhaps the primary reason that musicians have generated a specific term for it. Shope harmony reaches far beyond the Shope region of Bulgaria; it is also one of the primary chord derivation approaches found in the folk music of neighboring Serbia. According to Bartók (1976: 191):

> As a general characteristic of about half of the Yugoslav melodies must be mentioned the so-called imperfect [half] cadences at the end of the melodies. To Western European ears it seems as if these melodies end on the dominant. ... As mentioned before, these imperfect cadences at the end of melodies are widespread among the Bulgarians, too. They occur less frequently among the Western and Northern Slavs, and among the Hungarians they are quite unknown. A remarkable fact must be mentioned: in the very old Yugoslavian melodies connected with traditional ceremonies, this kind of final cadence is not to be found. In some ways, the melodies with the final imperfect cadence have a modern character.

As it will become evident in Chapter 5, at the time when Bartók wrote his essay (1942), Shope harmony was also a preferred ("modern") approach to harmonizations in Bulgaria.

Makam Hicaz

Makam Hicaz is a widely popular scale in Bulgarian music. Versions of Hicaz are also found in Macedonia, Serbia, Romania, Greece, Turkey, and the Middle East. In his essays, Bartók refers to Hicaz as "the oriental scale" (1976: 191). Bulgarian Hicaz does not use microtones. Hicaz is the most widely distributed makam in

---

[4]   A half cadence is an inconclusive cadence on the dominant.

Bulgaria and can be observed in the majority of the repertoire analyzed in this book (Example 4.8).

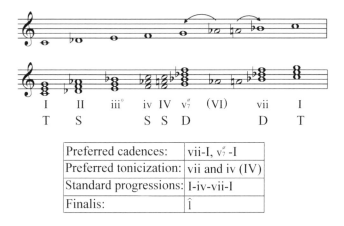

	I	II	iii°	iv IV	v⁷ᵍ	(VI)	vii	I
	T	S		S S	D		D	T

Preferred cadences:	vii-I, v⁷ᵍ -I
Preferred tonicization:	vii and iv (IV)
Standard progressions:	I-iv-vii-I
Finalis:	î

Example 4.8   Makam Hicaz

The preference for a final cadence of vii-I could be related to the drone tradition (î-ŷ [subtonic]-î). A half-diminished dominant is extremely difficult to play on accordions and tamburas (the primary accompanying instruments prior to the 1970s). This is another possible reason that the final cadence vii-I is preferred.

Hicaz harmonizations involve a chord which is not included in the chordal vocabulary listed in Example 4.8. This chord lies a tritone away from the tonic and is frequently used as a subdominant. In wedding music repertoire from the late 1970s and 1980s, this chord is followed by a half-diminished dominant built on the 5th scale degree. In C Hicaz, seen in Example 4.8, this chord would be an F♯ (G♭) or F♯7 (G♭7) followed by a G7 half-diminished. During the socialist period, Bulgarian musicians used this chord with caution because, from the viewpoint of socialist censorship, it implied a Turkish influence. Ironically, this chord does not exist in Turkish music. Similar caution was applied to the use of 7th chords built on the 2nd scale degree. Reminiscent of these prohibitions, even today Bulgarian musicians continue to avoid these chords in official contexts such as concerts, festivals, television shows, and recording sessions.

Harmonizations in Bulgarian Hicaz differ from those in other countries. According to Peter Manuel (1989: 78):

> Hicaz-type scales are generally harmonized in ways similar to those employed
> in Andalusian harmony. The major chord on the flat second degree functions
> essentially as a dominant, with the minor chord on the flat seventh degree as an

important lower neighbor. The minor iv chord serves as an important secondary tonal center, paralleling the importance of that pitch in the makam Hicaz itself.

Similar to Manuel's observations, in Bulgarian music iv has the important role of a secondary tonal center. The functional organization of the triads surrounding the tonic is different than that observed by Manuel. In Bulgarian music the II is used as a predominant and avoided as a penultimate chord in cadences; vii and $v_7^{\sharp}$ are used as dominants.

From a jazz studies perspective, Hicaz may be classified as the "fifth mode harmonic minor." An alternative scale name could also be hypoharmonic minor, i.e. a harmonic minor with the upper tetrachord shifted down an octave. From a Western music theory perspective, Hicaz can also be perceived as a permanent dominant pedal in harmonic minor starting on scale degree $\hat{5}$. If compared to harmonic minor, however, Bulgarian Hicaz chord progressions illustrate several phenomena which are strictly prohibited in Western common practice theory. These are retrogressions, augmented seconds, or ending on the leading tone (scale degree $\hat{7}$ in harmonic minor is scale degree $\hat{3}$ for Hicaz). Example 4.9 compares the Roman numerals of Hicaz to these of harmonic minor.

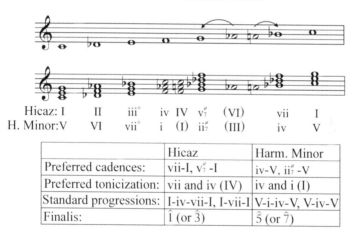

| Hicaz: I | II | iii° | iv IV | $v_7^{\sharp}$ | (VI) | vii | I |
| H. Minor: V | VI | vii° | i (I) | ii$_7^{\sharp}$ | (III) | iv | V |

	Hicaz	Harm. Minor
Preferred cadences:	vii-I, $v_7^{\sharp}$ -I	iv-V, ii$_7^{\sharp}$ -V
Preferred tonicization:	vii and iv (IV)	iv and i (I)
Standard progressions:	I-iv-vii-I, I-vii-I	V-i-iv-V, V-iv-V
Finalis:	$\hat{1}$ (or $\hat{3}$)	$\hat{5}$ (or $\hat{7}$)

Example 4.9   Chordal vocabulary in makam Hicaz compared to harmonic minor

As a person, who teaches Western tonal theory to undergraduate students and plays Bulgarian Hicaz melodies outside of the theory classroom, I have attempted numerous times to adapt Western harmonic minor progressions to Bulgarian Hicaz melodies. Theoretically, this should have been possible considering that Hicaz and harmonic minor share the same pitch collection. Contrary to my initial projections, all my efforts in this direction have been highly unsuccessful. In my opinion, this is due to the reversed harmonic logic of Hicaz, which prevents any successful hybridization with harmonic minor progressions. Furthermore, I began to realize that a significant portion of the rules taught in Western music theory prevent Western harmonic minor from becoming makam Hicaz.[5] Surprisingly, an examination of the Hicaz chordal vocabulary from a harmonic minor perspective provides possible explanations for some "exotic" chords found in makam Hicaz. The first pair of such chords is the F♯ (G♭) and F♯7 (G♭7) mentioned above, which in harmonic minor are labeled as Neapolitan chords. A second pair is built on the 2nd scale degree. In C Hicaz, such chords would consist of the pitches D♭-F-A♭-C♭ and D♭-F-G-C♭. In Western tonal harmony, these chords are labeled as German and French augmented 6th chords (spelled with B instead of C♭). I find it remarkable that Western music theory devotes a significant amount of time in the theory classroom to discussing the proper use of the Neapolitan and augmented 6th chords, and the Bulgarian socialist censorship targeted the same chords in Bulgarian harmonized folk music.

Minor Scales

The minor scales in Bulgarian folk music are more complex compared to the major collections. This is a result of frequent polymodality. The following classification is an attempt to group all minor scales into practical categories. Common characteristics in all minor scales are a preference for plagal over authentic cadences and tonicizations of the relative major.

Aeolian (Natural Minor)

Aeolian in its pure form is present in all styles of Bulgarian music; however, it is more frequently blended with other diatonic modes (polymodes). In Aeolian the dominant (v) chord is minor and the preferred cadences are predominantly plagal iv-i or IV-iv-i (Example 4.10).

---

[5]   A basic T-D-T progression in Hicaz (I-vii-I) from a Western music theory perspective is considered a retrogression (V-iv-V) that also contains a restricted linear augmented second, the defining interval of Hicaz.

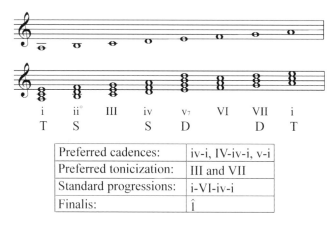

Preferred cadences:	iv-i, IV-iv-i, v-i
Preferred tonicization:	III and VII
Standard progressions:	i-VI-iv-i
Finalis:	$\hat{1}$

Example 4.10   Aeolian mode

From a Schenkerian perspective, progressions excluding dominants are considered examples of tonic prolongation. In Bulgarian folk music, the concept of tonic prolongation parallels the concept of a steady drone on tonic. If a song in Aeolian involves tonicizations of III or VII, these tonicizations would parallel the two main types of variable drone found in Bulgarian traditional polyphony ($\hat{3}$-$\hat{1}$ and $\hat{1}$-$\hat{7}$-$\hat{1}$).

Harmonic Minor (Makam Sultani Yegah)

Harmonic minor is a typical scale for Northern Bulgarian music. It is one of the two minor scales that involve a Western V_7-i cadence (Example 4.11). As previously stated, Bulgarian harmonic minor is identical to the Turkish makam Sultani Yegah without microtones.

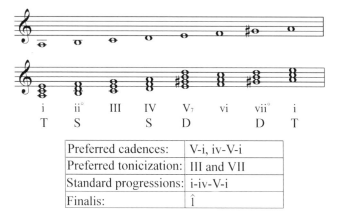

Preferred cadences:	V-i, iv-V-i
Preferred tonicization:	III and VII
Standard progressions:	i-iv-V-i
Finalis:	$\hat{1}$

Example 4.11   Harmonic minor

Phrygian

The Phrygian scale (Example 4.12) is typically found in music from the regions of Thrace and Strandzha (Southeastern Bulgaria; Map 4.5).

Map 4.5   The regions of Thrace and Strandzha

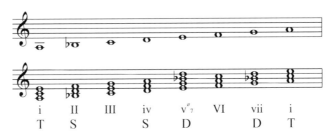

Example 4.12   Phrygian scale

After World War II, Phrygian was gradually displaced by polymodes. Phrygian is difficult to harmonize, as the lowered 2nd scale degree restricts tonicizations of III or VII. The most typical Phrygian cadence is II-vii-i.[6] As will become evident in the chapters devoted to the analysis of harmonized repertoire, accompanists often struggle with harmonizations in this particular scale.

---

[6]   In this book, I define the typical Bulgarian cadence in Phrygian mode, vii-i, II-vii-I, as well as the atypical but still used II-i cadence as Phrygian cadences. This departs from the standard meaning used in Western music theory (a half cadence iv_6-V in minor).

Minor Polymode #1: Aeolian and Phrygian (Variable 2nd Scale Degree)

One of the most widely distributed minor scales in Bulgaria is the combined Aeolian/Phrygian collection with a variable 2nd scale degree. As previously suggested, the variable degree could be a remnant of a microtonal inflection between a major and minor second. Today, a scale with a half-flat 2nd scale degree still exists in Southeastern Bulgaria (Strandzha region).

In this polymode, the raised 2nd scale degree acts as a leading tone in the tonicization of the relative major. This is a standard harmonic modulation present in thousands of Bulgarian songs and instrumental pieces in this polymode. The raised 2nd scale degree allows musicians and arrangers to harmonize the greater portion of these songs and melodies in the relative major to the point that ♭2 implies a return to the minor tonic (Example 4.13).

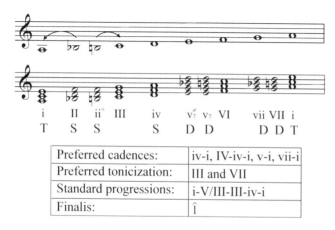

Preferred cadences:	iv-i, IV-iv-i, v-i, vii-i
Preferred tonicization:	III and VII
Standard progressions:	i-V/III-III-iv-i
Finalis:	$\hat{1}$

Example 4.13   Minor polymode #1 (Aeolian/Phrygian)

The most typical harmonic framework for this type of polymode is the juxtaposition of relative major and tonic as tonal areas. The juxtaposition can occur within one measure or over a 3–4 minute-long performance of a slow, free-rhythm melody.

Minor Polymode #2: Aeolian, Phrygian, and Makam Karcigar (Variable Scale Degrees $\hat{2}$ and $\hat{5}$)

This collection incorporates two variable scale degrees, $\hat{2}$ (Phrygian/Aeolian from above) and $\hat{5}$ (Makam Karcigar/Aeolian) (Example 4.14).

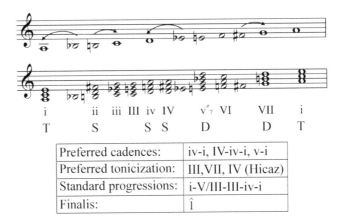

Preferred cadences:	iv-i, IV-iv-i, v-i
Preferred tonicization:	III,VII, IV (Hicaz)
Standard progressions:	i-V/III-III-iv-i
Finalis:	$\hat{1}$

Example 4.14   Minor polymode #2 (Aeolian/Phrygian/Makam Karcigar)

The lowered 5th and raised 6th scale degrees can be considered part of Makam Karcigar (Example 4.15).

Makam Karcigar

Example 4.15   Makam Karcigar

However, if the raised 6th scale degree is not paired with a flat fifth, the scale could be considered Dorian.

As in the Aeolian/Phrygian polymode, the raised 2nd scale degree assists in modulation to the relative major, III, while the flat 5th and raised 6th scale degrees create a tetrachord of Hicaz starting on scale degree $\hat{4}$. As a result, the typical tonicizations are III and IV Hicaz. The harmonic transition from Hicaz on scale degree $\hat{4}$ to the tonic is accomplished by a plagal cadence (IV-iv-i).[7] Tonicization of VII, stemming from the $\hat{1}$-$\hat{7}$-$\hat{1}$ drone tradition, is also possible, since the 6th scale degree is the third of V/VII and therefore serves as a leading tone in tonicization of VII.

---

[7]   A plagal cadence is the cadence IV-I (iv-i in minor). A typical Bulgarian plagal cadence includes major subdominant (IV) followed by a minor subdominant (iv) and tonic (i or I).

Minor Polymode #3: Variable Scale Degrees $\hat{2}$, $\hat{5}$, and $\hat{6}$

Similar to the major polymode #3 with variable $\hat{2}$, $\hat{4}$, $\hat{6}$, and $\hat{7}$ scale degrees,[8] there is an equivalent minor polymode that combines all diatonic modes. It includes a variable $\hat{2}$ (Phrygian/Aeolian), $\hat{5}$ (Makam Karcigar/Aeolian), and $\hat{6}$ (Makam Karcigar/Aeolian/Dorian) scale degrees (Example 4.16).

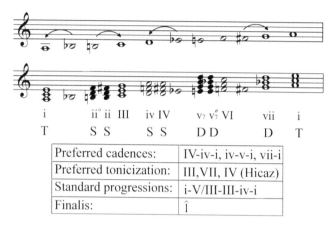

Preferred cadences:	IV-iv-i, iv-v-i, vii-i
Preferred tonicization:	III,VII, IV (Hicaz)
Standard progressions:	i-V/III-III-iv-i
Finalis:	$\hat{1}$

Example 4.16   Minor polymode #3: variable scale degrees $\hat{2}$, $\hat{5}$, and $\hat{6}$

The chordal vocabulary in this scale involves more chords than the previous minor collections. Its variable nature likely contributes to its popularity among certain musical traditions such as wedding music, since it allows for an extended harmonic vocabulary.

Minor Pentatonic Collections

Minor pentatonic scales (Example 4.17) are typical of the music of the Rhodope region in Southern Bulgaria (Map 4.6). The natural 7th scale degree and the minor tonic triad imply an Aeolian mode for the accompanists and the arrangers. In most harmonizations of minor pentatonic the "missing" pitches of the scale are considered implied.

---

[8]   See Example 4.6.

Map 4.6   The Rhodope region

Preferred cadences:	iv-i, VI-iv-i
Preferred tonicization:	III, VII
Standard progressions:	i-V/III-III-iv-i
Finalis:	$\hat{1}$

Example 4.17   Minor anhemitonic pentatonic

The harmonic vocabulary is that of Aeolian with the most likely tonicizations of III and VII. In the obrabotki repertoire, however, there are pentatonic examples harmonized only with verticals derived from the pitches of the pentatonic scales. During socialism, composers were encouraged to limit their harmonic vocabulary to verticals strictly derived from the scale of the original songs which served as the source for obrabotki.

Makam Mustear

Makam Mustear, with its characteristic inflection of a raised fourth, is typical for wedding music and the music of the Bulgarian Vlachs. Mustear is one of the two minor scales harmonized with a major-minor 7th chord on the 5th scale degree. Even though the 7th scale degree is a subtonic, Mustear is harmonized with a major V (Example 4.18).

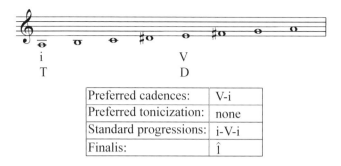

Preferred cadences:	V-i
Preferred tonicization:	none
Standard progressions:	i-V-i
Finalis:	$\hat{1}$

Example 4.18   Makam Mustear

Abrashev has written "No!" above an example with a V-i cadence in Mustear (Abrashev 1995: 59).[9] Contrary to his idea to avoid an authentic cadence, Bulgarian musicians employ a Western V₇ chord in Mustear cadences. My observations of the repertoire support this and confirm that the V-i cadence in Mustear is the most preferred, despite the minor v suggested by the pitch collection, the overall Bulgarian preferences towards plagal cadences, and the exclusion of dominant 7th chords from final cadences.

The only study of modal harmony in Eastern European music—"Modal Harmony in Andalusian, Eastern European, and Turkish Syncretic Musics" by Peter Manuel—provides different names for makam Mustear and its versions (1989: 78):

> Another common scale throughout much of the area in consideration here has the following structure: D E F G♯ A B C D. Slobin (1980: 314–17) and Beregovski (1967: 549–59) have summarized some aspects of the distribution of this scale throughout Eastern Europe, noting that it is common in Rumania (especially Moldavia), the Ukraine, and in traditional Yiddish folksong (the scale also forms the basis of the Turkish makam Nikriz, although that mode differs in its characteristic melodic patterns.) We shall note further uses of this scale below. Scholars have variously labeled the scale 'Ukranian Doric' (Idelsohn 1967: 185) and 'altered Dorian' (Beregovski 1967: 549ff); Greek and Yiddish musicians, meanwhile, refer to it as piraiotiko minore and misheberakh, respectively.

Besides the observations above, Manuel does not adequately explain how this scale is harmonized in the geographical areas he observed.

---

[9]   See Example 2.2 in Chapter 2.

Scales with Two Possible Tonics (Major and Minor)

I have provided several transcriptions and harmonizations of the song *Katerino Mome Sevda Golema* (Katerina, My Great Love), which illustrates a harmonic ambiguity caused by two different drones. The tambura accompaniment provides a drone a fifth below the finalis.

Example 4.19   Katerino Mome, tambura part

Although the drone a fifth below the finalis is very typical for music in the Pirin region of Southwestern Bulgaria (Map 4.7), due to the construction of the tambura (three strings tuned in fifths), the drone illustrated in Example 4.19 is often combined with a second drone on the finalis.

Map 4.7   The Pirin region

Performed in this manner, the drone from Example 4.19 implies B major as the scale with the melody ending on scale degree $\hat{5}$.

The vocal part, however, uses a variable drone of the type $\hat{1}$-$\hat{7}$-$\hat{1}$ where $\hat{1}$ (F♯) is the finalis. If performed without the tambura accompaniment, the vocal diaphony suggests F♯ as the tonal center and F♯ Aeolian as the mode (Example 4.20).

Example 4.20   Katerino Mome, vocal part

If the F♯ drone is maintained, the following basic harmonization can be applied in F♯ Aeolian.

Example 4.21   Katerino Mome harmonized in F♯ Aeolian

As seen in the Example 4.21, this harmonization follows a standard Aeolian harmonic progression involving a v-i cadence. A cadence of this type can be easily substituted with plagal cadences such as iv-i or IV-iv-i.

Example 4.22 presents a possible harmonization in B major, the second tonic suggested by the tambura part.

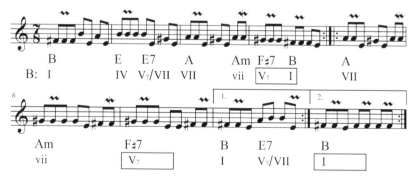

Example 4.22   Katerino Mome harmonized in B major

The functional logic of the two harmonizations is quite similar. It involves tonicizations of VII surrounded by primary chords in the main key, either B major or F♯ minor. Although both harmonizations sound aesthetically pleasing to experienced listeners, the B major example is more "appropriate" from the standpoint of harmonic rhythm.[10] However, due to the inconclusive sound of the final cadences in the B major harmonization, in recent decades performers typically prefer harmonizations in Aeolian (Example 4.21), which in this case is F♯ minor.

Shope Major or Aeolian?

The Shope major scale, with a finalis on scale degree $\hat{2}$, introduced a significant harmonic dilemma for Bulgarian accompanists, arrangers, and composers. As a scale, it stems from the tradition of a drone a fifth below the finalis. As previously explained, harmonizations in Shope major commonly conclude with a half cadence of the type V₇/V-V, which never resolves to the tonic. The melody shown in Example 4.23 can be harmonized with the chordal vocabularies of Shope major or Aeolian. The kolyano is from a Shope dance tune often heard in compositions based on Shope motives. The name Shope itself anticipates which harmonization and tonic would be more appropriate. Besides the regional characteristics and preferences for tonic, the ultimate determining factor for accompanists is the harmonic rhythm. Example 4.23 is harmonized in Aeolian from F♯, the finalis.

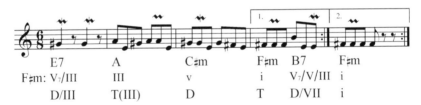

	E7	A	C♯m	F♯m	B7	F♯m
F♯m:	V₇/III	III	v	i	V₇/V/III	i
	D/III	T(III)	D	T	D/VII	i

Example 4.23   Shope kolyano harmonization in F♯ Aeolian

The harmonization involves tonicization of the relative major, which is common in Aeolian mode. The final cadence in the example involves a minor dominant, v-i. If C♯ minor (v) is replaced with B minor (iv), the progression would sound more "Bulgarian" due to the preference for plagal cadences previously described. Example 4.24 illustrates a harmonization in E Shope major ending with a half cadence, which is typical in this scale.

---

[10]   The rate at which harmonies change in a piece (e.g. one chord per measure or one chord per beat).

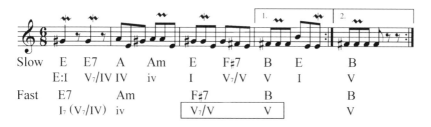

Example 4.24   Shope kolyano harmonization in E major

The harmonization in E Shope major fits the melody more appropriately. In spite of that, however, the finalis, scale degree $\hat{2}$, confuses Bulgarian musicians harmonizing instrumental tunes and songs in Shope major, especially if the melody instruments conclude an entire performance with a kolyano in this scale. From a harmonic standpoint, the entire piece would end on a half cadence. In order to avoid the inclusive effect of Shope major cadences, accompanists often reharmonize final phrases in Aeolian concluding with IV-iv-i or v-i cadence.

According to accompanists (tambura and guitar players) and composers with whom I have worked,[11] the judgment for harmonizations in Shope major or Aeolian depends on practice and experience. Clues can be found in the drop notes of the melody.[12] If the drop notes are a fifth below the finalis, the likely harmonization will be in Shope major. If the drop notes are a fourth below the finalis, the likely harmonization will be in Aeolian.

For the purposes of this book, I will refer to Shope major as a scale ending on scale degree $\hat{2}$ and concluding with half cadences. From a Bulgarian perspective, there is no need for resolution to the tonic chord. If tonic-dominant relationships are not taken into consideration, it can be also suggested that the drone pitch is the tonic and the finalis is scale degree $\hat{5}$. In this case the Roman numerals and functional analyses would be different, yet representative of the harmonic progression (Example 4.25, lower Roman numeral analysis).

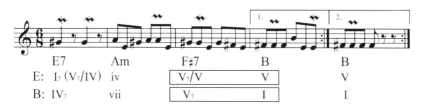

Example 4.25   Shope kolyano with two possible tonics

---

[11]   Stoyan Kostov, Dimitŭr Hristov, Nikolai Baldaranov, and Neshko Neshev.

[12]   Scale degrees $\hat{1}$ and $\hat{5}$ are typically used as drop notes in all scales and modes found in Bulgarian music.

Shope Major Polymodes

I consider the Shope major polymode to be a blend of Shope major and makam Mustear. Melodies using this polymodal collection develop in Shope major first, accompanied by the chordal vocabulary described above, and transition to makam Mustear, which is a minor scale. There are two possible tonics, major and minor respectively, which never appear as part of harmonic resolutions in a Western sense. Example 4.26, a fragment taken from Petŭr Ralchev's Bulgarian Suite, illustrates this issue.

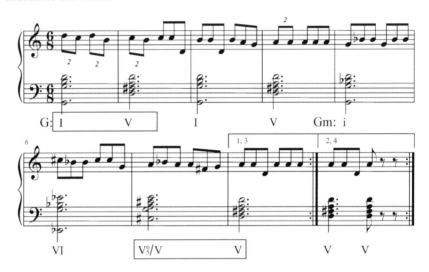

Example 4.26   Excerpt from Petŭr Ralchev's Bulgarian Suite #44

As seen from the example, both G major and G minor triads can be considered tonics. There is an additional issue in another excerpt from Ralchev's piece (Example 4.27).

The scale used in this excerpt is makam Mustear on G ending on scale degree $\hat{2}$. Scale degrees $\hat{1}$-$\hat{3}$-$\hat{5}$ (G-B♭-D) form a minor tonic triad. The final cadences throughout the example are of the type V/V-V with the exception of the last chord, which is V/V. Thinking backwards, however, and accepting the final chord (A) as tonic, the excerpt is reminiscent of a complete Hicaz scale from A (A-B♭-C♯-D-E-F♯-G-A) with a raised 6th scale degree. Moreover, if the accompaniment is reduced and the drop note D (a fifth below the finalis) in m. 90 is changed to E (the drop note for A Hicaz, a fourth below the finalis) a complete satisfactory harmonic progression in Hicaz can be applied. The last observation creates another Shope dilemma: Shope Mustear ending on scale degree $\hat{2}$ or Hicaz with a wrong drop note? Rather than expanding on Shope harmonic dilemmas, I can clarify them with the solution used by accompanists from the oral tradition: they harmonize tunes from the Shope region with V/V-V final cadences, but avoid them while performing music from other regions of the country. Although Shope major and its polymodes are typical for the Shope region of Bulgaria, they occasionally appear in the music of Dobrudzha, the Vlach region, and even Thrace. Final half cadences are also very typical for the music of neighboring Serbia. This is why Bulgarian musicians sometimes refer to Shope-type harmonizations ending on half cadences as "Serbian harmony."

Example 4.27   Excerpt from Petŭr Ralchev's Bulgarian Suite #45

Primary Characteristics of Bulgarian Harmonic Style

American musicians frequently ask me, "What makes Bulgarian harmony sound Bulgarian?" While the question requires a lengthy explanation of scales and chord derivations, there are certain elements that typify the Bulgarian harmonic practice regardless of the scale.

References to the Drone Tradition

The drone tradition of Bulgaria served and continues to serve as the foundation of the harmonic vocabulary. It coexists with harmony and has become a characteristic feature of Bulgarian harmonic style. The primary influences of melody and drone can be seen in the preference for plagal cadences (tonic prolongations) and cadences VII-I versus root motion by fifth.[13] Drones are

---

[13]   According to Schenkerian analysis as part of modern Western music theory, tonal music is driven by dominant (major-minor 7th) chords leading to resolutions at cadences.

still present in Bulgarian music. In wedding music and obrabotki they are not necessarily constant or sustained, but rather pedal voices inserted in harmonic progressions. Even in choral arrangements involving clusters[14] and chords with extended tertian verticals, pedal voices that obscure the harmonic progression are often inserted in the middle of the chordal texture.[15]

Seconds and Clusters

Major and minor seconds and stacks of these intervals are another essential mark of Bulgarian harmony. While a student at the Academy of Music, Dance, and Fine Arts in Plovdiv, Bulgaria I was taught the following chord definition by my theory professor, Dr. Plamen Arabov: "A chord is every vertical sonority of two or more voices which can be extrapolated and distinguished as a separate structural and definable unit" (Arabov 1992: 5–6). In other words, the current Bulgarian definition of chords incorporates diaphony, clusters, and quintal-quartal harmony, i.e. all non-triadic verticals found in Bulgarian harmonized repertoires.

The Bulgarian preference toward seconds and close spacing is rooted in the drone traditions as well. After World War II, musicians and composers appropriated this characteristic. As a result, seconds and clusters became a defining attribute of Bulgarian harmony.

Ambiguous Dominant Function

Harmonized Bulgarian music sounds quite unusual to Western audiences because a significant portion of instrumental melodies and songs do not have the expected Western cadences as conclusive progressions.[16] While touring with Ivo Papazov in 2003, an American musician shared with me that one of our pieces, in Hicaz, sounded to him like an endless dominant pedal in a minor key which never resolved to the tonic. The Bulgarian composer Karastoyanov also refers to Hicaz as an "exotic-harmonic" scale and provides an alternative interpretation of Hicaz as harmonic minor ending on a half cadence (1950: 81). Forty years later, in his book *Obrabotka i Orkestratsia na Bŭlgarskata Narodna Muzika*, Abrashev still elaborates on the possibility of Hicaz being a harmonic minor scale. According to Abrashev (1990: 52–3):

Major-minor 7th chords and their tendencies to resolve cannot be considered the driving force in Bulgarian harmony. The half cadences in Shope major illustrate that point well.

[14]   Clusters are non-triadic chordal verticals (typically stacks of major and minor seconds).

[15]   The incorporation of pedals in village style, wedding music, and obrabotki will be discussed in relation to particular examples in chapters 5–7.

[16]   In Western tonal music, half cadences, deceptive cadences, and authentic cadences are usually placed at the end of phrases or periods.

[W]hich version of Hicaz [harmonic interpretation] we will accept is a theoretical question without much practical application. Still, it is more appropriate to stop [the discussion] on the version of makam Hicaz [with tonic scale degree $\hat{1}$] not only because it is the true, 'lawful' mode of the songs but also because the constant underlining and 'circling around' the dominant of harmonic minor, as well as the dominant ending of the song, makes suspicious the real presence of harmonic minor.

A similar observation to Abrashev's can be made about melodies and songs in Shope major as well.

An analysis of chord progressions in Bulgarian folk music shows that the primary harmonic motion is not driven by a V_7-I(i) relationship. In the first volume of his book, Abrashev states (1990: 47):

> [W]e can conclude that the dominant function is generally foreign to our [Bulgarian] folk music and in many occasions (more specifically in pentatonic and diatonic scales) it should be avoided. Major dominants in the diatonic modes can be used in Ionian, temporary tonicizations, and modulations (it is recommended that the last one of which should be used with caution) …

The lack of major-minor 7th chords in the harmonic vocabulary creates major difficulties for Bulgarian composers using Bulgarian folk music as source material for classical compositions.

Plagal Cadences: Preference for Minor iv

Bulgarian musicians—both classically trained and within the oral tradition—prefer plagal cadences, especially these involving a minor subdominant. Even if the melody implies a Phrygian cadence in minor (due to the flat 2nd scale degree), accompanists often prefer the plagal iv-i instead of the Phrygian vii-i.[17] Abrashev makes the following observations and suggestions regarding the Bulgarian preferences for subdominant chords (1990: 47):

> Contrary to the dominant function, the subdominant is characteristic for melodies in diatonic modes and generally for our [Bulgarian] music. It was noted a long time ago that in most cases plagal chord connections (S-T) have advantages over the authentic (D-T). The plagal sound is an important quality of Bulgarian folk melodies which should be reinforced and brought to the foreground.

---

[17]   All pieces analyzed in this book, which include Phrygian as a scale or a part of a minor polymode, demonstrate the above interchange of cadences.

Tonicizations and Modulations

Most of the examples analyzed in this book that are in minor modes or scales involve tonicizations of the relative major. The following formulas emerge as standard procedures in minor modes and polymodes, regardless of mode and variable scale degrees:

1. Main Minor Key → Relative Major → Main Key
2. Relative Major → Main Minor Key

In addition to the primary tonal plans listed above, Aeolian mode also allows for the tonicization of VII.

1. Main Key →VII → Main Key
2. VII → Main Key

Makam Karcigar, as part of a polymode, also allows tonicization of IV with a Hicaz progression.

1. Main Key → IV (Hicaz) → Main Key
2. IV (Hicaz) → Main Key

In Hicaz the most likely plans for tonicization are:

1. Main Key →VI → Main Key
2. IV (requires a variable 6th scale degree) → Main Key
3. Main Key →iv → Main Key

The rest of the modes, makams, and scales involve tonicizations and modulations on a lesser scale. As will become evident in the following chapters, all the formulas listed above constantly repeat. The musical complexity is not achieved through patterns that are difficult to extrapolate, but rather through a high speed of pattern interchange.

Key Relationship and Music Structure

In Bulgarian music, keys and scales change more often than in Western tonal music. Each kolyano in an instrumental performance can be in a different scale and tonal center. In most examples of Bulgarian instrumental music, there is no overall tonal plan. Each new scale brings its own harmonic vocabulary, typical cadences, and standard progressions. On the other hand, tonal plans are found in songs with strophic structure and obrabotki.[18]

---

[18]   Tonal plans of choral arrangements are discussed in Chapter 7.

Harmonizing Bulgarian Music

Performing contexts and audience preferences are the two main factors determining the types of harmonization. For example, the same musicians would perform the same tune radically differently at a concert versus an event involving dancers.

Harmony–Dance Relationship

In Bulgarian music, dance restricts phrase lengths, phrase manipulations, and rhythm to a great extent. The same phenomenon is observed in terms of harmonic vocabulary. The music for folk dance ensembles, the wedding music played for dancers, and the folk music played on folk instruments all have simpler harmonic vocabularies than concert music. According to musicians, simpler harmonic vocabulary, regular phrasing, and steady harmonic rhythm all contribute to a better dance experience. While touring with Ivo Papazov and his wedding band, I experienced the differences in style, phrasing, performance, and accompaniment when our band performed for concerts versus dance events. Due to the interactive nature of dance events, wedding musicians gradually lead the dancers into the dance with simpler harmonies; they save challenging harmonic practices until the dancers are stabilized. Musicians observe the competence of the dancers and judge if dancers are able to appreciate higher levels of music complexity.

Interactive Harmonizations

Bulgarian instrumental folk music in the oral tradition is generally improvisatory or semi-improvisatory. Musicians make decisions about harmonic accompaniment and its complexity while live performances are taking place. Prior to a performance, there may be some limited arrangement between soloists and accompanists of what will be played in a set. Accompanists make their harmonic choices as the music goes along, drawing on the formulas listed so far.

The interactive process of harmonization involves several steps. The first involves hearing, anticipating, and identifying the scale, as well as applying a basic (standard) chord progression. The second step focuses on embellishing harmony in phrase repetitions through chord substitutions and proper placement of temporary tonicizations. The third and final step focuses on harmonic variety involving a huge spectrum of tools, from simple drones and pedal harmonies to tritone substitutions,[19] depending on the accompanist's skills and experience with interactive harmonization.

---

[19]   Tritone substitution is used primarily in jazz music. It involves the use of a dominant 7th chord which is a tritone away from the original dominant chord.

Mastering the above principles of harmonic accompaniment takes between 10 and 20 years, depending on the accompanist's musicianship, musical memory, and ability to derive harmonic patterns from oral repertoire. It is noteworthy that harmony in Bulgarian instrumental music is not taught in any music school or academic establishment. The patterns of harmonization described in this chapter, the harmonic vocabulary for each scale, and the skills for accompanying interactively are learned through practice only.

In concert music, the improvisatory elements are reduced to the solo sections. If the pre-composed material has been rehearsed, an accompanist may have a set of progressions to choose from in advance. Regardless of the rehearsals, however, interactive accompanists constantly search for better progressions during performances. In wedding style, for example, it is often impossible to find two identical harmonizations of the same piece. The process of constant invention and reinvention generates variety in harmony and stimulates the creativity of the soloists.

Harmony in Compositions and Arrangements

The process of harmonizing Bulgarian folk music in a non-interactive environment (obrabotki repertoire) follows the same steps as listed above. However, in such a "passive" environment, a composer (or arranger) may produce more eloquent progressions, due to the advantage of multiple repetitions and the lack of an actively participating audience. While each scale offers a colorful palette of chords, progressions, and cadences, composers chose different progressions depending on their musical training, exposure to accompaniments and arrangements, relation to the socialist state, etc.

Expanding the Boundaries: Jazz Harmony

Extended tertian verticals first appeared in choral obrabotki in the 1970s, and entered wedding style and folk music performed on folk instruments about a decade later. After mastering the triadic vocabulary explained in this chapter, both musicians from the oral tradition and classically trained composers began experimenting with listeners' expectations and expanded chordal vocabularies. This direction of harmonic expansion continues to the present day.

In the mid-1990s, wedding-style musicians released recordings with jazz accompanists, and classical composers coming from the folk tradition, such as Georgi Andreev, began incorporating more jazz chords in compositions and obrabotki. I was not aware of the shift in harmonic languages in wedding music until I toured the United States with Ivo Papazov in 2003. While I was fluent in the styles from the 1980s and the early 1990s, I was not able to provide chordal accompaniment in the "free jazz" styles upon which Papazov insisted with his constant remarks "jazz, jazz."[20]

Non-Triadic Harmony and Twentieth-Century Techniques

Since a system for harmonizing Bulgarian folk music was never formalized, many composers took the freedom to experiment with chordal vocabularies different from the ones described thus far. Although these alternative systems were never fully accepted by Bulgarian audiences, certain examples will be presented in the chapters on choral obrabotki as an illustration of this tendency.

A different approach to building chordal vocabularies can be seen in some choral arrangements, where composers experiment with harmonic verticals based on fourths and fifths. Examples of quintal-quartal harmony can be found in the choral arrangements of Krassimir Kyurkchiiski, one of the leading composers of obrabotki seeking unconventional solutions for harmonization and reharmonization.[21] Other composers have also sought unconventional harmonic languages, attempting to distinguish themselves from the core body of arrangers who use conventional triadic harmony.

Another approach to harmony taken by composers and arrangers in the 1980s and 1990s is related to twentieth-century aleatory or chance techniques. The most innovative composer in these styles is Ivan Spasov, whose choral arrangements extend the limits of the harmonic language. During socialism, avant-garde arrangements were discouraged by the socialist censorship due to their contradiction with the ideology that "music should be accessible to the audience." On the other hand, the formulaic sound of hundreds of obrabotki allowed Spasov's innovations to enter the repertoire of world-famous choirs such as Le Mystère des Voix Bulgares.

This chapter is the last one to address general characteristics of Bulgarian harmonic practice. The content of Chapter 4 will serve as a main reference for the following three chapters devoted to the analysis of repertoire. In the subsequent chapters, I take a historical approach, starting from the earliest, simpler examples and moving to the later, more complex ones.

---

[20]   Papazov's Balkan jazz style is illustrated with the piece *Hitŭr Petŭr* (Clever Petŭr) in Chapter 6.

[21]   Reharmonization is a term frequently used in jazz harmony for alternative harmonizations of familiar tunes.

Chapter 5
Harmony and Accompaniment in Village Style

In this chapter I trace the development of harmonic accompaniment in the village music style. I begin my analyses of repertoire with village music because its harmonic vocabulary is simpler than wedding music and choral obrabotki. In addition, the village style developed earlier and served as a foundation for all other styles.

The village style incorporates professional (individuals who earn their livelihood through music) or amateur musicians who participate in bands with regular members or with a random selection of musicians. Most village-style performers have no formal musical training and do not use notation. Accompanists apply chords intuitively and by ear. Since village musicians have no concept of chordal functions and patterns for harmonization, such as IV-V-I or ii-V-I, they frequently have difficulties transposing chord progressions to new keys.

Harmony in Village Music between World War I and World War II

Early examples of village-style accompaniment are limited to two or three primary triads per scale, a transitional stage from drone-based harmony to basic chordal accompaniment. The following musical examples are taken from the compilation CD *Song of the Crooked Dance* (2000), which contains some of the oldest recordings of Bulgarian folk music from 1927 to 1942. The harmonic vocabulary of the examples I have selected is very limited and represents the local musical aesthetics of that time period.

Pristanala Ganka

Pristanala Ganka (Ganka Got Engaged) is a song performed by Masha Byalmustakova (singer) and Radi Angelov's orchestra (CD, Track 8). The song is in D Ionian. Accompaniment is provided by tuba and includes the alternating roots of two chords, tonic and dominant. At this point in the development of harmony in Bulgarian village music, predominant chords were not a part of the harmonic vocabulary. The placement of the dominant bass notes is closely related to the melody. In the instrumental breaks, the rest of the ensemble joins the tubist, playing the melody in parallel thirds, which is characteristic for Bulgarian folk music in Ionian, Hicaz, and Shope major. The meter of the song is $\frac{9}{8}$ (2+2+2+3).

Ya Stani Milke

Ya Stani Milke (Get up Milka) is a song sung by Yordan Bonev and accompanied
by the Bistrishkata Chetvorka (Bistritsa Quartet), one of the first groups to include
the tambura as an accompanying instrument (CD, Track 9). The meter of the
song is $\frac{5}{8}$ (2+3) and the mode is A Aeolian. The tambura player, Deyan Stefanov,
provides interesting (though still very basic) harmonic variety by varying the drone
from scale degree $\hat{1}$ to scale degree $\hat{4}$ (a fifth below the finalis, A), and therefore
anticipating the later confusion with the finalis of this particular scale (Shope
major with finalis scale degree $\hat{2}$ or Aeolian ending on scale degree $\hat{1}$). During the
instrumental breaks between verses, Stefanov uses D as a drone, while during the
song he drones on A. Occasionally, while droning on A, Stefanov plays a D major
triad, "reminding" the audience of the alternative Shope major harmonization of
this scale. Despite the use of some triads, the overall accompaniment of the piece
is primarily in the melody and drone framework.

Plevensko Horo

Plevensko Horo (A Dance from Pleven; CD, Track 10) is a dance tune in $\frac{9}{8}$
(2+2+2+3) performed by *Grupata na Tsvyatko Blagoev* (Tsvyatko Blagoev's
group). Being one of the first recordings of a dance tune in non-microtonal makam
Hicaz, this tune illustrates multiple features of harmonic practice that would later
become standard. First, it uses I-vii-I as the basic harmonic progression in Hicaz.
Second, it illustrates the model of pre-composed melodies followed by solos and
a restatement of the opening material at the end of the piece. Predominant chords
are not present in the accompaniment, although the melody frequently suggests
a predominant iv. While the accompaniment is limited to I-vii-I, one particular
kolyano provides the standard harmonization for Shope major described in
Chapter 4: G-C-A-D (G: I-IV-V/V-V), ending on a half cadence.

   Wedding musicians from later generations often entertained themselves by
joking about the harmonic vocabulary used by the "pioneers" of harmonized
village music. The next recorded selection contains an altered version of the tonic
triad that does not correspond to the mode.

Selska Svatba

Selska Svatba (Village Wedding) is performed by the clarinetist Demir Cholakov
(CD, Track 11). Selska Svatba begins with a traditional wedding song, *Ela Se Vie
Previva* (A Fir Tree Bends and Twists), still performed at Bulgarian weddings
today. On the recording, the harmonic accompaniment is provided by an accordion
and bass. I have provided a transcription of the beginning of the recording, which
gives an idea of the harmonic language used by the musicians (Example 5.1).

Example 5.1   Ela Se Vie Previva

The chord symbols in parentheses indicate the triads played by the accordion when different from the bass. This example clearly illustrates the process of applying chords in the 1930s. The second phrase is an interesting take on the major-minor dilemma described earlier as viewed by accompanists in the 1930s. The scale could be defined either as Shope major on A with finalis scale degree $\hat{2}$ (B) or as B minor polymode with a variable 2nd scale degree, Aeolian/Phrygian. Example 5.1 presents a mixture of both types of harmonization. In the first phrase, mm. 1–12, the bass player has chosen a progression which would later become common practice for the Aeolian/Phrygian polymode, i.e. temporary tonicization of the relative major (D). The chords played by the accordion player for the same excerpt are D-A-E (a Shope major progression IV-V/V-V). The most intriguing point is the final chord, B major. This chord can be interpreted as the accompanist's desire to provide a more conclusive chord built on the finalis. While many accompanists from later decades would experience the same "desire" to resolve the Shope major final half cadences, the question remains unanswered as to why the triad is B major when the scale has a D natural.

After repeating the melody in Example 5.1 twice, the performers continue with a slow, non-metered melody. In the clarinet solo, a clear B minor scale is defined, while the accordion player continues to accompany with a B major triad. This could be due to the fact that accordions in the 1930s were mainly of the type *dvuredki* (button accordions with two rows of buttons), which allowed chordal accompaniment (in the left hand) only with major triads.[1]

In order to see the difference between the harmonization from the 1930s recording and a 1980s accompaniment, I will present the two harmonizations side by side (Example 5.2).

1930s   D   D (A)   A (E)
1980s   D   Em   Bm

            A (E)   D   A
            A7   D   E7

            A
            A

            D   E   A
            D   E   Em

            E   B (tonic)
            Bm (or G)   Em   Bm (tonic)

Example 5.2   Ela Se Vie Previva as harmonized in the 1930s and 1980s

The modern harmonization follows a typical harmonic framework for a song in Aeolian/Phrygian minor polymode as described in Chapter 4. The final cadence (mm. 14–16) in the 1980s harmonization is plagal (IV-iv-i).

In the Shope region and other parts of Western Bulgaria (along the Serbian border), this song may be still harmonized in Shope major following the regional

---

[1]   Modern 120 bass accordions have two vertical rows for playing bass notes (chordal roots), a vertical row with major triads, a vertical row with minor triads, a vertical row with major-minor 7th chords, and a vertical row with diminished 7th chords. The dvuredki had only one vertical row for chordal roots and one with major triads.

harmonic preferences for accompaniment and final half cadences. I have also encountered recordings of a Macedonian version of Ela Se Vie Previva where the song is in Phrygian mode paired with a chordal accompaniment in Ionian, a third below the finalis of the song.

In the summer of 2014, I played at a Macedonian wedding[2] at the Naval Academy in Annapolis, Maryland. Just before the bride and groom exited the church, the moment when we were supposed to perform Ela Se Vie Previva, I said to my colleagues: "Wait a minute, these are Macedonians. The tonic is different. Play the song in Phrygian." From a scholarly perspective it is hard to speculate why ethnic groups give preferences to different tonal centers. Ultimately, the three completely different harmonizations of the same song (in Aeolian, Shope major, or Ionian) that are still applied today contribute to the harmonic variety and further complicate ethnographic questions such as "Whose song is this?"

Village Style Music from the 1950s

Recordings of the famous Bulgarian accordion player, Boris Karlov, from the 1950s illustrate a gradual expansion of the harmonic vocabulary. Most of Karlov's recordings of the early 1950s have two chords per scale, tonic and dominant. During this time period parallel motion in thirds was prevalent. Later in the 1950s, most of his recordings include predominant chords, even in scales such as Hicaz (Example 5.3).

Example 5.3   Pravo Horo by Boris Karlov

The example shows the opening kolyanos of Pravo Horo recorded by Karlov (CD, Track 12). The scale is E Hicaz (E-F-G♯-A-B-C-D-E). Primary triads in this scale are E (T), Am (S), and Dm (D). The chords are placed in an aesthetically

---

[2]   Bulgarian musicians label weddings according to the ethnicity of the wedding parties involved. These designations also imply different repertoires, ways of harmonization, and differences in traditional wedding protocols.

pleasing position corresponding to the melody. The slow harmonic rhythm is characteristic for the accompaniment from this time period.

Analysis of the majority of Karlov's recordings in the compilation CD *Boris Karlov: Legend of the Bulgarian Accordion* (2003) suggests a number of stylistic traits from the 1950s: a correspondence between the primary triads and the mode; a slow harmonic rhythm; and the incorporation of predominant chords in both makams and diatonic modes. In Karlov's style, the harmonic dilemma Shope major-Aeolian is solved with an aesthetic preference for Shope major.[3]

Even nowadays, many bands limit their harmonic vocabulary to primary triads, particularly for dance music. This applies to most American groups performing Bulgarian music as well. Perhaps, this is partially due to Americans' fascination with older layers of Bulgarian music, as described by Mirjana Lausevic in her book *Balkan Fascination: Creating an Alternative Music Culture in America* (2006). Another reason could be a lack of experience and understanding of Bulgarian harmonic practice.

Village Style from the 1960s–1970s

The recording of *Kopanitsa* made by Yves Moreau in March 1970 at a festival in the Sofia region (CD, Track 13) shows that not all accompanists had embraced the newly formed harmonic progressions and vocabularies. Similar to Selska Svatba, the tambura player from the village of Bistritsa (Sofia region) accompanied kolyanos in minor modes with major triads.

Analysis of the harmonic vocabulary, as captured by the field recordings (*Beyond the Mystery*, volumes 1–3) of Yves Moreau from 1966 to 1972 at Bulgarian folk festivals, suggests that in the early 1970s, many of the village ensembles still performed in the traditional melody and drone fashion. The harmonic accompaniment (if any) is reduced to primary triads, and there are examples of chords that are not normally seen in later harmonized repertoire. In summary, the non-professional village music-makers recorded in the *Beyond the Mystery* CD series have not yet adopted the harmonic vocabulary of professional recording artists. Harmonic accompaniment, when added, is basic, or even in disagreement with the melody. Disagreements can be labeled as such only if perceived from a theoretical point of view. From a performer's standpoint, or in the context of village harmonic practice, such "disagreements" may be perceived as fully accurate, and even style-defining harmonic gestures.

---

[3]   Prior to the 1950s, most instrumental pieces in Aeolian were harmonized with Shope major progressions.

Village-Style Music with Ensemble Influence from the 1970s

As Bulgarian harmony developed, many non-professional musicians and accompanists did not extend their accompaniment beyond the traits described above. A natural question arises: who continued the models heard in Karlov's recordings? The answer is that professional musicians associated with state ensembles and national radio extended accompaniments to more complex levels.

Pazardzhishka Kopanitsa

Pazardzhishka Kopanitsa (Kopanitsa dance from Pazardzhik) was performed by the *Trakiiskata Troika* (Thracian Trio), formed by performers of folk instruments who were employed in state ensembles (CD, Track 14). These musicians were professionals, as opposed to village amateurs, and they were exposed to Western models of harmony in orchestral settings. The harmonic accompaniment in this recording is provided by the tambura player Rumen Sirakov. As seen in my transcriptions,[4] kolyanos are labeled as numbers.[5] Rather than analyzing the entire piece, I will select numbers that are representative of Sirakov's chordal vocabulary in particular scales.[6]

Numbers 1–5 are in A Mixolydian, followed by a number in A Hicaz (#6). Numbers 7 and 8 are in F♯ minor, and, to the end of the piece, the subsequent numbers are in A Hicaz. As a piece, Pazardzhishka Kopanitsa is representative of the accompaniment style of Thrace, which has a preference toward plagal cadences.[7] The harmonic vocabulary used by Sirakov is limited when compared to the wedding-style harmonizations of the same period. As seen from the excerpt shown in Example 5.4, the opening number (1) is harmonized with a plagal cadence of the type I-IV-iv-I.

---

[4] Due to their density, the upper ornaments are not written in any of my transcriptions, but are implied between repeated notes. Only lower mordents are indicated in the scores.

[5] This numbering system was adopted in scores and transcriptions of Bulgarian music in the 1950s, and is used currently as well.

[6] Sirakov's style is representative of the interactive accompaniment, as described in Chapter 4.

[7] Depending on the region, there is a difference in the general accompaniment style of the musicians. As mentioned above, plagal cadences predominate in Thrace, and final half cadences are avoided.

Example 5.4   Pazardzhishka Kopanitsa #1

If the plagal cadence is considered a tonic prolongation, the harmonization of the entire kolyano can be reduced to one chord only and even compared to a drone on A. The last two measures (mm. 3–4) from the excerpt illustrate a process that is often observed in harmonizations of Bulgarian folk music: the notes of the melody do not correspond to the chords. In other words, preferences for certain cadences frequently overpower what the melody suggests.

The chordal vocabulary chosen by Sirakov for #1 does not reinforce the Mixolydian mode. In the subsequent number (2), the harmonic progression reinforces the mode in agreement with the melody (Example 5.5).

Example 5.5   Pazardzhishka Kopanitsa #2

The chords characterizing Mixolydian are the minor dominant (v) and VII. In the second kolyano, Sirakov uses both mode-defining chords. The following number (3) features a reharmonization of #1 with characteristic chordal vocabulary for Mixolydian (Example 5.6).

Example 5.6   Pazardzhishka Kopanitsa #3

The natural question of why only #1 is harmonized with a plagal cadence (tonic prolongation), regardless of Mixolydian, is related to the drone tradition. Beginning pieces with a symbolic acknowledgment of the older drone tradition is a characteristic of Bulgarian harmonized music. This symbolic gesture is present in the opening measures of most of the repertoires analyzed in this book.

Example 5.7 summarizes Sirakov's chordal vocabulary in Hicaz, which is restricted to vii and I (dominant and tonic).

Example 5.7   Pazardzhishka Kopanitsa #10

More elaborate harmonizations of Hicaz can be heard in the village style of the 1980s and in wedding music.[8]

In Phrygian on F♯ (kolyano #8), Sirakov does not apply the chords characterizing this mode, ♭II and vii. He replaces the characteristic final Phrygian cadence vii-i with a plagal cadence, iv-i (Example 5.8).

Example 5.8   Pazardzhishka Kopanitsa #8

The temporary tonicization of the relative major is another typical feature of Bulgarian harmony. A natural 2nd scale degree typically assists with the temporary tonicization of the relative major, but in cases such as Example 5.8, where the melody develops in the upper tetrachord, a temporary tonicization of the relative major in Phrygian is also possible.

Krivo Horo

Krivo Horo (Crooked Dance) is a concert tune (CD, Track 15). The term "crooked dance" in Bulgarian has two meanings: a dance in ¹¹⁄₈ (2+2+3+2+2) and a non-danceable tune involving mixed meters. As in the previous piece, Krivo Horo is performed by the Trakiiskata Troika with Sirakov on tambura.

Krivo Horo involves melodies in Hicaz, Ionian, Dorian, and minor polymode with variable 2nd scale degree (Aeolian/Phrygian). The opening numbers are composed in a combined metric group ¹³⁄₈ (2+2+2+2+3+2+2) + ⁹⁄₈ (2+3+2+2)

---

[8]   Refer to the analyses of *Mominska Rŭchenitsa* (Rŭchenitsa Dance of the Unmarried Girl) and Kopanitsa later in this chapter.

balanced by an ending section in a different combined metric group $\frac{7}{8}$ (3+2+2) + $\frac{11}{8}$ (2+2+3+2+2). The middle solo section is in $\frac{13}{8}$. Sirakov's chordal vocabulary in Krivo Horo is similar to that of Pazardzhishka Kopanitsa. The beginning of the tune (#1), in minor polymode with a variable 2nd scale degree, has a short drone reference (Example 5.9) similar to that of #1 in Pazardzhishka Kopanitsa.[9]

Example 5.9   Krivo Horo #1 and 2

Measures 3 and 4 involve an almost chromatic accent, C-C♯-D-E, while E is kept as a pedal voice (drone). D♯ is omitted due to a reference to the drone-type cadence $\hat{7}$- $\hat{1}$.[10] The following number 2 initiates the same melody in Hicaz. Sirakov's accompaniment preserves the opening drone reference for mm. 5–6 while the end of the kolyano is modified to iv-vii-I, a standard Hicaz cadence (S-D-T).

Numbers 4, 5, and 6 are transpositions of 1, 2, and 3 up a perfect fourth. Transposition, another typical feature for Bulgarian music, became a standard practice in obrabotki. In order to achieve variety, the musicians in Trakiiskata Troika have rearranged the transposed numbers as 2-1-3. The chordal vocabulary is expanded and the transposed numbers do not have the drone reference. Sirakov uses standard cadences IV-iv-i for the minor kolyanos with the expected temporary tonicizations of the relative major. The Hicaz kolyanos introduce a new chord, II, in an elaborated version of the standard Hicaz cadences vii-I involving the two predominants, iv-II-vii-I (Example 5.10).

---

[9]   See Example 5.4.

[10]   There are no variable drones in Bulgaria of the type $\hat{1}$-♯$\hat{7}$-$\hat{1}$.

Example 5.10   Krivo Horo #4

Sirakov's harmonic vocabulary in Ionian is limited to the tonic triad. The last number (12) is in A Dorian harmonized with v-i progressions (Example 5.11).

Example 5.11   Krivo Horo #12

Melodies in Dorian are rare in the repertoire and can be traced to ascending melodic motion in minor polymodes. If present, accompanists harmonize them as Aeolian/Phrygian polymodes with final cadences IV-iv-i or v-i.

Village-Style Music with Ensemble Influence from the 1980s

It is difficult to define village-style music from the 1980s. This is a period characterized by the strong influence of wedding music and its expanded harmonic vocabulary. In terms of harmonic accompaniment, the village style and the wedding style are difficult to separate, since most tambura players also played guitars in wedding orchestras. However, as heard in recordings, the village accompaniment from the 1980s more closely follows the aesthetic and harmonic models of ensemble, rather than wedding music.

My selection of examples for analysis from the 1980s includes two recordings of the *Harmanliiskata Troika* (Harmanli Trio) made for the Bulgarian National Radio. The accompanist Stoyan Kostov,[11] a tambura player, currently resides in the United States. In 2005, he explained that the melodies were either composed by the gŭdulka player Dimitŭr Lavchev or assembled from preexisting repertoire. The performances of the Harmanliiskata Troika, like those of the Trakiiskata Troika, cannot be considered pure examples of village music. All of the musicians had professional training and performed in state-sponsored ensembles or wedding bands. Nevertheless, the music-making process in their band resembles the process of creating music and performing in the villages—there is no notation involved, and the harmonization varies from performance to performance.

Mominska Rŭchenitsa

Mominska Rŭchenitsa is a dance tune in ⅞ (2+2+3) beginning with a short introduction (CD, Track 16). The introduction is built on an open-fifth chord, a remnant of the drone tradition (Example 5.12).

The introduction sets the mode of the opening kolyanos, E Phrygian. In the following kolyano, #1, Kostov gradually transitions to a full chordal accompaniment (Example 5.13). As seen in the Roman numeral analysis, the temporary tonicization of III is accomplished with a ii-V₇-I cadence (in G major) in which A minor serves as a pivot chord, if the tonicization is viewed as modulation. The second ending (mm. 9–11) involves an incomplete Phrygian cadence in which D minor (vii) is omitted. As previously mentioned, Phrygian

---

[11] Stoyan Kostov graduated from the Kotel high school of folk music. He obtained a bachelor's degree in tambura performance from the Academy of Music, Dance, and Fine Arts in Plovdiv, Bulgaria.

cadences are generally problematic for accompanists in the oral tradition, who frequently substitute these cadences with v-i or plagal iv-i.

Example 5.12   Mominska Rŭchenitsa, Introduction

Example 5.13   Mominska Rŭchenitsa #1

The second number of Mominska Rŭchenitsa also lacks a complete Phrygian cadence, although the melody suggests such a cadence (Example 5.14).

Example 5.14   Mominska Rŭchenitsa #2, mm. 19–26

Measure 25 includes a chord built on the fifth scale degree with an F♯. A chord corresponding to the scale would be a B diminished triad. Such conflicting verticals are frequently observed among tambura, guitar, and accordion players who are not used to building diminished and half-diminished chords. In the repetition of the phrase, Kostov substitutes his final v-i cadence with a plagal one (Example 5.15).

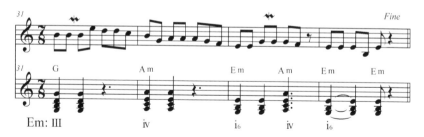

Example 5.15   Mominska Rŭchenitsa #2, mm. 31–34

The variable scale degrees in #2 are $\hat{2}$ and $\hat{5}$. While the 2nd variable scale degree implies the Aeolian/Phrygian polymode typical of Thracian music, flat $\hat{5}$ implies Makam Karcigar or even Locrian. Rather than precisely defining the mode responsible for the lowered 5th scale degree, I suggest an analysis of the harmonic areas in #2. The opening measures are harmonized as an A minor polymode (variable 2nd scale degree), which for the main key of E minor is a temporary tonicization of iv. From this perspective, the first and second phrases tonicize iv and III, the third iv and i, and the last phrase (Example 5.15) closes the kolyanos with a plagal cadence in the main key, E minor.

Number 4 shows another interesting polymode involving variable 2nd, 6th, and 5th scale degrees (Example 5.16). The antecedent phrase ends on a half cadence, while the consequent concludes with a Phrygian vii-i. The final cadence sounds like an extension of the preceding standard plagal cadence IV-iv-i.

Example 5.16   Mominska Rŭchenitsa #4

In numbers in Aeolian, such as #6, Kostov uses cadences of the type iv-v-i (Example 5.17).

Example 5.17   Mominska Rŭchenitsa #6, mm. 64–70

From the observations made on Mominska Rŭchenitsa, Kostov's harmonic preferences in minor modes and polymodes include: v-i or iv-v-i cadences in Aeolian; plagal cadences (iv-i or IV-iv-i) for minor polymodes; tonicizations of relative major (ii/III-V₇/III-III or V/V/III-V/III-III) or iv (v/iv); and occasional Phrygian cadences of the type vii-i.

Kopanitsa

Kopanitsa, a dance tune in $\frac{11}{8}$ (2+2+3+2+2), is also performed by the Harmanliiskata Troika (CD, Track 17). Although the piece melodically sounds quite different than Mominska Rŭchenitsa, Kostov uses a similar harmonic vocabulary.[12] I will focus on several excerpts from my Kopanitsa transcription: the harmony at the beginning of the piece, and certain atypical harmonizations found in the middle of the piece.

The introduction and following kolyano (#1) explore the harmonic ambiguity of Shope major-Aeolian (Example 5.18). The chord played by Kostov (B-E-F♯-B) is unusual for the repertoire outside of obrabotki.[13] As a chord, B-E-F♯-B combines the open fifths of the two possible harmonizations, A (Shope major) or B Aeolian. F♯ and B form a $\hat{1}$- $\hat{5}$ drone supporting F♯ minor as a key center while B and E represent the drone a fifth below the finalis, which later developed in Shope harmony concluding with half cadences.

Example 5.18   Kopanitsa, Introduction and #1, mm. 1–6

---

[12]   According to Kostov, both recordings of the Harmanliiskata Troika were made during the same recording session.

[13]   Quintal-quartal harmony is typical for the choral obrabotki discussed in Chapter 7.

This quintal-quartal harmonic vertical, supported by the gŭdulka part as well, can be interpreted as a challenge for the listener to guess which harmonization (tonal center) will be chosen for the continuation of the piece. In the following number, #2 (mm. 11–14), Kostov clearly states his choice of scale and tonal center as B Aeolian with plagal cadences, which are typical of Thracian music. Rather than stating his key of preference at the beginning of m. 11, Kostov gradually leads the listener to the chosen key with a summary of the cadential vocabulary used later in the piece (Example 5.19). Measure 11 involves a standard plagal cadence in B minor, iv-I; m. 12 involves an embellished version of the same cadence IV-iv-I; and mm. 13–14 a third type of plagal cadence, VI-iv-i.

Example 5.19   Kopanitsa #2

Example 5.20 is illustrative of an expanded version of the tonicization of the relative major in a minor polymode with a variable 2nd scale degree. For the greater part of the kolyano, the melody develops primarily in the relative major and cadences in the main key at the very end.

As the harmonic language developed, soloists and composers modified the melodies according to the harmony. Whereas prior to the 1980s temporary tonicizations of the relative major occurred within one or two measures, during the 1980s tonicization models expanded to several kolyanos in which the last one concluded with a cadence in the main key.

The next excerpt from Kopanitsa involves a typical Western chordal progression in a modal context (Example 5.21).

Example 5.20   Juxtaposition of relative major and main key

Example 5.21   Kopanitsa #7

In mm. 27–28 Kostov employs a typical plagal cadence of the type IV-iv-i. The rest of the kolyano, however, has a progression that does not match the melody, i-VI-iv-v-i. In this context, Kostov and other accompanists think on a larger scale, where the logic of the chordal progression overpowers the conflict between chords and melody. This is a departure from the established "harmony follows melody" model.

Following the traditional approaches of harmonizations, #7 should be harmonized in Shope major (suggested by the drop notes, A). In Example 5.22, I have provided an alternative harmonization of #7 in Shope major, a harmonic possibility not explored by Kostov.

Example 5.22   Alternative harmonization of Kopanitsa #7 in A Shope major

Although in the Shope major harmonization there is a tight relationship between melody and harmony, Kostov favors an Aeolian harmonization (B minor is tonic), as shown in Example 5.21. This four-measure example illustrates a process that in the 1980s divided accompanists and arrangers into two main categories. The first group (like Kostov) consisted of musicians thinking of harmony on a larger scale; for them, melody did not determine each chord. The second group of musicians built their progressions according to a close agreement with the melody.

Two more excerpts from this piece are representative of the 1980s ensemble-influenced village style, and illustrate patterns that can be observed in the rest of the repertoire. Pre-harmonic Bulgarian music involves a rare major-minor polymode[14] that was not mentioned in the scale classification. This polymode occurs within kolyanos in a call-and-response manner, in which pairs of measures in major (Ionian) alternate with the same number of measures in the parallel minor (Aeolian). Polymodes of this type are disliked by contemporary Bulgarian accompanists. Perhaps this was the reason why kolyanos of this type gradually

---

[14]   In one of his 1943 Harvard lectures, Bartók says that "not only different modes can be superposed; the same can be done with the major and minor scale or, to be more exact, with a major and minor pentachord. As a result, we will get a triad with a doubled third; one minor, the other major" (1976: 368).

began to disappear from the repertoire. Today, major-minor kolyanos still exist, and often catch accompanists by surprise. Kostov's harmonic solution in such a situation is illustrated by Example 5.23.

Example 5.23   Kopanitsa #8: A major-minor alternation

Kostov avoids the alternation of major and minor tonic triads by treating C natural in the second and fourth repetitions as an upper neighbor to the fifth of the dominant (E7). This allows him to remain in A major for the entire kolyano.

Occasionally, cotemporary accompanists use the major-minor juxtaposition as a musical joke. Instead of applying creative solutions, such as Kostov's, they exaggerate the major-minor juxtaposition ($\hat{3}$-$\flat\hat{3}$-$\natural\hat{3}$-$\flat\hat{3}$ etc.), "telling" the soloists through the accompaniment that such pre-harmonic kolyanos should be removed from contemporary harmonized repertoire.

The last analyzed excerpt from Kopanitsa is kolyano #9 (Example 5.24). The mode of this kolyano is hard to define since the scale is incomplete. The "missing" 6th and 7th scale degrees, and probably the inertia from the harmonization in #8 (V7-I), has led Kostov to "supply" a G♯ to the scale and harmonize it as A harmonic minor.

Example 5.24   Kopanitsa #9 in harmonic minor

Kolyano #9 can also be harmonized with a minor v chord, yet for variety Kostov inserts a short example of Western harmony (V_5^6-i).[15] The rest of the piece follows the standards for Bulgarian harmony as outlined in Chapter 4.

Village-Style Music with Ensemble and Wedding-Style Influence from the 1990s

In the 1990s, the style of accompaniment in bands of folk instruments followed the models established in the 1980s. Although the socialist regime collapsed in 1989, socialist aesthetics and conventions of ensemble-influenced folk music continued to dominate recorded material. While village music in the rural areas declined, several bands, such as *Bulgari* (Bulgarians) and *Maistori* (Masters), toured successfully in Western Europe and the United States, and continued to release new recordings. Due to the fact that the tambura players in these bands had a strong educational background[16] and expertise in a variety of styles, the harmonic language of their recordings is far more advanced in comparison to the 1980s style of accompaniment.

In order to summarize the harmonic style of the 1990s, I will analyze a piece performed by the band Maistori. Their tambura player, Angel Dimitrov, is one of the most respected tambura players in Bulgaria, a renowned guitar player in the wedding style, and one of the best rock-guitar performers. On the recording, Dimitrov plays a modern eight-string tambura. Compared to his predecessors, Dimitrov's accompaniment is quite enriched in terms of rhythm, bass lines, and chordal vocabulary in each scale.

Vodeno Horo

Vodeno Horo (CD, Track 18) is one of several terms for a line dance in a metric pattern of $\frac{9}{8}$, and typifies the music of Thrace. The melody of Vodeno Horo is composed by Nedyalko Nedyalkov, the kaval player in Maistori. The tonal plan of the piece is A Hicaz, F♯ minor, B minor (solo tambura), F♯ minor (solo gŭdulka), and E Hicaz (solo kaval and concluding kolyano).

The introduction of the piece involves an open fifth chord, a feature observed in examples from previous decades (Example 5.25).

---

[15]   In the Bulgarian modal context, quotations from Western harmony sound "exotic."

[16]   Most tambura players from the 1980s–1990s had a college degree in tambura performance from the Academy of Music, Dance, and Fine Arts in Plovdiv. The Academy's curriculum—both in the past and in the present—does not include classes devoted to harmonizing Bulgarian music. Instead, the focus is on performance, conducting, and Western music theory.

Example 5.25   Vodeno Horo, Introduction

Even Dimitrov, a rock guitar player, starts his accompaniment with a reference to the drone tradition, similar to that of his predecessors. However, a tremendous change in rhythm and accompaniment becomes obvious immediately after the introduction. Dimitrov uses a wide chordal vocabulary and avoids any repetitions of cadences or rhythmic patterns. This is a feature of the late wedding style.

The first kolyano is in A Hicaz. The structure of the kolyano is 5+5 measures, another reference to older layers of Thracian music. Example 5.26 illustrates the first statement of the kolyano.

Example 5.26   Vodeno Horo #1, mm. 5–14

Dimitrov's progression for the first five measures involves a descending bass line I-I$_2^4$-iv$_6$-v" answered by I-I$_2^4$-I-I$_2^4$-iv-II-vii-I. In the next five measures, from the standpoint of Western theory, the antecedent phrase ends on a half cadence, and the consequent with iv-II-vii-I. In the repetition of the kolyano, Dimitrov makes a number of changes (Example 5.27).

Example 5.27   Vodeno Horo #1, mm. 15–24

The stepwise descent to iv₆ is preserved with a different rhythm, while the half cadence in m. 20 is transformed into a leading bass line to the final cadence, II-vii-v⁸₇ -I. From the viewpoint of melody, the harmonic progression is not a perfect match (a trend first observed in Kostov's Kopanitsa). Measures 20–21 imply tonic, m. 22 a predominant iv, and m. 24 a return to tonic. Rather than using the chords implied on strong beats, Dimitrov uses the repeated B♭ in m. 20 as the pitch supporting II, and in m. 21 as a common pitch between II and the two dominants. Furthermore, in m. 23 he uses the D to hold vii instead of supplying a cadence. Dimitrov reserved the remaining two measures for his final cadence. Compared to his predecessors, Dimitrov's preferences for the cadences in Hicaz are v⁸₇-I versus vii-I. This is evident in the following kolyano #2 (Example 5.28). Dimitrov utilizes vii-I as a weaker Hicaz cadence and applies v⁸₇ -I for structurally significant moments, such as his final cadences.

Numbers 1 and 2 repeat as 3 and 4, and the melody remains unchanged. The harmonization, however, not only draws on previously asserted patterns, but it also explores new possibilities. In examples 5.29a and 5.29b, I have layered all four harmonizations of the melody (as #1 and its repetition as #3). Reharmonizations of the same melodic material underline which chords interchange, as well as the processes leading to such changes.

Example 5.28   Vodeno Horo #2, mm. 25–28

Example 5.29a   Vodeno Horo #1, antecedent phrase reharmonizations

Example 5.29b   Vodeno Horo #1, consequent phrase reharmonizations

The side-by-side comparison shows that the overall structure of the harmonic progression is preserved in terms of the placement of cadences and the opening descent. At the first repetitions of the kolyano, Dimitrov uses the standard Hicaz vii-i cadence, while at his final cadences, he prefers a root motion by fifth (v⁷–I).

Dimitrov's chordal vocabulary in minor modes is innovative and complex. The scale of #5 is an F# minor polymode with a variable 2nd scale degree. From the previously analyzed examples, a tonicization of III is likely to occur. While the temporary tonicizations in Kostov style in the 1980s were limited to either a secondary dominant, or ii-V-I, Dimitrov's tonicizations are far more complex. Example 5.30 contains a reharmonization of the same melody. In the first harmonization, Dimitrov applies a descending line from i to iv (i-i⁴₂-♭vi⁶ -iv₆). In mm. 77–78, similar to Kostov's approach from the 1980s, Dimitrov uses iv as a pivot chord (m. 79).

Example 5.30   Vodeno Horo #5, antecedent phrase

The difference in Dimitrov's style is the altering of the predominant ii of the relative major (A), which makes a stronger cadence in the relative major, ii-iiₒ₆-V₇-I. The temporary tonic, A major, also has an inserted pitch producing a chordal vertical of A-B-C♯-E. Surprisingly, the second harmonization of the same passage goes back to the drone tradition: F♯ is held as a pedal while the bass chromatically descends. The insertion of this chromatic descent postpones the temporary tonicization of III by one beat (m. 81).

The consequent phrase in both harmonizations has the role of reestablishing the main tonic, F♯ minor, and concluding the period with a strong cadence (Example 5.31).

The first harmonization of the consequent phrase initiates the same descending line observed in the first harmonization of the antecedent phrase (Example 5.30). The difference is that Dimitrov builds a new vertical on D♯—a B6—which is a IV₆ chord, enabling him to apply a standard plagal cadence of the type IV-iv-i.

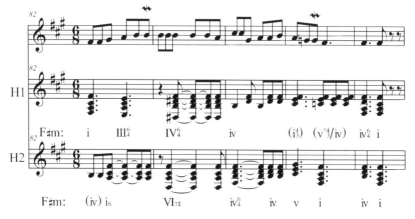

Example 5.31   Vodeno Horo #5, consequent phrase

Dimitrov uses the standard IV-iv elaborated by a pedal formula often used by accompanists and arrangers in the 1980s–1990s (Example 5.32).

F♯m: (i⁴₃)   (v°₃/iv)   (iv₄⁶)   i

Example 5.32   Cadential formula in F♯ Aeolian

In this particular case, the cadential formula substitutes for the Aeolian v-i cadence.

The second harmonization (Example 5.31) is the last repetition of the consequent phrase, and therefore should contain the strongest cadence. Dimitrov applies i-VI₇- iv₄⁶-v°-i with a plagal extension iv-i. Once again, regardless of the modal context, the order of chords follows the Western cadential pattern iv-v-i (iv-i). What makes this phrase stronger in comparison to the previous ones is also the rhythm chosen by Dimitrov. While the first two measures involve accented off-beats, the final cadence is placed with block chords matching the melody.

The next excerpt typifying Dimitrov's style of chord progressions is a transition from F♯ minor to a new key, B minor (Example 5.33).

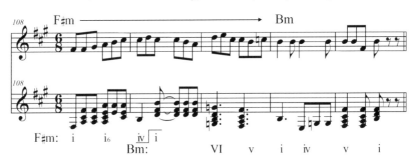

F♯m: i   i₆   iv⌐i
         Bm: VI   v   i   iv   v   i

Example 5.33   Vodeno Horo, mm. 108–112 (transition)

In order to have a strong modulation, Dimitrov pulls the cadence of the new key forward, anticipating the melody. Although the melody of m. 109 suggests an A major chord, Dimitrov plays B minor (the new tonic) and reinforces it with syncopation. He establishes B minor with two cadences, the first of which is accented (VI-v-i), and the second is elaborated with a standard predominant (iv-v-i).

The major features observed in Dimitrov's accompaniment confirm that the 1990s accompaniment style is far more complex than those of the 1970s and 1980s. In the 1980s, if a satisfactory harmonization is achieved, it was repeated for each repetition of the melody with minimal changes. In the 1990s, melodies repeat while harmonizations do not. Even if a satisfactory harmonization is produced, accompanists from the 1990s continued to search for different versions. In Dimitrov's style, bass, chords, and rhythm are indispensable parts of the chordal accompaniment. Whereas in the 1970s and 1980s these three components were often separated, in the 1990s they formed a unified entity, pushing the musical performance forward. Another signifier of the 1990s accompanimental style is a preference for root motion by fifth at final cadences. However, despite all of these different innovations, accompaniments of the 1990s still reference older layers of the tradition (drones and pedal harmony) at the beginning of pieces or after segments with high harmonic intensity.

The accompanists of village music from the 1980s and 1990s also performed with wedding bands. For example, Stoyan Kostov and Angel Dimitrov are both recognized as two of the best wedding-style guitar players. This suggests inevitable similarities between the harmonic vocabularies of the village style and those of the wedding style, as discussed in the following chapter.

Chapter 6

Harmony in Bulgarian Wedding Music: Trakiya's Dance and Concert Repertoire from the 1970s–1990s

In this chapter, I analyze the development of harmony in Bulgarian wedding music from the 1970s to the 1990s. My choice of repertoire for analysis focuses on that of Ivo Papazov's band *Trakiya* (Thrace), which was the most influential wedding band. As in the previous chapter, I will start my analysis with early, less complex repertoire and proceed with more harmonically complex pieces. I will analyze a dance medley from the 1980s and four pieces from the advanced wedding concert repertoire.

Wedding music came to the foreground in the late 1970s. In the early 1980s, wedding music challenged traditional music to an unprecedented level through amplification, the incorporation of electric guitars, synthesizers, and a heavy emphasis on improvisation. Created mostly live in front of hundreds or thousands of dancers, the arrangements of wedding tunes introduced new approaches to improvisation, harmony, and ornamentation. According to Silverman (1996: 239):

> Wedding music emerged in the 1970s as a countercultural, mass youth movement complete with superstars and inflated prices. In Bulgaria, wedding music—with its loudness, electric amplification, Western instruments, daring speed and technique, rock and jazz influences, and eclectic borrowings from film, classical, and pop music—epitomized youth culture even more than rock music.

The wedding style as a phenomenon has its roots in village music, but is characterized by the use of Western instruments and amplification. In socialist Bulgaria, wedding musicians had the same function as village musicians. They provided musical accompaniment for life-cycle celebrations and community events. Wedding-style improvisations, filled with chromaticisms and arpeggios, stem from the solos of village-style musicians and their approach to kolyano variation. Following an unwritten rule of "do not repeat the same thing twice," wedding accompanists (guitarists, keyboardists, and accordionists) also developed new ways of harmonizing Bulgarian music; they even eventually influenced socialist composers to borrow harmonic patterns from wedding repertoire. Potential reasons for the rapid development of harmonic languages in wedding-style accompaniment were the freedom of experimentation and a lack of training in Western harmony. While classically trained Bulgarian composers often struggled with applying basic progressions to traditional songs, musically uneducated wedding musicians were capable of providing multiple harmonizations of any Bulgarian song or melody.

The Wedding Style of the 1970s

The harmonic accompaniment of wedding music in the 1970s parallels to a great extent the accompaniment with primary triads observed in the village style from the same time period. Gradually, wedding-style guitarists developed an innovative accompaniment technique, "bass and rhythm," in which bass notes were played on downbeats and chords were strummed on offbeats. Accompanists produced walking bass lines with the thumb of the left hand while holding a basic chord position. The most challenging feature of this type of accompaniment was that both bass and chords were played with downstrokes, which also required a demanding right-hand technique. The "harmonic revolution" in the wedding style began after the formation of Ivo Papazov's Trakiya wedding band in the mid-1970s.[1] According to Buchanan (1996: 203):

> Contemporary wedding orchestras became popular following the establishment of Ivo Papazov's band, Trakiya, in 1974 in the Thracian town of Stara Zagora. Papazov credits himself as the originator of the wedding music style, which combines highly eclectic and improvisatory renditions of Bulgarian *narodna muzika* with stylistic elements of Greek, Macedonian, Serbian, Romanian, Turkish, and Rom (Gypsy) traditional music, and American rock and jazz.

The Wedding Style of the 1980s: Dance Repertoire

In the 1980s, wedding music bloomed and reached its climax of popularity. An alternative to the socialist-controlled "authentic" music and obrabotki, wedding music performances attracted audiences of thousands. Silverman writes (1989: 155):

> The popularity of this contemporary 'wedding music' is enormous and a few musicians and singers are as famous as rock stars in the West. The few times these famous contemporary folk musicians are permitted to perform live on television, the viewer turnout is staggering. People crowd around televisions in

---

[1] Recordings of Ivo Papazov's band from the 1970s are not available. Therefore, precise observations of how wedding style progressed from primary triads to the elaborated accompaniment of the 1980s cannot be made at this point.

hotel lobbies to hear and see the improvised music they adore but rarely hear through the official media. A well-known contemporary wedding musician can earn as much money playing at a two-day wedding as an ensemble musician can make in two months.

For analysis, I chose pieces from the repertoire of Ivo Papazov's orchestra, since this band set the standards for the genre. Most of Trakiya's musicians were Roma born into families of musicians. Roma musicians have played an important historical role in Bulgarian music. Their eclectic repertoire allowed them to perform for all ethnic groups, therefore complicating all nationalist and official party narratives about culture and "pure" Bulgarian music.[2]

In the early 1980s, Papazov included the guitar player Yuri Kamzamalov in his band. A Turkish-speaking Rom (whose Romani name is Gyurai), Kamzamalov became renowned for his rhythmic precision and harmonic rhythm. His accompaniment style, imitated to the present day, influenced wedding musicians, tambura players associated with socialist state ensembles, and even state-sponsored composers and arrangers. In a conversation about Kamzamalov's style, Nikolai Baldaranov (a renowned Bulgarian tambura and guitar player) shared with me: "It is not about what he plays. His chords are simple. It is about when and where he places his chords."

Trakiiski Temi

Trakiiski Temi (Thracian Themes) is a medley of four themes. Normally, Papazov would insert improvisation sections after each theme using the themes as head-ins and head-outs. In this unique performance, Papazov combined four independent themes.[3] I chose this particular medley to illustrate Kamzamalov's wedding harmonic progressions imitated by hundreds of guitar players. The themes are in a slow, danceable tempo allowing for careful selection of chords and cadences by the accompanist.

Trakiiski Temi: First Theme
The opening kolyano of the first theme is based on a minor polymode from E. As seen in Example 6.1, the modes are: Aeolian for the opening measures, Locrian ($\flat\hat{5}$) in mm. 4–11, and Aeolian for the first and second endings.

---

[2] For more information, refer to Silverman (2012).
[3] Due to the poor quality of the recording, which was made at a wedding without professional equipment, I have not included it on the attached CD compilation.

Example 6.1   Trakiiski Temi #1

It is common knowledge that Locrian is rarely used in modal practices. That is why I suggest searching for an alternative scalar interpretation from the abundance of modes and makams in Bulgarian music. If harmony may be considered to be a clue to scale derivation, mm. 4–5 (and their repetition in mm. 7–8) are based on makam Hicaz from A. G minor is the vii in A Hicaz and the commonly applied Hicaz dominant; therefore, the mm. 7–8 segment can be viewed as a Hicaz tonicization of IV within the larger framework of an E minor polymode. With respect to harmony, a Hicaz tonicization of IV fits the standard minor progressions observed in Example 6.1, i.e. tonicization of III followed by a plagal cadence in the main key (IV-iv-i) where vii/IV is inserted as a connective chord between III and IV.

An alternative interpretation of the mode in #1 is as a minor polymode of makam Karcigar (Example 6.2) and Phrygian.

Example 6.2   Makam Karcigar

As previously stated (see Chapter 3 and the concept of "movable Hicaz"), makam Karcigar involves a Hicaz pentachord starting from scale degree $\hat{4}$. The existence of this pentachord explains the tonicization of IV with vii/IV.[4]

The first ending of #1 plays the role of bringing the harmonic progression from the Phrygian cadence (vii-i in E Phrygian) back to the relative major tonal center, G major. Kamzamalov's choice of chords in this excerpt is one of the most suitable tonicizations observed in the entire repertoire. Kamzamalov places a chord on every beat in mm. 10–12: Dm-Em-C-Am-D7-G. Functionally, he cadences in E Phrygian with a standard Phrygian cadence (vii-i) and builds his tonicization as VI-iv-V$_7$/III-III. Analyzed in retrospect from the newly tonicized III (G), the progression is ideal from the viewpoint of Western functional harmony, IV-ii-V$_7$-I. One of the unique features of Kamzamalov's style is his application of standard Western cadences without any formal education in Western harmony.

The second kolyano (#2) of the first theme is harmonized with progressions similar to those found in #1 (Example 6.3).

Example 6.3   Trakiiski Temi #2

The melody of #2 involves a C♯, the highest pitch (climax) of the melody, which supports the previously made suggestion that the Gm-A chord connection is a vii-I Hicaz tonicization of IV as a result of a Phrygian/Karcigar minor polymode.

My discussion of the modes and harmony in the first two kolyanos of Trakiiski Temi raises the question: "how do accompanists orient themselves in such complex polymodality?" In attempting to provide an answer, I harmonized several songs in different minor polymodes, and asked myself: "why did I do that?" and "what in the music suggested this particular tonicization?" The analysis

---

  [4]   Based on this conclusion, I will refer to the flat 5th scale degree in minor polymodes as being part of makam Karcigar rather than Locrian.

of my own accompaniment revealed the following interesting conventions for harmonizing minor polymodes in the wedding style. For example, the natural 2nd scale degree in ascending motion acts as a leading tone to III and the third of the V$_7$/III secondary dominant. Therefore, when scale degree $\hat{2}$ is raised, a tonicization of III can be applied at any time. The flat 5th and raised 6th scale degrees are markers for a tonicization of IV in Hicaz (makam Karcigar). The tonicization of IV is optional, and can be applied as a vertical displacement of IV, an embellishment of a IV-iv-i plagal cadence, or as a practical tool for postponing the final cadence in longer phrases. The flat 2nd scale degree is a marker for a return to the main key in Phrygian. It is also an indicator for applying Phrygian cadences of the type vii-i (D-T) or the more elaborated II-vii-i (S-D-T). In summary, variable scale degrees provide important clues for tonicizations in minor polymodes. Raised scale degrees act as leading tones, while lowered ones assist in descents. Another conclusion can be derived by further examining Kamzamalov's accompaniment in minor polymodes. When melodies develop higher than the variable scale degree $\hat{2}$, wedding-style harmonizations are predominantly in the relative major key area.

Besides drawing on patterns and formulas, harmony in wedding music is also predetermined to a great extent by the melody. A detailed look at the score of the first theme reveals a model for Papazov's thematic construction. After numbers 1 and 2, which are 24 measures long and developmental in nature, Papazov inserts a short, condensed kolyano (#3) that is only eight measures long. The third kolyano is in an E Aeolian/Phrygian polymode and contains motivic repetition. From a harmonic perspective, the two-measure phrasing of #3 does not allow for tonicizations or extended chordal vocabulary (Example 6.4).

Example 6.4   Trakiiski Temi #3

Most wedding musicians who imitated Papazov's style did not adopt the above scheme of alternating long developing kolyanos with short summarizing ones. Perhaps Papazov's well-balanced approach to thematic construction is one of the primary reasons why his music is still extremely popular compared to the music of other wedding bands.

After the condensed kolyano #3, Papazov changes the mode to E Aeolian, which opens new possibilities for harmonization. The raised 2nd scale degree no longer requires the insertion of a Phrygian cadence (vii-i) at the end of a phrase, but rather a v-i cadence, or the standard substitute for all modal minor cadences, a plagal IV-iv-i (Example 6.5).

Example 6.5   Trakiiski Temi #4

In the opening measures of #4, the melody develops in the upper tetrachord of E Aeolian. Following the formulas described up to this point, Kamzamalov initiates a progression in the relative major, G (mm. 33–34). Measures 35 and 36 involve a tonicization of iv (A minor) followed by a tonicization of VII (D). Although mm. 41–42 resemble a deceptive cadence in Western terms, in the context of E Aeolian this cadence is a short segment in B Hicaz (I-II). In later recordings of the same theme, the B major triad is replaced by a B minor triad, which preserves the diatonic chordal vocabulary of Aeolian. Both endings of #4 conclude with a plagal cadence.

Number 5 (Example 6.6) is built on thematic material from #4, following the principle of a successive "kolyano chain," as described by Buchanan earlier in this book (Chapter 3).

Example 6.6   Trakiiski Temi #5

Number 5 is conclusive and built on a descending 5-line.[5] The mode is E Aeolian harmonized with plagal cadences separated by a tonicization of III. The C major triad in m. 52 does not match the melodic content. My interpretation is that Kamzamalov follows the inertia of the root motion by 5th (D7-G) and extends it for one extra measure.

Kamzamalov's accompaniment in #1–5 illustrates general preferences for plagal cadences in both minor polymodes and Aeolian. His tonicizations of III and IV (Hicaz) often involve secondary dominants preceded by secondary subdominants. In Phrygian, Kamzamalov makes little use of Phrygian cadences (vii-i), preferring the standard plagal IV-iv-i cadence. In Aeolian, Kamzamalov also utilizes IV-iv-i as his final Aeolian cadence rather than v-i. In summarizing kolyanos, Kamzamalov applies a reduced chordal vocabulary and avoids tonicizations.

Trakiiski Temi: Second Theme
The second theme is similar to the first in terms of harmonic vocabulary. Its opening kolyano (#6) is in E Aeolian/Phrygian polymode and contains standard tonicizations of IV (Hicaz) and the relative major, III (Example 6.7).

Example 6.7   Trakiiski Temi #6

The tonicization of IV seen in Example 6.7 is not in agreement with the melody. While in the first theme makam Karcigar suggests a tonicization of IV (Hicaz), in this particular excerpt, G minor is a secondary dominant, embellishing IV in a plagal cadence (IV-iv-i). However, the question remains: is Gm-A a tonicization borrowed from Karcigar, or only a secondary (Hicaz) dominant to IV?

The following number 7 contains the first v-i cadence in Aeolian observed thus far in *Trakiiski Temi* (Example 6.8).

---

[5]   The term 5-line refers to the typical fundamental descent $\hat{5}$-$\hat{4}$-$\hat{3}$-$\hat{2}$-$\hat{1}$, or *Urlinie*, found in tonal music according to Schenkerian theory.

Example 6.8   Trakiiski Temi #10

Kamzamalov uses a descending bass line (E-E♭-D-C-B), which is followed by a major dominant (V₇) and a Western deceptive cadence. Once again, the deceptive cadence in this particular modal harmonic context should be viewed as an embellishment for the harmonic vocabulary of Aeolian, rather than a structural, Western-type deceptive cadence.[6]

Number 11 (in E minor polymode with a variable scale degree $\hat{2}$) involves a different type of tonicization of IV that is not found in Hicaz (Example 6.9).

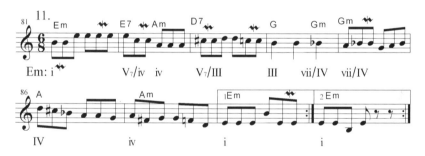

Example 6.9   Trakiiski Temi #11

The initial chord of #11 (m. 81) is the tonic triad, E minor. Measure 82 tonicizes IV (V₇/iv-iv), and is followed by a two-measure tonicization of III (V₇/V/III-V₇/III-III). Measures 85 and 86 involve a tonicization of IV (Hicaz), which leads to a standard plagal cadence of the type IV-iv-i. From a broader perspective, #11 illustrates the entire expansion of harmonic vocabularies in the wedding style in the 1980s, characterized by an increasing number of tonicizations (a tonicization in almost every measure, particularly in antecedent phrases) and the expansion of temporary tonicizations into modulations. In my opinion, this last feature became one of the reasons that audiences for wedding music declined in the

---

[6]   A parallel can be drawn to Kostov's use of an authentic cadence (V⁶₅-i) in Aeolian (Chapter 5, Example 5.24).

1990s: harmonic accompaniment became too independent and preoccupied with tonicizations such that they often overshadowed the melody. As my colleague Stoyan Kostov remarked: "some people just do not know when to stop."

Trakiiski Temi: Third Theme

The third theme of Trakiiski Temi is in makam Hicaz from E. As noted in Chapter 4, the most common progression for Hicaz is iv-II-vii-I with vii-I as a typical final cadence. Example 6.10 illustrates the first number of the third theme, marked as #13 in my transcription.

Example 6.10   Trakiiski Temi #13

The first three measures establish the key with a I-vii-I (T-D-T) progression. The presentation of the tonic (E) as a major-minor 7th chord (m. 95) is a common observation for tonic presentation in Hicaz.[7] Wedding musicians employ I_7 even as a tonic resolution in final Hicaz cadences.[8]

The following number (#14) is a concluding kolyano where the melody suggests the ♭V chord, characteristic of Hicaz (Example 6.11).

Example 6.11   Trakiiski Temi #14

---

[7]   From the perspective of harmonic minor, this chord is V_7, a chord that, in Western music theory, would not be considered tonic under any circumstances.

[8]   In harmonic minor, this progression is equivalent to iv-V_7.

The flat 5th scale degree could be a remnant of a makam that is no longer in use, or an uncommon major polymode based on Hicaz. In Hicaz harmonic accompaniment, ♭V is typically applied at cadences preceding the dominant (♭V-vii-I or ♭V-v$_7^♯$-I). In longer progressions, ♭V is often preceded by II (its secondary dominant).[9]

The rest of the third theme follows the standards for harmonizing melodies in Hicaz. As outlined in Chapter 4, the most likely tonicization found in a Hicaz kolyano is that of the subdominant, iv. An example of this type of tonicization is evident in #17 (Example 6.12).

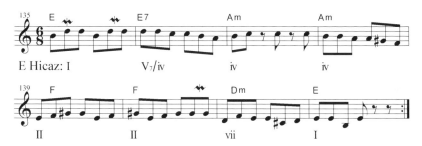

Example 6.12   Trakiiski Temi #17

Trakiiski Temi: Fourth Theme

The fourth theme is in E minor polymode with a variable scale degree $\hat{2}$. This theme differs from the first two themes by the predominance of the Phrygian mode over Aeolian. In the opening kolyano of the theme (#19), Kamzamalov acknowledges the Phrygian mode with a complete Phrygian cadence (iv-II-vii-i) in the opening measures of the kolyano (Example 6.13).

---

[9]   Measure 12 in Chopin's Prelude in C minor, Op. 28 contains the same chord progression. Often provided as a rare example in classical music of the tonicization of the Neapolitan chord, Chopin's progression completely matches a Hicaz tonicization of ♭V. From a Western-theoretical perspective, Chopin's progression is V$_7$/N-N-V$_7$-i. In G Hicaz, the same progression would interrupt immediately after the V$_7$ chord. The corresponding Roman numerals for Hicaz are II$_7$(V$_7$/♭V)-♭V-I$_7$.

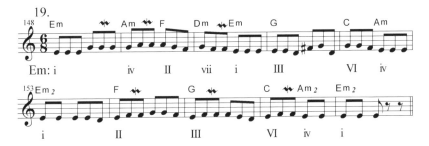

Example 6.13   Trakiiski Temi #19

The final cadence of #19 is an elaborated version of the II-vii-i Phrygian cadence. Although the progression II-III-VI sounds like a tonicization of VI, I suggest that this progression is a cadential substitution for the standard Phrygian II-vii-i. The II-III-VI-iv-i cadence type and the Aeolian plagal cadences (IV-iv-i and iv-i) are the preferred ones for Phrygian in the 1980s. More elaborate Phrygian cadences emerge in the wedding style in the late 1980s. These cadences, such as VII₇-III₇-VI-VI₇-II-vii-i, are based on a circle of fifths subordinated to Phrygian. On rare occasions, a complete circle of fifths progression in Phrygian (i-iv-VII₇-III7-VI-VI₇-II-vii-i) can be heard in the wedding music of the 1990s.

Number 20 of the fourth theme is still primarily in Phrygian, with the exception of m. 163, where a raised 2nd scale degree permits tonicization of III. An earlier tonicization of III is not possible due to ♭2̂ and the development of the melody in the lower tetrachord (Example 6.14).

Example 6.14   Trakiiski Temi #20

The last kolyanos of the fourth theme follow the standard chordal vocabulary of Phrygian combined with plagal cadences typical for Aeolian. The tonicizations applied by Kamzamalov are limited to the relative major, III.

Some of the main observations made about the chordal vocabulary in Trakiiski Temi apply to a vast repertoire of the styles discussed in this book. The harmonic language used by Kamzamalov in Trakiiski Temi, as well as other pieces from the 1980s, became an archetype for wedding-style harmony, and has remained such to the present day. This style of accompaniment was named after the Turkish name of Yuri Kamzamalov, Gyurai, and is presently known among Bulgarian accompanists from the oral tradition as "Gyurai's style."

Accompaniment for Improvisations and Solos

In the wedding music of the 1980s, the accompaniment of improvisatory/ solo sections is simpler than that of opening themes. In fast tempos, harmonic accompaniment focuses on rhythmic precision rather than elaborate tonicizations and sophisticated cadences. The faster the tempos, the more restricted the chord vocabulary becomes.

My observations show that most of the improvisations in wedding music are based on major polymodes that vary from a combination of two modes to an almost complete chromatic scale.[10] In order to balance the polymodal complexity found in melodic improvisations, accompanists apply basic chordal progressions of the type I-IV-V-I or I-V-I. If the melodic improvisations are in makam Hicaz (entirely or as a part of a polymode), the most commonly applied progressions are I-iv-vii-I, I-II-vii-I, or I-vii-I for Hicaz.

In wedding-style improvisations, major modes and keys interchange constantly (CD, Track 19). Bulgarian wedding musicians prefer to improvise in $\frac{6}{8}$ (Pravo Horo) and $\frac{7}{8}$ (Rŭchenitsa), the two most common Thracian dance meters. Example 6.15 illustrates typical accompaniment formulas in $\frac{6}{8}$ used by Kamzamalov and other accompanists based on four-bar megameasures.

---

[10] See Chapter 4.

Example 6.15   Typical accompaniment formulas in Pravo Horo ($\frac{6}{8}$)

The same four-bar megameasure formulas adapt to improvisations in asymmetrical meters. Example 6.16 illustrates the accompaniment patterns from Example 6.15 adjusted to $\frac{7}{8}$ meter.

Example 6.16   Typical accompaniment formulas in $\frac{7}{8}$

The incorporation of megameasures and megameters[11] is what distinguishes the accompaniment of improvisations in the wedding style from the accompaniment of improvisatory sections in village music. Megameasures in wedding improvisational accompaniment have the important role of providing a phrase length reference for the improvising soloists. For example, a megameasure of four measures assists a soloist to conclude his phrases at the end of a megameasure cycle (at the end of the fourth or the eighth measure). The achieved result is that improvisers have the freedom to focus on melodic variety, as opposed to counting measure cycles.

Solo improvisations in minor modes and minor polymodes are atypical for wedding music. If inserted, such minor improvisations have symmetrical kolyano structure. Improvised kolyanos in minor serve as stability anchors ("micro themes") between large improvised sections in major polymodes. In terms of harmony, improvised minor kolyanos have similar chordal progressions to those of themes. Their harmonic complexity, however, is often reduced, due to the overall faster tempos of the improvisational sections.

The harmonic concepts described above became standard for dance repertoire in the oral tradition from the 1980s and 1990s. Kamzamalov's accompaniment formulas for wedding dance repertoire are still performed and recorded today.

Wedding Style of the 1980s: Concert Repertoire

In the 1980s, wedding music was recontextualized from wedding parties to the concert stage. In an attempt to restrict wedding music, the Bulgarian communist government organized festivals in which wedding music could be performed in censored venues. According to Silverman (1989: 156):

> For the first time in 1985, the [Bulgarian] government organized a 'Festival of Wedding Music' and offered a prize for the best band. A few hundred bands entered, but no band won first prize. The rationale for withholding the first prize was that no one played 'pure' Bulgarian music. Moreover, all band members were required to attend a meeting after the festival in which an ethnomusicologist lectured them about how they have allowed foreign elements to corrupt Bulgarian music. Their mission should be to purify the music to its original state.

Timothy Rice further elaborates on the Stambolovo (Thrace region) wedding music contests.[12] The festivals were the primary impetus for new wedding music concert repertoire (1994: 251):

---

[11]   For more information regarding megameters and megameasures, refer to Chapter 3.

[12]   The Stambolovo festivals were marketed as *Natsionalna Sreshta na Instrumentalni Grupi za Bŭlgarska Narodna Muzika* (National Meetings of Instrumental Groups for

The festival proved so successful that by 1988 it had been 'nationalized,' controlled by the central 'concert direction' in Sofia, and augmented by preliminary regional festivals all over the country. By taking control of the festival and its aesthetics, the state apparatus tried to alter, defuse, and diminish the anti-establishment challenge of wedding music.

While participatory dance events restricted dance repertoire, concert settings provided a new stage for wedding-style experimentations and innovations, regardless of government control. Stylistically, wedding concert music places an emphasis on mixed meters (combined metric groups and heterometric rows), innovative tonal plans and progressions, non-danceable fast tempos, improvisations in megameasure structures, and expansions of traditional kolyano structures. Wedding concert music also embraced versatile source material (Indian music, music of countries neighboring Bulgaria, Russian music, Arabic/Middle Eastern music, and Western classical music) and incorporated Western jazz and rock elements.

The earliest examples of wedding concert repertoire stemmed from the opening tunes performed at weddings while guests sat at banquet tables. These opening pieces, called *otkrivane* (opening),[13] had the purpose of impressing the audience by displaying the technical virtuosity of the wedding performers. These early non-danceable compositions became the model for the entire wedding-style concert repertoire. In the mid-1980s, at music festivals such as Stambolovo, wedding orchestras performed their otkrivanes, dance tunes from their dance repertoire, and wedding-style songs. Later in the 1980s, most of the concert repertoire consisted of suites and medleys featuring fast tempos, thematic contrasts, improvisations, and mixed meters. All of these pieces were modeled after Papazov's First Otkrivane.

Ivo Papazov's First Otkrivane from the Early 1980s

The authorship of the piece First Otkrivane is questionable. Petŭr Ralchev, Ivo Papazov's accordion player in the early 1980s, released sections of First Otkrivane in an official Balkanton LP.[14] In my personal interactions with Papazov, he claimed authorship of most of the music performed by the Trakiya orchestra. The recording of the piece (CD, Track 20) was made at an actual wedding by a musician or guest holding a tape recorder close to a speaker, a standard practice for recording and disseminating wedding music in the 1980s.

Bulgarian Folk Music). For fuller descriptions of the Stambolovo festivals, see Silverman (1989), Buchanan (1991: 541–50), and Rice (1994: 250–55).

[13]   Lowercase otkrivane (singular) or otkrivanes (plural) refers to the genre. Uppercase Otkrivane, as it appears in First Otkrivane and Second Otkrivane, refers to Papazov's opening pieces from the early and late 1980s, which are analyzed in this chapter.

[14]   Peter Ralchev, *Accordion*, Balkanton: BHA 12268 (1988).

First Otkrivane is approximately 10 minutes long; its middle section and solo improvisations vary tremendously from one performance to another. I will focus my harmonic analysis primarily on the opening themes, since the improvised sections have a simpler accompaniment of the type described in the previous section of this chapter. Similar to Trakiiski Temi, the harmonic accompaniment in First Otkrivane is provided by Yuri Kamzamalov on electric guitar.

The opening kolyano of First Otkrivane is in D Aeolian, which, for the majority of the kolyano, develops in the relative major, F (Example 6.17).

Example 6.17   First Otkrivane #1

Since the mode of kolyano #1 is D Aeolian as opposed to an Aeolian/Phrygian minor polymode with a variable scale degree $\hat{2}$, a tonicization of III (F major) becomes possible at any time. Moreover, it can be suggested that the composer took into consideration the III-i tonal juxtaposition while composing the opening kolyano. The melody in mm. 1–6 repeatedly emphasizes F and its fifth, C, which also implies that the composer was thinking harmonically. The metric organization of #1 is rather complex; mm. 1–6 are based on a combined metric group $\frac{7}{8}$ (3+2+2) + $\frac{11}{8}$ (2+2+3+2+2); after m. 6, the metric organization is an example of a heterometric row ($\frac{6}{8} + \frac{6}{8} + \frac{6}{8} + \frac{7}{8}$).

Motivically, the opening kolyano can be divided into four motives (Example 6.18).

Example 6.18   Phrasing in First Otkrivane #1

The second motive repeats a variation of the first. The third motive is an extended version of the second with an additional measure of $\frac{6}{8}$. The last motive has a completely different metric organization ($\frac{6}{8}+\frac{6}{8}+\frac{7}{8}$). This model resembles a "kolyano chain" accomplished at a motivic level.

In this particular performance of First Otkrivane, Kamzamalov's harmonization of the first kolyano is limited to tonicizations of the relative major (V_7/III-III) and a v-i. In later performances of the First Otkrivane, Kamzamalov substitutes certain chords, which serves to illustrate how changes of harmony can cause a piece to transform over time. In subsequent performances, Kamzamalov also elaborates the C7-F (tonicization of III) with the insertion of secondary subdominants: B♭m-C7-F or Gm-C7-F (F: iv-V$_7$-I or ii-V$_7$-I).[15] In addition, Kamzamalov substitutes his final cadence, Am-Dm, with D7-G. As a result, he reinterprets the mode through harmonization from D Aeolian to C Shope major, and applies a standard Shope major half cadence (V_7/V-V).

The second kolyano (#2) of First Otkrivane has the same overall tonal plan as #1, but uses a different final cadence of the type ii-v-i (Example 6.19).

---

[15]   Temporary tonics in wedding music are often established through longer progressions that involve not only secondary dominants, but also subdominant chords (secondary subdominants) preceding the secondary dominants.

Example 6.19   First Otkrivane #2

A cadence of the type ii-v-i is atypical for Aeolian mode; this is probably the reason Kamzamalov substitutes ii-v-i (Em-Am-Dm) with the more commonly used iv-v-i (Gm-Am-Dm) in later performances of First Otkrivane. Another reason is the B♭ in the melody, which conflicts with the B♮ as the fifth of the E minor triad (m. 17). Motivically, the second kolyano follows the general structure of the first. There are four motives: the first two are eight beats long, the third and fourth are six beats long (Example 6.20).

Example 6.20   Phrasing in First Otkrivane #2

Number 7, which comes after the repetition of #1–3, is in D Aeolian and includes tonicizations of VII (accomplished by V/III) and III. After the tonicizations, the harmony gradually leads to a final cadence (IV-v-i) of the first repetition. The second repetition is a transition to a new key area, A minor (Example 6.21).

Example 6.21	First Otkrivane #7

Kolyano #8 is difficult to define in terms of mode. Modally ambiguous melodies of this type exist only in the pre-composed repertoire of the wedding style (Example 6.22).

Example 6.22	First Otkrivane #8

The primary key center determined by the final cadence is G Hicaz. At the same time, the melody suggests three different chords: m. 35 arpeggiates an A minor triad; m. 36 arpeggiates a C diminished 7th chord; and m. 37, along with the following first and second repetitions, are in G Hicaz. Rather than searching for a functional explanation of A minor and C minor (or C diminished) in G Hicaz, I suggest that in pre-composed kolyanos of this type, functional harmonic logic is difficult to apply.

The primary mode of #9 is an A minor polymode, but A minor as a tonal center is not established until the end of the second repetition, m. 45. The measures prior to that can be interpreted as being in G major polymode harmonized with I-V₇/ ii-ii-iv-I (Example 6.23).

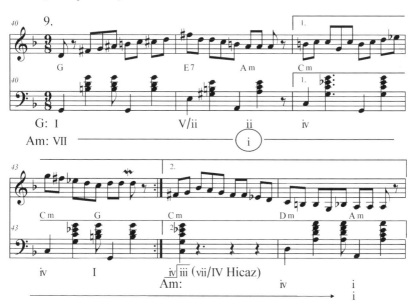

Example 6.23   First Otkrivane #9

The most important observation that can be made from #9 is that concert wedding repertoire moves beyond the standard tonicizations in minor modes. VII is tonicized for the majority of #9 and involves its own tonicization of ii (in the key of VII). The temporary tonic ii (E7-Am) is not perceived as a cadence in the main key (A minor polymode) due to the raised 6th scale degree and natural 2nd. The return to the main key is accomplished through a plagal cadence iv-i at the end of the second repetition. The C minor triad in m. 44 (first measure of the second repetition) is interpreted as vii/IV, since melodically m. 44 is in Hicaz from scale degree 4̂. Number 10, which follows, develops a standard juxtaposition of III and i in A Aeolian (Example 6.24).

Example 6.24   First Otkrivane #10

The overall harmonic plan for kolyanos #9–10 explores the likely tonicizations for Aeolian and minor polymodes, VII and III. Both kolyanos have a developmental character. Following the thematic construction logic from Trakiiski Temi, the composer would insert a condensed, summary-type kolyano after #9–10 with no melodically implied tonicizations. Such a kolyano appears next as #11 (Example 6.25).

Example 6.25   First Otkrivane #11

Number 11 is based on an A minor polymode of Aeolian and makam Karcigar. Rather than tonicizing IV (Hicaz), Kamzamalov applies a diminished chord (F#dim) and avoids the IV Hicaz tonicization. This is due to the fact that experienced Bulgarian accompanists generally avoid tonicizations in condensed kolyanos. As a result, the general harmonic plan of #11 is reduced to emphasizing the main key, A minor. The first cadence is weak, F-Am (VI-i), while the second one is a standard plagal cadence, iv-i. In such a harmonic context, due to the presence of F♯ in the scale, a IV-iv-i final cadence can be applied as well. A v-i cadence would create a clash with the ♭$\hat{5}$ in Karcigar, and this is perhaps the reason why Kamzamalov avoids applying it.

The following number 12 is in an Aeolian/Phrygian polymode and involves the characteristic tonicization of III (Example 6.26).

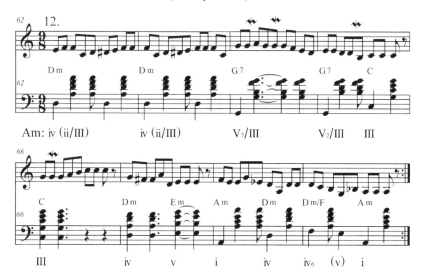

Example 6.26   First Otkrivane #12

The tonicization is accomplished through a progression ii-V$_7$-I followed by a plagal cadence in the main key. Although the melody in mm. 62–63 suggests an F major triad and IV-V-I type of tonicization of III, Kamzamalov substitutes it with ii-V-I, most likely for harmonic variety.

The segments of First Otkrivane and Trakiiski Temi analyzed above, which are in minor modes or minor polymodes, suggest the existence of several general patterns of tonal organization involving tonicization of the relative major (III), VII, IV, and IV Hicaz as a result of polymodality including makam Karcigar. These basic formulas constantly repeat not only in Trakiiski Temi and First Otkrivane, but throughout the entire repertoire. In spite of their simplicity, these formulas are difficult to detect, due to fast tempos and rapid change of keys and modes. Moreover, even the most experienced accompanists of Bulgarian music are not cognitively aware of the existence of such formulas. In my conversations with Stoyan Kostov, Nikolai Baldaranov, and the American bass player Paul Brown, I mentioned the above repetitive tonicization patterns as being foundational for all harmonizations in minor modes and polymodes. All three of my colleagues agreed that such patterns may exist, but due to the fast tempos and improvisatory nature of the music, there is no time to calculate chords and intellectually approach progressions and tonicizations. Rather, what seems to be most important for the proper execution of a performance is the accompanist's ability to memorize melodies, hear instant mode changes suggested by variable scale degrees, and adjust to the changes instantaneously. Therefore, the complexity of the accompaniment in wedding music is not a result of complex formulas, but rather the proper placement and rapid interplay of formulas. Perhaps it is the fact that Bulgarian interactive accompanists constantly search for new ways of harmonizing each kolyano that harmonizations in Bulgarian music are so attractive, innovative, and inventive.

The faster tempo in the continuation of First Otkrivane limits the chordal vocabulary to primary triads and standard cadences. Nevertheless, I have highlighted several segments of the $\frac{6}{8}$ section of First Otkrivane that differ from the harmonic formulas described thus far. Example 6.27 (#17) is based on an ascending melodic sequence.

Example 6.27   First Otkrivane #17

Even though sequences are atypical for the traditional repertoire in the 1980s, they entered concert wedding music as an additional tool for enriching melodic material. Number 17 is in C major polymode (Ionian/Mixolydian) and contains several secondary dominants in the harmonization, something unseen until this piece. Sequential segments become evident in numbers 16 and 21, balanced by kolyanos with standard harmonic frameworks.

Numbers 22 (Example 6.28) and 23 are unique for First Otkrivane, since they are in harmonic minor, an atypical scale for wedding music. These numbers come with standard Western authentic cadences of the type V_7-i.

Example 6.28   First Otkrivane #22

The number-by-number analysis so far has explained the harmony on a micro level. At this point, however, I find it crucial to pull back and look at the larger picture. First Otkrivane deviates from the established standards for Bulgarian wedding music in a number of ways. The opening numbers (1–6) have standard tonicization plans, but are placed in a context of mixed meters and asymmetrical phrasing. Numbers 7 and 8 have unstable harmonic frameworks and changing meters. The following numbers (9–15) are in $\frac{9}{8}$ of the type 2+3+2+2, an uncommon meter for fast tempos. Numbers 16–21 are atypical of Bulgarian wedding music sequences. Numbers 16 and 17 are motivically related, but differ in terms of meter: number 16 is in the asymmetrical $\frac{5}{8}$, whereas number 17 is in the symmetrical $\frac{6}{8}$. Numbers 22 and 23 are based on harmonic minor, which, again, is unusual for wedding music. Number 24 balances these by inserting standard Aeolian plagal cadences combined with Western authentic cadences in harmonic minor. In short, when standardized harmony is used, other structural elements deviate from the standards. When phrasing is regular, the composer uses atypical modes. Applied ascending sequences build tension, especially when combined with metric changes. When a plateau is finally reached (#22), it is placed in the atypical harmonic minor.

After number 25, First Otkrivane continues with a fast Pravo Horo ($\frac{6}{8}$) harmonized using standard progressions corresponding to the specific modes. The only unusual kolyano with respect to harmony is #30, which is in makam Mustear from G. Makam Mustear is typically harmonized with a V_7-i progression. In order to deviate from the standards, Kamzamalov alternates i and VI^{16} (Example 6.29).

Example 6.29   First Otkrivane #30

Papazov's First Otkrivane encouraged almost all wedding bands to create impressive otkrivanes of their own. However, with few exceptions—such as the otkrivanes of Ivan Milev's *Mladost* (Youth) orchestra and Georgi Yanev's *Orfei* (Orpheus) band—these failed. In order to give a comparison between Papazov's First Otkrivane and otkrivanes of other wedding bands, I have provided an excerpt from Ivan Milev's otkrivane from the mid-1980s (CD, Track 21), recorded at a concert.

Otkrivanes provided an important model for all concert suites in the wedding style featuring mixed meters, megametrical structures, and improvisations in incredibly fast tempos. In my opinion, the overexploitation of the otkrivane-type suites produced a sort of "virtuosity overload" that contributed to the gradual decline in audience size for wedding music in the mid-1990s.

Jazzing up Bulgarian Harmony

Considering that both jazz and Bulgarian folk music are modal, a successful harmonic hybridization of jazz harmony and Bulgarian wedding music accompaniment would be relatively easy to envision. Contrary to this assumption,

---

[16]   In later performances of First Otkrivane, Kamzamalov changes this progression to i-VI₆-♯vi°₆-VI₆, a chord progression found in the soundtracks of James Bond movies.

however, a successful and complete hybridization of jazz harmony and Bulgarian folk music has not yet occurred. In my opinion, this is due to several factors. During the peak years of wedding music (1980s), communist censorship suppressed all Western musical influences, including jazz harmony. A hybrid between Bulgarian melodies, which lie at the core of socialist nationalism, and jazz harmony, a musical symbol of the capitalist West, would have potentially endangered the careers of wedding music performers.

Another factor could be rooted in the established listeners' expectations of wedding music's patrons, the people providing income for wedding musicians by hiring orchestras to perform at weddings. Traditional Bulgarian weddings follow a protocol that allows wedding musicians to perform only a limited number of non-danceable tunes, such as otkrivanes, free-rhythm melodies played during exchanges of wedding gifts, or pieces by special requests. If a wedding orchestra wished to maintain a good position on the market, it had to provide danceable tunes, restrain its use of megameters (which might lead dancers to confuse the dance steps), use only limited improvisation, and adapt its entire performances to the tastes of wedding guests. An exploration of jazz harmony does not fit well into this performance context.

The short phrasing of Bulgarian folk melodies may have become another obstacle preventing a successful merger between jazz harmony and wedding music accompaniment. When combined with fast tempos and listeners' expectations for standard Bulgarian cadences, short phrases limit chord progressions to several chords, simply due to the lack of space.

One final reason is related to the fact that in Bulgarian wedding music, harmony always had a supporting role. Wedding musicians never learned how to improvise over longer chord progressions. Soloists are accustomed to leading, determining key changes, and inventing sophisticated chromatic modulations intended to keep accompanists always on high alert. In Papazov's own words, in wedding music, "soloists run and accompanists chase them."

Despite the factors listed above, more and more examples of jazz progressions began to surface in the wedding music concert repertoire of the 1980s. Gradually, they created and established a new framework for improvisations and accompaniment that Papazov labeled "Balkan jazz."

Western Influences in Papazov's Concert Music in the Early 1980s

It is difficult to suggest an approximate date of when jazz chords and progressions first appeared in wedding music accompaniment. Recordings made at weddings from the early 1980s illustrate either the use of single extended tertian chords (9th chords or 11th chords) or direct quotations from rock music progressions. A recording I made while attending one of Papazov's concerts illustrates the early incorporation of rock and jazz elements in Yuri Kamzamalov's guitar accompaniment (CD, Track 22). On the recording, Papazov plays the clarinet and the saxophone at the same time. In his concerts in the 1980s, Papazov often included this ostentatious display of virtuosity, which was typically preceded by the disassembling of his clarinet one part at a time. As heard from the recording, Yuri Kamzamalov applies a 12-bar blues progression (I-I-I-I-V-IV-I-I-V-IV-I-V) embellished with 7th and 9th chords. Certain elements of Kamzamalov's rhythmic accompaniment are also reminiscent of Gypsy jazz. This musical excerpt provokes a question: if Kamzamalov knew jazz chords and progressions, why did he not incorporate them into his dance music accompaniment, or in contexts other than that of "mocking" Western musical styles? Potential answers might relate to the socialist censorship restrictions from the 1980s, or Papazov's aesthetical and accompanimental preferences from this particular period.

Papazov's Concert Music in the Late 1980s

1986 was a year of change in Papazov's band. The renowned accordion player Petŭr Ralchev left Trakiya. Ralchev's place was taken by the accordion player Neshko Neshev, who was also a gifted composer and arranger. Shortly after Ralchev's departure, Papazov replaced his guitar player, Yuri Kamzamalov, with two guitar players: Radi Kazakov on bass and Yuri Kamzamalov's brother, Andrei Kamzamalov,[17] on rhythm guitar. The addition of an electric bass was not an innovation, as other wedding bands—such as Ivan Milev's Mladost orchestra and Filip Simeonov's wedding band *Sever* (North)—had two guitars long before Papazov incorporated the bass guitar in Trakiya.[18]

It is debatable whether Papazov's Balkan jazz inspirations occurred before Radi and Andrei joined Trakiya, or if he developed his jazz ideas after seeing the potential in his new accompanists. In either case, the addition of a bass guitar significantly changed Trakiya's sound and accompaniment.

Before proceeding further, I find it necessary to provide a brief comparison between the single-guitar and two-guitar accompanimental styles. In "bass and rhythm" single-guitar accompaniment, bass lines are limited by the nature of the left hand position. A specific neck grip with a thumb on top of the strings allows a guitar player to "walk bass lines" around the chords being held. Despite the limitations in terms of possible bass patterns, this type of guitar accompaniment sounds particularly strong due to the full agreement between bass lines and chords. An accompaniment split between two guitar players provides several harmonic advantages, such as jazz chords, elaborated bass lines, an additional lower octave (or more, for a five-string bass) added to the texture, fuller chords in the rhythm guitar, more syncopations, and transparent harmonic textures. One persistent problem with two-guitar accompaniment is the lack of perfect agreement between bass lines and chords. This results from the mere fact that there are two performers

---

[17]   Andrei Kamzamalov's Romani name is Aidŭn.
[18]   Ivan Milev's otkrivane (CD, Track 21) features a two-guitar accompaniment.

involved. Although Radi Kazakov and Andrei Kamzamalov became well synchronized in terms of harmonic choices, they could not completely suppress their desire to experiment and explore different harmonic progressions.

Trakiya's Second Otkrivane

Shortly after the incorporation of Radi Kazakov and Andrei Kamzamalov in Trakiya, Papazov changed his otkrivane. The new piece became popular among musicians as Papazov's Second Otkrivane (CD, Track 23). Second Otkrivane paved the road for Papazov's Balkan jazz style and reshaped all the pieces in Trakiya's concert repertoire.

The first innovative element in Second Otkrivane emerges from the very beginning of the piece: a fanfare quintal-quartal chord, an atypical feature of Bulgarian wedding music (Example 6.30).

Example 6.30   Second Otkrivane, introduction

Similar to the opening chord of Kopanitsa by the Harmanliiskata Troika discussed in Chapter 5, the chord found in mm. 5–9 of Second Otkrivane contains the open fifths of the two possible final triads, A-E (if the triad is built upwards) and A-D (if the triad is built downwards). The introduction, in ⅜, also involves a change of grouping (boxed in the example) from the asymmetrical 2+2+2+3 to compound 3+3+3, a feature that will be further explored in Second Otkrivane.

The opening numbers (#1 and #2) of Second Otkrivane introduce an Aeolian/ Phrygian polymode along with its typical cadences and expected tonicization of III (Example 6.31).

Example 6.31   Second Otkrivane #1 and 2

It is interesting to examine the harmonic clash in m. 16 resulting from the different harmonic preferences of the two accompanists. The Aeolian/Phrygian polymode has two typical cadences, IV-iv-i and v-i. As seen in Example 6.31, the bass player prefers the root motion by fifth (v-i), while the rhythm guitar player prefers a plagal cadence (IV-iv₇-i). Sometimes, such disagreements unintentionally produce extended tertian verticals.

After #2, Second Otkrivane continues with an "asymmetrical-compound-asymmetrical" change of grouping riddle followed by jazz-style fanfares reminiscent of the introduction (Example 6.32).

Example 6.32   Second Otkrivane #3

Similar to First Otkrivane, Second Otkrivane contains a large section in $\frac{6}{8}$, or Pravo Horo. The transitional kolyano between the two meters ($\frac{9}{8}$ and $\frac{6}{8}$), however, involves melodic and harmonic material quite atypical of Bulgarian wedding music (Example 6.33).

Example 6.33   Second Otkrivane, transition to $\frac{6}{8}$

In my opinion, Example 6.33 captures one of the best examples of Papazov's early Balkan jazz aspirations.

The improvised section of Second Otkrivane (CD, Track 24) also features significant innovations. Example 6.34 illustrates a guitar rhythm that set a new standard for accompaniment in wedding concert music improvisations.

Example 6.34   Guitar rhythm in $\frac{6}{8}$

A modal disagreement stands out from the accompaniment pattern. The presence of both D7 and Dm7 chords in the rhythm guitar accompaniment allows Papazov not only to switch between major and minor in his improvisation, but also to utilize the entire palette of modes, scales, major polymodes, and makams in his solos. I consider this a departure from the established model of "accompanists chasing soloists." In the new accompanimental context, guitar players establish a plateau of stability. The progression illustrated in Example 6.34 is ultimately perceived as a tonic prolongation. From the viewpoint of Bulgarian traditional polyphony, this progression may even be explained as a highly rhythmicized drone on scale degree $\hat{1}$.

Similar to most wedding concert tunes, in the improvised section of Second Otkrivane, all musicians take solos. The beginning of the two-guitar solo, however, takes many listeners by surprise. As heard from the recording of this particular segment of Second Otkrivane (CD, Track 25), Andrei Kamzamalov plays rock (in minor pentatonic) mixed with Bulgarian wedding music elements. At the end of the rock solo, the two guitars gradually transition into a Bulgarian melody, followed by a megameasure-based accompaniment, setting the stage for Papazov's clarinet improvisation.

New Megametrical Accompaniment Patterns

Second Otkrivane not only provided a framework for new compositions; it also inspired ideas for rearranging older repertoire. Freed from restrictions imposed by dancers and dancing patterns, Trakiya musicians began to perform Rŭchenitsas in megameters of $\frac{14}{8}$, Kopanitsas in $\frac{22}{8}$, and Pravo Horos in $\frac{12}{8}$ or $\frac{24}{8}$. These megameasure structures opened space not only for elaborate, free jazz-style improvisations but also for experimentation within the accompaniment and the incorporation of longer jazz chord progressions.

The accompaniment patterns first introduced in Papazov's Second Otkrivane began to transform, appearing in other meters. For example, by adding one extra eighth note per measure, the accompaniment pattern shown in Example 6.34 transformed from $\frac{6}{8}$ into a $\frac{7}{8}$ accompaniment formula (Example 6.35).

Dm: (i)

Example 6.35   Guitar rhythm in $\frac{7}{8}$

Track 26 on the CD further illustrates how the improvisation accompaniment patterns from Second Otkrivane adapted to the rhythm of $\frac{7}{8}$. As heard from the recording, the chordal vocabulary of the accompaniment remains almost identical.

Track 27 on the CD illustrates the largest megametrical structure I have observed in wedding concert repertoires. A $\frac{24}{8}$ megameasure groups four measures of $\frac{6}{8}$ united by an accompaniment pattern. This accompaniment pattern became the foundational idea of one of the most influential concert pieces from the repertoire of Ivo Papazov's Trakiya orchestra: *Hitŭr Petŭr* (Clever Peter).[19]

Hitŭr Petŭr

The composer of Hitŭr Petŭr is Radi Kazakov, Papazov's bass player. The recording (CD, Track 28) that I used for my transcription was made in the spring of 1988 at a wedding in the Romani settlement of Bukovlak, Northern Bulgaria. In this particular performance, Hitŭr Petŭr is preceded and followed by slow (free-rhythm) melodies. In the opening kolyanos of the piece, Kazakov has portrayed Hitŭr Petŭr riding his donkey across the countryside.

Hitŭr Petŭr is the first piece with fluctuating rhythm in its improvisatory section, a departure from the rhythmicized, kolyano, and megameasure-structured improvisations observed so far. The formal structure of the piece is as follows:

1. Introductory kolyanos (#1–2)
2. Primary theme (#3–4)
3. Unstable middle section (kolyano) with developmental character (#8)
4. Second theme in $\frac{6}{8}$ with swing-type accompaniment (#9–10)
5. Transition (#11)
6. Free improvisation (#12)

The tonal plan of the piece is as follows:

1. #1–3—C Ionian
2. #4—D minor
3. #8—E minor (tonicizations of G, B, and F# minor)
4. #9–10—E minor
5. #12—A major polymodes

A distinctive feature of Hitŭr Petŭr is a gradual introduction of ideas. Kazakov guides his listeners rather than overwhelming them with mixed meters in the opening measures.[20] The most metrically and tonally unstable segment (#8) is balanced on both sides by areas of greater metric and tonal stability.

---

[19]   Hitŭr Petŭr is the name of a popular Bulgarian folktale trickster character.

[20]   This is a different compositional approach that illustrates a departure from the otkrivane models.

In this particular recording, Hitŭr Petŭr starts with a melodic motive combining groupings of twos and threes in a large megameasure produced by two measures of $\frac{15}{16}$ (Example 6.36).

Example 6.36   Hitŭr Petŭr #1

The opening motive, which is in C Ionian, is supported by a bass line underlining a I-IV-ii-V progression. The motive repeats twice (mm. 1–4), ending with a sustained dominant 7th chord (mm. 5–6). It is intriguing how Kazakov resolves the V₇ chord. As mentioned above, one of the characteristics of this piece is a gradual layering of ideas. In this case, while the V₇ chord is sustained in the bass, the third of the tonic triad, E, is supplied in the middle voice (m. 5). In m. 6 Kazakov adds a second layer of resolution for the tonic triad (in the rhythm guitar part) and also supplies the root of the tonic, C, in the middle of an ascending bass line (Example 6.36). This overlapping of a dominant pedal with a gradual resolution to the tonic in a crescendo leads to the complete resolution in m. 7, the rhythmic pattern of Hitŭr Petŭr's primary theme (Example 6.37).

Example 6.37   Hitŭr Petŭr #2

The rhythmic complexity of this segment is a result of polyrhythm. On top of the texture, a tonic pedal provides the expected resolution of the dominant pedal from mm. 5–6. While the expected resolution takes place, Kazakov sets a rhythmic juxtaposition of 3+3+3+3+2+2 in the rhythm guitar against 4+4+4+2+2 in the bass. Alternatively, the bass could be notated with the rhythm of the guitar based on the motives bracketed in Example 6.37. However, the accents, which Kazakov applies on C2, imply that he is thinking in 4+4+4+2+2. As heard on the recording, the drummer, Salif Ali, provides a steady pulse of eighth notes, which assists both guitar players in establishing a steady polyrhythm. The harmonic vocabulary, limited to three chords, shows another departure from the standards previously discussed. The progressions observed—C-Dm7 (I-ii₇) and C-Dm7-Em7 (I-ii₇-iii₇)—show that, as a composer, Kazakov thinks from a non-traditional harmonic viewpoint.

After the rhythm is stabilized in mm. 7–10, Kazakov introduces the primary theme in fast triplets, which adds another layer to the polyrhythm (Example 6.38):

Melody	2+2+2+2+2+2+2+2	¹⁶⁄₁₆ (triplets normalized)
Guitar	3+3+3+3+2+2	¹⁶⁄₁₆
Bass	4+4+4+2+2	¹⁶⁄₁₆

Additional rhythmic complexity is achieved by rhythmic shifts from triplets to normal subdivision in the melody and placement of embellishing auxiliary notes (transcribed only in the first measure of the excerpt). The embellishments further subdivide the fast triplets into smaller note values (Example 6.38).

Example 6.38   Hitŭr Petŭr #3

The next segment (#4), a continuation of the primary theme, has an expanding character, which is accomplished through the interplay of mixed meters (heterometric rows) and accents (Example 6.39).

Example 6.39   Hitŭr Petŭr #4

The first three measures (transcribed in simple meters) create a megameasure of $\frac{16}{16}$ ($\frac{4}{4}$). The second and fourth repetitions of #4 expand the phrase length.

Number 4 is in D Aeolian. The observed progression is i-VI-iv-v for repetitions 1 and 3, and a fanfare-type sonority for repetitions 2 and 4 (Example 6.39). Such fanfare-type non-tertian verticals set a trend still followed by many Bulgarian musicians today.

After the repetition of Hitŭr Petŭr's main theme as #5–7, #8 brings about the culmination of the metric changes, key explorations, and phrase expansions. The mode of #8 is E Aeolian. Kazakov avoids cadencing several times, and creates a looping effect (Example 6.40a and Example 6.40b) that is not resolved until the beginning of #9.

Example 6.40a   Hitŭr Petŭr #8, mm. 28–40

Example 6.40b   Hitŭr Petŭr #8, mm. 41–48

The phrasing of #8 is asymmetrical, which contributes to the perception of evaded cadences. At the end of the last phrase (m. 48) the entire kolyano is repeated for a second time.

Number 8 is preceded by one measure of transition (m. 27) in $\frac{14}{16}$. Typical for Bulgarian folk melodies in Aeolian, mm. 28–31 (#8) tonicize the relative major, G. Melodically, mm. 32–33 have the potential for a cadence in the main mode. In order to evade the cadence, Kazakov does not harmonize m. 33 at all. Measures 34–35 lead away from the tonic, tonicizing the relative major (G: ii-V₇-I) and continuing to a deceptive cadence in the main key, iv-V-VI; mm. 37–38 repeat the deceptive cadence, V₇-VI, and lead to a plagal cadence in the main key (iv-i). The tonic triad at the beginning of m. 40 does not sound conclusive, due to the fact that the melody circles around scale degree 4̂. When the melody finally descends to scale degree 1̂ at the end of the measure, the note in the bass is the fifth of the tonic triad. This is the second evasive cadence. Measures 41–42 tonicize F♯ minor (ii) with the progression iv-v-i followed by a tonicization of the relative major of F♯ minor, A, with a cadence ii-V₇-I (mm. 43–44). Measures 45–46 bring back the deceptive cadence V₇-VI in the main key, which precedes the final III-iv-v of the number. The lack of a tonic triad in the final measure (m. 48) allows Kazakov to repeat the entire number once again.

Number 9 is an area of metrical stability in comparison to #8. It establishes E minor with a pedal (similar to #2), introduces a slower tempo ($\frac{6}{8}$), a different rhythm, and the progression i-i$^4_2$-VI-iv-v (Example 6.41).

Example 6.41   Hitŭr Petŭr #9

This example is quite different from the entire repertoire analyzed thus far. Number 9 anticipates the new style of accompaniment, which Hitŭr Petŭr introduces for the first time. There is far less synchrony between bass and rhythm guitars in comparison to the previous numbers. The disagreement is in terms of both rhythm and harmony. The megameasures combine four measures of $\frac{6}{8}$ in a swing rhythm.

Harmony and rhythm tighten once again in #10, which introduces a song-like second theme in E minor polymode with variable 2nd, 5th, and 7th scale degrees. In the upper octave, scale degree $\hat{7}$ is raised, and serves as a leading tone, whereas in the lower octave it functions as a subtonic (Example 6.42).

Example 6.42   Hitŭr Petŭr #10

Although the melody in m. 64 suggests a Western half cadence (D♯ in the melody), the leading tone is disregarded in favor of a minor v which is a more typical dominant for minor polymodes. Perhaps Kazakov's initial compositional idea was to incorporate a Western half-cadence in m. 64. Knowing Papazov's harmonic preferences from my experience as his accompanist, I think that Kazakov's initial idea might have been "censored" by Papazov.

Number 11 is one of the most challenging transitions in the entire wedding repertoire (Example 6.43). While touring with Papazov in 2005, I noticed that the first four measures of this particular transition were a frequent topic of conversation and jokes associated with musical memory and aging.

Example 6.43   Hitŭr Petŭr #11

Number 12 marks the beginning of Papazov's solo improvisation. Hitŭr Petŭr is the first piece to include a jazz-type riff (boxed in Example 6.44) setting the stage for improvisations. Although the riff is in Hicaz from A, the chords and the bass line do not follow the chordal vocabulary typical for this scale.

Example 6.44   Hitŭr Petŭr riff in #12

In the transcribed improvisatory section, the guitar player, Andrei
Kamzamalov, employs the following chordal vocabulary to accompany
Papazov's improvisation in A major polymodes: A, A7, A/G, Em/D, A7♯9, D,
Am, C, Em7, and inversions of the same chords (Example 6.45).

Example 6.45   Hitŭr Petŭr clarinet improvisation

The bass line, although walking and syncopated, maintains a basic symmetrical structure by supplying the root of the tonic triad, A, on a downbeat at the beginning of a four-measure cycle (Example 6.45). The four-measure framework (megameasure) is also marked by the rhythm guitar. Later in the improvisation (not transcribed) both rhythm and solo become more fluid, where free-jazz style sections interchange with sections containing a four-measure-long megameasure similar to the one discussed above.

Although in Hitŭr Petŭr Andrei Kamzamalov and Radi Kazakov do not incorporate tritone substitutions and modern jazz harmony, this piece opened the door for incorporating advanced jazz harmony into wedding music.

Kopanitsa

Kopanitsa is essentially a rearrangement of Papazov's First Otkrivane from the early 1980s, analyzed earlier in this chapter. The recording of Kopanitsa (CD, Track 29) used for my transcription is taken from Papazov's CD *Orpheus Ascending* (1989) released in the United States. I chose to compare the 1989 Kopanitsa to First Otkrivane in order to illustrate how concert wedding repertoire changed over time.

Prior to comparing the structure of Kopanitsa to that of First Otkrivane, it is important to mention how the concert setting affected the structure of Kopanitsa. First Otkrivane was designed as an opening piece to be performed at weddings. As a concert piece, Kopanitsa is designed to fit in a set concert program adapted to Western audiences.

A comparison of the recordings of Kopanitsa and First Otkrivane highlights several differences. In Kopanitsa, the opening suite is significantly shortened. After #14 of the new arrangement (#15 for First Otkrivane), a new kolyano has been inserted that summarizes meters played up to this point. The section in $\frac{6}{8}$ of First Otkrivane has been removed from the new arrangement and replaced by a section in $\frac{11}{8}$ (Kopanitsa dance). This section has provided the new name of the concert piece. The improvisations in Kopanitsa lack the closed structures observed in First Otkrivane, and can be related to the improvisational style of Hitŭr Petŭr.

Surprisingly, the harmonic accompaniment in the opening suite of Kopanitsa is similar to First Otkrivane. Differences are found primarily at cadences, or at segments where Yuri Kamzamalov's chord choices in First Otkrivane are ambiguous. I will highlight several such moments.

The first dissimilarity is at the final cadence of #2. In D Aeolian, Yuri Kamzamalov concludes #2 of First Otkrivane with a ii-v-i cadence (atypical for Aeolian), where the fifth of the ii chord (B♮) conflicts with the B♭, which is part of the D Aeolian scale. The same measure in Kopanitsa (m. 17) is harmonized with a tonicization of VII (v/VII-VII), which fits the Aeolian mode (Example 6.46).

First Otkrivane, Harmonization of #2

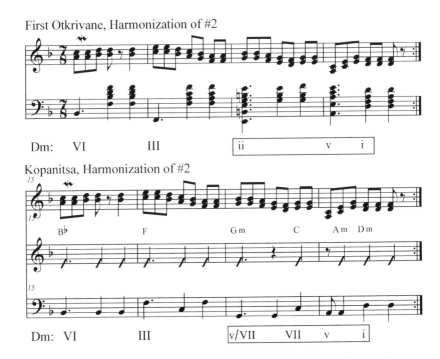

Example 6.46   Comparison between #2 in First Otkrivane and Kopanitsa

Differences are also found in the concluding #11 of First Otkrivane melodically identical to #10 of Kopanitsa (Example 6.47).

As seen in the excerpts, harmonic differences are evident, but they are not structurally significant. The disagreement between bass and rhythm guitars in the Kopanitsa excerpt (m. 57 and m. 59) shows that when the recording was made, the guitar players had not yet reached a complete agreement on the harmonic progression of #10.

After #14 of Kopanitsa (#15 for First Otkrivane), Kopanitsa discontinues the quotation from First Otkrivane and introduces a new kolyano (#15) that is one of the most metrically intricate kolyanos in the entire wedding concert repertoire (Example 6.48).

First Otkrivane, Harmonization of #11

Example 6.47   Comparison between First Otkrivane #11 and Kopanitsa #10

Example 6.48   Kopanitsa #15

The metric intricacy is achieved through non-standard groupings of twos and threes. In Bulgarian music, ¹⁵⁄₈ is typically grouped as 2+2+2+2+3+2+2. The asymmetrical ¹⁵⁄₈ seen in Example 6.48 is an artificial meter created through the reappearance of a group of three notes, two of which are repeated, followed by a stepwise descent. This grouping and rests at the end of motives allow for the accurate transcription of #15. In the first motive, the group of three notes repeats twice. In the second motive, it occurs only once (in the middle of a symmetrical ¹¹⁄₈). In the third and fourth motives, the grouping is repeated three times. As a result, the composer achieves asymmetrical phrasing. The antecedent phrase is 10 beats long, whereas the consequent is 12.

With respect to harmony, m. 80 contains a deceptive cadence in Aeolian involving a minor v. Another non-standard chord in this kolyano is the insertion of IV, which is not followed by iv as part of a standard plagal cadence. Rather, Andrei Kamzamalov uses IV at cadences first as part of IV-v-VI (deceptive) and, second, as part of IV-v-i.

The improvisation section of Kopanitsa starts after the end of #15 with the establishment of a syncopated ¹¹⁄₈ rhythm in the guitars that is reminiscent of the accompaniment in the popular jazz piece Take Five by Paul Desmond, but adapted to an ¹¹⁄₈ meter (Example 6.49).

improvisation

Example 6.49   Kopanitsa rhythm for improvisation

The improvisation contains both metrically structured and free-rhythm segments. The end of Kopanitsa brings back the metrically intricate #15.

The comparison between First Otkrivane and Kopanitsa highlights several points. While in the early 1980s the same piece had a longer pre-composed section continuing into improvisation in the most common danceable rhythm (Pravo Horo), in the late 1980s the piece follows a different model. The pre-composed section has been shortened in lieu of a longer improvisation section in a different meter. Similarly to Second Otkrivane and Hitŭr Petŭr, Kopanitsa's improvisation section is based on long megameasures and accompaniment formulas, giving Papazov enough space to showcase his Balkan jazz improvisations. The model observed in Kopanitsa defines Papazov's style to the present day. While touring with Papazov's band in 2003 and 2005, we often "refreshed" tunes from the early 1980s by rearranging them in the style of Kopanitsa. We used the opening kolyanos from old tunes; inserted rhythmically complex kolyanos mirroring the idea of Kopanitsa's #15; set the stage for improvisation with a riff; and continued with improvisations until Papazov gave us a cue for a closing kolyano or closing section.

Wedding Concert Music from the 1990s

After the collapse of the socialist regime in November 1989, Bulgarian society entered a post-socialist period. Most Bulgarians also perceived the 1990s as a period of transition from a totalitarian regime to a democratic society.

In the early 1990s, most of the political agencies in charge of music censorship were disbanded. On the one hand, after decades of suppression, wedding music quickly began to carve its niche in the national media; on the other, hyperinflation and the declining economy impoverished the real sponsors of wedding music: the patrons hiring wedding orchestras to perform at family celebrations. In the winter of 1994, hyperinflation reached its peak. Within a year, many Bulgarians lost their life savings, including funds set aside for elaborate weddings. After losing its patronage, wedding music entered a period of gradual decline.

The standards for concert wedding music during the 1990s were once again set by Papazov's band. After touring the United States and Australia in 1994, Papazov stopped playing at weddings and community celebrations, focusing instead on concert performances. Papazov kept gaining recognition in the West as a star on the World Music scene. However, during the 1990s, Trakiya's style and repertoire did not change significantly beyond the trends and pieces discussed to this point. In terms of harmonic vocabularies, Radi Kazakov and Andrei Kamzamalov continued their jazz harmony explorations, following the path charted by Second Otkrivane, Hitŭr Petŭr, and Kopanitsa.

This chapter concludes the discussion of wedding music, even though many excellent and influential examples from the wedding repertoire remain outside of its scope. Further studies should pay particular attention to the compositions of Ivan Milev, Petŭr Ralchev, Georgi Yanev, Peyo Peev, Nedyalko Nedyalkov, and other innovators of contemporary Bulgarian wedding music.

Chapter 7

Harmony in Choral Obrabotki:
Choral Arrangements and Compositions
from the 1950s–1980s

This chapter traces the development of choral obrabotki as a genre, starting from the earliest examples and concluding with choral obrabotki from the "avant-garde" period. The general selection of repertoire for this chapter was made with the help of Tsvetanka Varimezova, a former soloist with the Bulgarian National Ensemble of Folk Song and Dance Filip Kutev, and choral conductor at the University of California, Los Angeles. I further reduced Varimezova's selection to the most influential pieces that served as models for the hundreds of choral obrabotki written from 1950 to 2000.

Historical Context

In the early 1950s, Filip Kutev wrote the first choral obrabotki. In her article "'Move over Madonna': Gender, Representation, and the 'Mystery' of Bulgarian Voices," Silverman elaborates on the formation of the first Bulgarian vocal choir and the role of Kutev (2004: 213):

> Kutev's brilliant idea was to take traditional village songs, which are monophonic in most of Bulgaria or have drone-based harmony in the southwest region of the country, and to arrange them into four- or five-part Western harmonies, to add dynamics and tempo changes while preserving the throat-placed vocal quality. With the goal of creating a national folk chorus, Kutev traveled around Bulgaria in the early 1950s to recruit the best female village singers and instrumentalists for the newly formed state-sponsored music ensembles.

Although in Kutev's early choral obrabotki some Western harmonic progressions are evident, the choral obrabotka genre evolved far beyond the adaption of chordal progressions typically found in Western tonal music.[1]

---

[1]   Most Bulgarian songs are modal. Silverman's use of the term "Western harmonies" is accurate only if it refers to triadic verticals not found in Bulgarian traditional polyphony, and not to a complete adaptation of Western cadences, harmonic vocabularies, and chord progressions.

During the socialist period, choral obrabotki were part of a nationalist enterprise closely monitored by socialist censorship. The unwritten rules of the censors can be summarized as follows:

1. Obrabotki should preserve the original song melody and text intact.
2. Harmony should enhance the qualities of the original song without overshadowing its melody.
3. Harmony should be modern (but not too modern) and definitely not too Western or Turkish.
4. Motivic developmental techniques should be avoided because they damage the authenticity of the song, which is considered the most valuable component of the obrabotka.

The rules outlined above dominated the genre decades after Kutev. They can be found even in the opening pages of Abrashev's *Obrabotka i Orkestratsia na Bŭlgarskata Narodna Muzika*, which was published in 1990.

Types of Choral Obrabotki

The choral obrabotki analyzed in this chapter are divided into three categories. The first category includes pieces that use a basic chordal language. The second category groups examples from the "golden period" of choral obrabotki, when composers experimented with different techniques of enriching the standard chordal vocabulary for each scale. The third category includes pieces typifying the avant-garde approach to choral obrabotki and the period of the "emancipation of dissonance."

The primary characteristics of choral obrabotki are close vocal spacing and the incorporation of drones, clusters, triadic harmony, and quintal-quartal verticals. While in traditional vocal music drones are distinct and predictable, in obrabotki from the 1970s–1980s, any pitch of the harmonic texture can be sustained as a drone (pedal voice). In order to analyze examples of this time period and seek the underlying harmonic progressions veiled by textural elements, I have often removed or "normalized" sustained pedals, added pitches, and stacks of seconds. In several choral obrabotki, I have compared the chordal progressions used by composers to a standard triadic harmonization, which is provided above each musical example. These comparisons enabled me to outline vertical displacements and chord substitutions used by the composers and arrangers who expanded the standardized progressions described in Chapter 4.

Pre-1990 Bulgarian scholarship differentiates between two main types of choral obrabotki. The first type prioritizes the original song and incorporates "characteristic harmonic models and combinations of seconds which are typical for Bulgarian folklore [traditional vocal polyphony]" (Kaufman 1977: 125). The second type encompasses *avtorski* (author's) obrabotki, which is characterized by an enhanced role for the arranger in modifying the original songs. Avtorski obrabotki were pioneered by Krasimir Kyurkchiiski.[2] Todorov elaborates on the avtorski obrabotki type (1978: 152):

> We can state that a new [avtorski obrabotki] style was pioneered by Krasimir Kyurkchiiski. The new style did not emerge from the tradition founded by Kutev with its preserved relationship original folk song—obrabotka. Kyurkchiiski set different goals for himself, i.e. to give a musical character to the original song texts in his avtorski obrabotki.

In the mid-1990s, Abrashev introduced a new categorization system[3] dividing choral obrabotki into three categories (1990: 11):

1. Harmonization—the melody of the song is preserved in its original state.
2. Genuine obrabotki—the composer creates a new form which continues, develops, and enriches the original melody.
3. Avtorska obrabotka—the composer creates his own piece using as a model songs or instrumental melodies from a particular region of Bulgaria.

Unlike Abrashev, who classifies obrabotki according to the degree of the arranger's intervention, I suggest a categorization based on the complexity of the applied harmonizations.

Early Choral Arrangements

The chordal vocabulary of early obrabotki is limited to basic triads and closely follows the harmonic formulas outlined in Chapter 4. Timothy Rice provides a detailed description of Kutev's choral obrabotki style, and explains how some of the first choral obrabotki were created (1994: 177):

> His [Kutev's] singers knew how to sing in unison, and some from the southwestern region of the country had sung with drone-based harmonies. He began by teaching them simple choral arrangements with little more than a drone accompaniment. Gradually his arrangements became more complex, with harmony at the third, homophonic textures, and some imitative counterpoint in a typically three-part texture with the introduction of an occasional fourth part.

---

[2] For more information about Krasimir Kyurkchiiski, refer to Appendix B.

[3] Abrashev's categorization system is probably based on Bartók's essay "The Influence of Peasant Music on Modern Music," which outlines similar categories while explaining how folk music is transmitted into modern music (1976: 341–3).

My first analysis focuses on an early choral obrabotka still performed today that established models for the later, more complex choral obrabotki.

Polegnala e Todora

Polegnala e Todora (Todora Lay Down) is a choral obrabotka that is considered "iconic" for the genre (CD, Track 30). Written in 1953, Polegnala e Todora typifies the earliest obrabotki created by Kutev, blending traditional diaphony with a limited chordal vocabulary. The obrabotka has preserved the original song intact with respect to mode (Ionian) and structure in the first section. According to Timothy Rice (2004: 65):

> Koutev began with a traditional song tune in four measures in a meter of 11 (2+2+3+2+2), but everything else about the piece is composed. First he added a second melody of four measures to lengthen the song's form. Then his wife, Maria Kouteva, composed a new text on a folk theme. The text tells of a girl who lies down to rest in the shade of a tree, but she becomes annoyed when falling leaves interrupt her dreams of a boyfriend … Koutev created a three-part choral score for the original melody and set his composed melody for a quartet of soloists.

As an obrabotka, Polegnala e Todora is in simple binary form, **AB**, in which each section is repeated. The opening section, **A**, involves antiphonic singing, a typical feature of traditional Bulgarian group singing that also became a cliché for early choral obrabotki. Kutev divides the female choir into two groups singing the same melodic and harmonic material. In traditional antiphony, when the second group enters, the first group sustains the last sonority, a feature also employed by Kutev. The mode of the song is D Ionian, which allows for the incorporation of Western chordal vocabulary. Example 7.1 illustrates the original song as used in the **A** section of the obrabotka.

Example 7.1   Polegnala e Todora, section **A**

Example 7.2 explains Kutev's compositional procedures by highlighting the elements added to the original folk song. Kutev's chordal vocabulary includes tonic prolongations and Western authentic cadences of the types ii-V-I and IV-V-I.

Example 7.2   Polegnala e Todora, compositional processes in section **A**

As seen from the example, Kutev embellishes the main melody in section **A** by adding parallel thirds over a tonic pedal (Example 7.2). At cadences Kutev interrupts the pedal, preserving the close vocal spacing. In m. 4, the motion in parallel thirds is transferred to the second and third voices, resulting in a IV₆-V-I cadence.

The second section of the song (a composed addition to the original song) has two repetitions that involve structurally insignificant differences in the final cadences. Kutev uses a four-voice texture, with the third voice sustained as a tonic pedal. The Roman numeral analysis (Example 7.3) lists the chord progressions. In many cases, the pedal voice is not part of the chordal verticals, but rather serves as a unifying force for the entire section.

Example 7.3   Polegnala e Todora, section **B**

The harmonization can be reduced to IV-I-ii°-I-V-I. The final cadences of **B** sound incomplete because of the sustained pedal voice, D, and the omitted leading tone (C♯) in the dominant. It is possible that the C♯ is omitted because it is not present in the scale. The only C seen in the melody, m. 10, is a C♮, which implies Mixolydian as the mode, or a major polymode with variable 7th scale degree. Rather than acknowledging the Mixolydian, Kutev omits the third of the dominant throughout the entire harmonization.

The literature during the socialist period often portrayed Kutev as the model of a composer who enriched original folk songs. In his book *May it Fill your Soul*, Rice also says (1994: 177):

> The most important principle, and one that distinguishes his arrangements from many treatments of folk song by classical composers, was that the song melody was always heard in its entirety and then repeated in full, retaining the strophic structure of ordinary village singing. The song tunes never collapsed into melodic motives to be 'developed' in the manner of classical composition. Motives might be used as countermelodies or in brief points of imitation, but the tune proceeded unbroken through a number of varied repetitions.

Ironically, Polegnala e Todora, which is frequently shown as a model for obrabotka with minimal composer intervention, contains an entire section which is composed.

Some of the key features of Polegnala e Todora became standards for the choral obrabotki genre. These standards include chordal functions blurred by pedals, ambiguous dominants at cadences, functional harmony intertwined with pedals, and a preference for close vocal spacing or small intervals (seconds, thirds, and fourths). Most of the features summarized above became guidelines for Kutev's followers and a formulaic model of how "authentic" songs should be properly enriched. Even today, Polegnala e Todora is one of the first pieces performed in concerts.

Choral Arrangements from the "Golden Period" of Choral Obrabotki

Each of the songs in this section illustrates a different trend in choral obrabotki from the 1970s. The songs selected for analysis are organized in order of increasing complexity rather than chronology.

Ergen Deda

Ergen Deda (Old Bachelor) is a choral obrabotka by Petŭr Lyondev[4] written in 1975 (CD, Track 31). Lyondev is primarily a classical composer who also wrote choral obrabotki. Ergen Deda is an arrangement that exemplifies key changes,

---

[4]   For more information about Petŭr Lyondev, refer to Appendix B.

contrasts, and instrumental imitation as obrabotka techniques. Unlike Polegnala e Todora from the early 1950s, Lyondev's obrabotka involves transitions between sections and a Coda.

The main key centers associated with sections are B minor (section **A**), F♯ minor (section **B**), F♯ major (section **C**), and C♯ major (Coda). The three main sections have the formal design **AA′A″**, since they are based on the same melodic material. For the purpose of this harmonic analysis, however, I will refer to them as sections **A**, **B**, and **C**.

Ergen Deda begins with a short introduction, mm. 1–3, which is a vocal imitation of the sound of tŭpan playing in the rhythm of Rŭchenitsa in $\frac{7}{8}$ (2+2+3). Later in the song, rhythmic accompaniment on wooden spoons and tŭpan join the vocal parts in a percussive dialogue. The incorporation of percussion vocal imitation, wooden spoons, and tŭpan relates to the lyrics of the song, which depict a funny story of a grandfather joining young girls at the village dance. The song is a parody of the old bachelor dancing, and the percussion elements refer to the musical accompaniment at the dance event. From a cultural perspective, the text of the song illustrates a culturally unacceptable setting of an old unmarried male attempting to attract the attention of young girls at a public event.

Section **A** (mm. 4–19) of the arrangement is in B minor and involves a twofold repetition of the original folk song. The first eight measures after the introduction (mm. 1–3) are monophonic (Example 7.4).

Example 7.4   Ergen Deda section **A**, mm. 4–12

For the repetition of the verse (starting in m. 12), Lyondev adds a steady drone on scale degree $\hat{1}$, which, as already mentioned, is a standard reference to the drone tradition not only in choral obrabotki, but also in performances of ensemble-influenced village-style and wedding music. After the end of section **A** (m. 19), Lyondev uses mm. 20–25 as a transition to section **B** and the new key center of F♯ minor (Example 7.5).

Example 7.5   Ergen Deda, mm. 20–25

Following classical models, Lyondev prepares the arrival of F♯ minor with a cadence, which, although blurred by suspensions and drones, follows the functional logic of Western cadences. In the transition, F♯ is held as a drone for mm. 20–23; a G♯ drone is added in m. 21 followed by a C♯ drone in m. 22. From a harmonic point of view, m. 20 is related to the old key of B minor (tonic), and also serves as a pivot chord (subdominant) to the new key center. The following measure contains a V/V (or ii$^{ø}_{7}$) to the new key F♯ minor. The vertical in m. 22 is a typical dominant for the choral obrabotki of the 1970s–1980s, a quintal-quartal V$^{5}_{4}$. Within such a vertical, the question remains open as to whether the dominant is major or minor. In mm. 22–23, a dominant pedal voice prepares the arrival of F♯ minor.

Section **B**, in F♯ minor, is a transposition of section **A** with a fuller chordal accompaniment. In a three-voice texture, Lyondev maintains the drone on scale degree $\hat{1}$ for the first two measures of the section, mm. 25–26; mm. 27–28 have quartal chords on downbeats. In the following decades, more non-tertian (quartal and quintal) harmony is evident in choral obrabotki, in which the fourth becomes a preferred vertical even for melodies in parallel motion. Example 7.6 contains a chordal analysis of section **B** (mm. 27–33).

Example 7.6   Ergen Deda, mm. 27–33

Measure 26 illustrates the vertical F♯-G♯-B, which on the one hand is perceived functionally as tonic due to the drone on scale degree $\hat{1}$, but on the other hand as an incomplete ii$^4_2$ chord.[5] The harmonic progression VI-VII-i can be interpreted as an inversion of the descending melodic motive C♯-B-A. Measure 30 blends two functions together. The C♯ and G♯ imply dominant, while B and G♯ imply predominant. The overlapping of subdominants and dominants is characteristic of later obrabotki, where the dominant at a cadence is often suggested by a single pitch within a plagal cadence.[6] The final authentic cadence of this section, mm. 31–32, is transformed into a deceptive cadence, allowing Lyondev to insert a $\hat{6}$-$\hat{7}$-$\hat{1}$ ascent in the lowest voice. As stated in chapters 3 and 4, a $\hat{7}$-$\hat{1}$ conclusion is typical of Bulgarian drone-type diaphony. If that were removed, the cadence in mm. 31–32 would sound Western, with a root motion by 5th. These two measures can be viewed as a summary of the harmonic organization of choral obrabotki as a whole, a blend of Western chordal logic (subordinated to modes) and Bulgarian textural elements.

Section **C** is preceded by a transition that prepares the arrival of a new key, F♯ major (Example 7.7).

---

[5]   In the 1970s–1980s, chordal verticals blending two functions become standard for choral obrabotki.

[6]   A similar phenomenon was observed in #1 of Papazov's Second Otkrivane (Chapter 6, Example 6.31).

Example 7.7   Ergen Deda, mm. 33–40

The second transition is diaphonic and concludes with a drone-type cadence, $\hat{7}$-$\hat{1}$. The transition can be considered a tonic prolongation, where the third of the tonic triad is held over from the previous section, and supplied in the melody only in m. 35.

Section **C** is a modified version of the original song in the parallel key, F♯ major (Example 7.8).

Example 7.8   Ergen Deda, mm. 41–44

Although section **C** is in Ionian, Lyondev continues to avoid standard Western cadences, as he did in previous sections. The C♯ (third voice) in m. 44 anticipates the pedal voice of the Coda that follows (Example 7.9). The Coda explores the F♯-G♯-C♯ sonority, a blend of the fifths of the dominant and tonic triads (V_4^5).

Example 7.9   Ergen Deda, mm. 45–51

In m. 48, the texture is intensified by the rhythm of the tŭpan, followed by the continuation of the Coda, which further increases the tension with a transposition of the same V_4^5 vertical (mm. 52–63). A culmination is reached in m. 60 (Example 7.10).

Example 7.10   Ergen Deda, mm. 52–62

Lyondev begins his preparation for the culmination in m. 57 by layering sustained voices, starting with C♯ in the alto. An F♯ pedal is added in the last beat of the measure. The next measure, m. 58, adds two more sustained pitches (drones), G♯ and B, followed by a C♯ doubling the second alto at the octave (m. 59). The vertical in m. 59 contains the fifths of all three primary triads, i.e. tonic, subdominant, and dominant. In the following measure (m. 60) the vertical is transformed into an ii°⁶₅ chord which leads to a dominant open fifth chord on the downbeat of m. 61. The third of the dominant is omitted even in the Coda.

Taken out of the context of previous key relationships, the final measures of the Coda (mm. 57–62) can be reinterpreted as being in makam Hicaz from C♯ (C♯-D-E-F-G-A♭-B♭-C). From such a perspective, the Coda does not end on a half cadence but with a v°⁶₅-I authentic cadence in Hicaz. Lyondev uses this type of ending both to create listeners' expectations for a return to the F♯ key areas (through a dominant pedal) and to explore the tension potential of makam Hicaz applied at a point of culmination. The use of makam Hicaz at the point of culmination is not a compositional innovation, but rather a phenomenon based on folk music practice.

After the Coda, the entire song is repeated with a different text. The singers have added expressive elements such as shouts and raised speech imitation to the culmination. This underlines the effect of the Coda, which ends on a high point of tension echoed by the tŭpan rhythm.

The Ergen Deda obrabotka reveals several conventions. It involves transposition of the original (or modified) song to a variety of keys, and features an expansion of the form. The harmonic vocabulary includes the exploration of quintal-quartal chords for textural intensification, complex harmonic verticals (clusters) at culmination points built through layering, bifunctional chords, and an expanded harmonic texture in the Coda. This last convention became a trademark of choral obrabotki, as it often expanded from a three- or four-voice texture to six, seven, or eight in the Coda. Climactic vocal Codas have their analogue in instrumental music. Instrumentalists prefer to end pieces with symmetrical *kolyanos*, frequently in makam Hicaz and at increased tempos. Although instrumental closing phrases do not feature choral clusters or particular complex chordal verticals, the idea of concluding a piece at the peak tension level is quite similar.

It is noteworthy that the vocal technique of singers in female choirs allowed composers/arrangers to use clusters in obrabotki. In the polyphonic vocal oral tradition, folk singers are typically praised for holding major and minor seconds perfectly in tune. The clusters at culminations in choral obrabotki are an expanded version of traditional diaphony, in which chords are perceived by the singers as layers of traditional diaphony.[7] The cluster at the culmination of Ergen Deda (mm. 57–60) is built additively. If the vertical from m. 60 is placed on the downbeat of m. 57, the singers would experience significant difficulties with intonation. One of the choral obrabotki analyzed later in this chapter, Kalimanku Denku by Krasimir Kyurkchiiski, involves similarly challenging chordal verticals; for this reason, this obrabotka has been recorded successfully only once.

Aida Tsŭfti Ruzho

Aida Tsŭfti Ruzho (Blossom Ruzha Flower) is a choral obrabotka by Kiril Stefanov,[8] former director of the Pirin State Ensemble based in the city of Blagoevgrad, Southwestern Bulgaria. I have chosen this song in order to illustrate how obrabotki of the 1970s began expanding in terms of form. Stefanov explores different textures that range from one soloist to five voices. The recording of this obrabotka (CD, Track 32) is taken from an album of the Pirin Ensemble. On this recording, Kiril Stefanov conducts the ensemble's female choir himself.

Aida Tsŭfti Ruzho is in E Aeolian; therefore, according to the conclusions derived so far about harmonizations in Aeolian, a III-i tonal juxtaposition, tonicization of VII, and use of standard cadences (IV-iv-i and v-i) can be predicted. In the previously analyzed obrabotki, both Kutev and Lyondev placed the original songs at the beginning of the obrabotka or after a short introduction (Ergen Deda). In Aida Tsŭfti Ruzho, Stefanov moves the original song to the middle of the obrabotka. The original song, which serves as a foundation for Stefanov's obrabotka, is illustrated in Example 7.11.

---

[7]   This is also the reason that, in many choral obrabotki, chordal tones are spelled incorrectly from the viewpoint of Western music theory. Bulgarian composers and arrangers accommodate the singers and their diaphonic/linear thinking.

[8]   For more information about Kiril Stefanov, refer to Appendix B.

Example 7.11   Aida Tsŭfti Ruzho, original song

The song is from the Pirin region, in Southwestern Bulgaria.[9] The meter of the song, an asymmetrical $\frac{7}{8}$ grouped as 3+2+2, is the most typical meter for the musical traditions of the Pirin region. As seen in the example, the range of the folk song is a perfect 5th. As previously stated, tonicizations of III occur primarily when the melody develops higher than scale degree $\hat{2}$. Therefore, the opening descent, $\hat{3}$-$\hat{2}$-$\hat{1}$, limits the harmonization to a great extent.

Stefanov begins this obrabotka with a long introduction (mm. 1–11) that is based on motives from the song and gradually prepares the arrival of a complete, harmonized verse. From a first listening to the introduction, two typical features for choral obrabotki stand out: drones and plagal cadences. The first subsection of the introduction, mm. 1–4, has two motives. The first motive (mm. 1–2) concludes with an arrival on scale degree $\hat{2}$, which is also seen in measures 2 and 4 of the original song, while the second motive concludes on the second sustained pitch of the original song (scale degree $\hat{4}$) (Example 7.12).

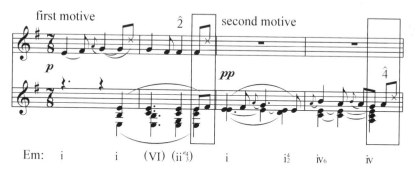

Example 7.12   Aida Tsŭfti Ruzho, mm. 1–4

The first motive is harmonized with a plagal cadence over a drone on scale degree $\hat{1}$. The chords in m. 2 are hard to distinguish harmonically, due to the $\hat{1}$- $\hat{5}$ drones sustained from m. 1. As mentioned in previous analyses, such blends of chords and drones are typical for later examples of choral obrabotki, in which the

---

9   See Map 4.7 in Chapter 4.

listener's ear is often presented with multiple choices for chordal functions. The first vertical in m. 2 combines i and VI. In the following vertical, E and G support the tonic; however, the overall perception of the sonority is ii⁴₃. The last vertical of the measure is almost identical to the previous one, but its function as ii⁴₃ is clearer. If reduced, the harmony of the first motive is essentially a move from tonic to ii°or, on a deeper level of structure, a tonic prolongation (drone on scale degree 1̂). The second motive (mm. 3–4) features harmonic motion from i to iv.

The second subsection of the introduction, mm. 5–8, combines the first two motives of the first subsection, and quotes the last two measures of the original song (Example 7.13).

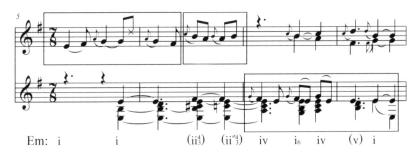

Example 7.13   Aida Tsŭfti Ruzho, mm. 5–8

This example is essentially a summary of the entire original song. Stefanov uses i₇-ii⁴₃-ii⁴₃ and a pedal voice, which is a slightly modified version of m. 2. This is followed by a predictable plagal cadence (iv-i₆) and a iv-v-i cadence.

The introduction is extended by three measures (Example 7.14) that serve as a transition between the reduced version of the song and the harmonization of a complete verse.

Example 7.14   Aida Tsŭfti Ruzho, mm. 9–11

From a harmonic point of view, Example 7.14 illustrates a combination of pedals and seconds that is ultimately perceived as tonic prolongation.

The harmonization of the original song occurs in mm. 12–19 of the obrabotka (Example 7.15).

Example 7.15 Aida Tsŭfti Ruzho, mm. 12–19

The first half of the verse contains an added drone on scale degree $\hat{1}$ and gradually expands to a four-voice texture. The antecedent phrase (mm. 12–15) arrives on a ii°⁴₃ chord (same as the introduction). Measures 16 and 17 of the consequent phrase also repeat verticals iv and ii°⁶₅ already explored in the introduction. The final cadence of the harmonized verse contains a clear V₇/v followed by an incomplete v (obscured by a tonic pedal in middle voice), VI⁴₂, an incomplete v, and i. As evident in the following analyses, VI is frequently used as a substitute for iv at cadences in Aeolian. The incomplete v is also representative of the "transparent" dominant chords used in choral *obrabotki* of this period. The drone on scale degree $\hat{1}$ is sustained throughout the entire verse.

The Coda contains a iv-v-i cadence and ends with a minor second (E-F), an atypical cadential device (Example 7.16).

Example 7.16 Aida Tsŭfti Ruzho, mm. 24–25

The v chord in the last measure lacks its fifth, which is replaced by an anticipated tonic pedal in the middle voice. The final minor second interval is not heard on the recording. Similar free interpretations of the score become evident in other recordings as well. This could be due to particular aesthetic preferences of the conductor (in this case the composer himself), or to the large umbrella of "folk music" in which all melodies and songs, whether arranged or not, could be subject to minor modification by conductors and performers.

Pilentse Pee Govori

Pilentse Pee Govori (A Nightingale Sings and Speaks) is a choral arrangement by Krasimir Kyurkchiiski (CD, Track 33).[10] Between 1968 and 1971, Krasimir Kyurkchiiski was the conductor of the State Radio Choir, which later became popular as Le Mystère des Voix Bulgares. Known among Bulgarian musicians as a radical innovator, Kyurkchiiski constantly pushed the limits of his singers. This obrabotka illustrates expanded choral texture (six voices) and quintal-quartal harmony combined with multiple drones. The recording of Pilentse Pee Govori is taken from an album by Le Mystère des Voix Bulgares.

Structurally, the original song, which serves as the foundation of this particular choral arrangement, is in a Phrygian/Aeolian polymode (Example 7.17).

Example 7.17   Pilentse Pee Govori, original song

Following Kutev's standards, Kyurkchiiski begins his obrabotka with the original song in a diaphonic, melody and drone-type setting (Example 7.18).

The next line of text surprises the listener with a six-voice texture involving four drones (on scale degrees $\hat{1}$ and $\hat{5}$) and a doubling of the melody a fourth below (Example 7.19a and Example 7.19b).

---

[10]   The author of this study is unable to provide precise or approximated years of when Kyurkchiiski's wrote some of the choral arrangements analyzed in this chapter. In a phone conversation with the composer that took place in the summer of 2007, Kyurkchiiski said: "I cannot specify years; all these obrabotki were written between 1970 and 1985."

Example 7.18   Pilentse Pee Govori, mm. 1–6

Example 7.19a   Pilentse Pee Govori, mm. 7–8

Example 7.19b   Pilentse Pee Govori, mm. 9–12

Motion in parallel fourths is unknown in the Bulgarian tradition. In the Balkans, melodies in parallel fourths are found in Greek Pontic music and musical accompaniment for fire-walking ceremonies in Southern Thrace (present-day Northern Greece). It is debatable as to whether or not Kyurkchiiski is imitating Pontic music in Pilentse Pee Govori or simply experimenting with dissonance.

In m. 10 (Example 7.19b), Kyurkchiiski interrupts his drones and cadences with a plagal Phrygian cadence of the type II6-i7. The II-i cadence in Phrygian, similar to the II-I cadence in Hicaz, is generally avoided by composers and accompanists. This is probably due to comparisons to Spanish music that typically cadences II-i (in Phrygian) or II-I (in the Spanish equivalent of Hicaz), or its associations with Balkan Romani music that cadences II-i or III-II-i (in Phrygian) and II-I or ♭III-II-I (in Hicaz). In the context of Pilentse Pee Govori, I suggest that Kyurkchiiski is using "unexplored" progressions in his choral arrangement.

In the following segment, the first half of the verse is placed in the dominant key, F♯ minor, followed by a return to the main key, B minor. In m. 15, Kyurkchiiski combines tonic and dominant in a four-voice texture. The next line of text is presented in mm. 13–18 (Example 7.20).

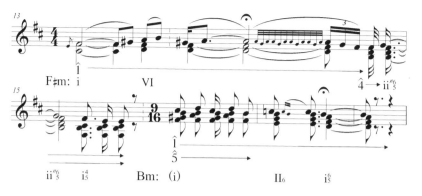

Example 7.20   Pilentse Pee Govori, mm. 13–18

In m. 19 (Example 7.21), Kyurkchiiski uses all the tools mentioned above to achieve contrast: changing the tempo, the key, the harmony, and the texture (from six voice to four voice). In the middle of m. 19, he brings back parallel fourth motion, this time with the doubling on top. From a harmonic perspective, voices 1 and 2 are in B minor, whereas the parallel melodic line is in F♯ minor, the dominant key. The supporting drones at the beginning of m. 19, C♯ and F♯ (scale degrees $\hat{1}$ and $\hat{5}$ for F♯ minor), confirm that Kyurkchiiski is juxtaposing two different key centers.

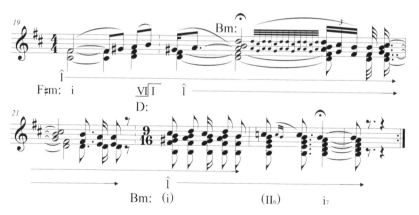

Example 7.21   Pilentse Pee Govori, mm. 19–24

Prior to the entrance of the top voices (in B minor with a drone on scale degree $\hat{1}$), the drones in the low voices change to D and F♯. For the key of F♯ minor, these drones support VI, but for B minor they imply III. In m. 20, although blurred by drones, the first vertical is perceived as ii$^{\sharp 4}_{3}$ in F♯ minor, followed by III at the end of the measure. The last vertical is III of B minor, or VI of F♯ minor. While it is highly debatable whether any of those functions predominate, I consider it worthwhile searching for explanations in order to trace Kyurkchiiski's compositional logic. The compositional technique used in this segment is the temporary overlapping of two key areas. From a purely Western theoretical perspective, the same segment can also be perceived as quintal-quartal harmony and dominant tension functioning as a half cadence.

The continuation of the line of text, mm. 22–24, is in B minor. Both harmonically and texturally, this segment is identical to its first six-voice presentation in mm. 10–12. For the next line of text, mm. 25–30, Kyurkchiiski juxtaposes F♯ minor and C♯ minor, and after m. 28, he returns to the main key of the obrabotka, B minor (Example 7.22).

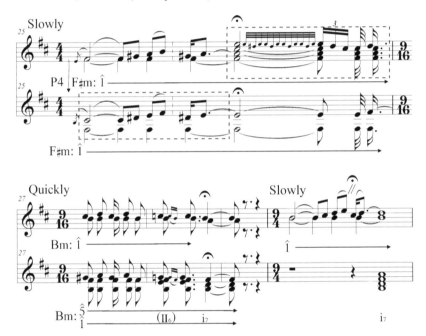

Example 7.22   Pilentse Pee Govori, mm. 25–31

The key of F♯ minor is presented by doubling the melody a fourth below with an added drone on scale degree 1̂. Halfway through m. 26, voices 1 and 2 enter by continuing the melody in the dominant key of F♯ minor (C♯ minor). The first six-voice vertical is perceived as an overlapping of F♯ minor and A major, or an F#m9. The drones in m. 26 are C♯, A, and F♯, which support both chords. The final vertical of m. 26 is D♯ half-diminished in first inversion, which is difficult to explain functionally in any of the key areas established in the excerpt. Measure 27 also contains an ambiguous quintal-quartal vertical (B-E-F♯-A). The F♯ and B from this measure can be viewed as an anticipation of the continuation of this section in B minor.

The following section is almost identical to previous presentations of the same melodic material with a slight modification in the fifth voice in which Kyurkchiiski adds an extra fourth to the overall vertical. The final cadence of the section restates the previously introduced Phrygian cadence II₆-i₇. The obrabotka ends with a two-voice restatement of the opening measures (mm. 1–2) presented as melody and drone followed by a i₇ vertical in a six-voice texture.

In Pilentse Pee Govori, Kyurkchiiski tests the limits of the singers in terms of texture and vertical sonorities. This particular obrabotka stands out in obrabotki repertoire for its unique exploration of quintal-quartal harmony and the incorporation of multiple drones juxtaposing different key centers. I suggest that Kyurkchiiski's quintal-quartal harmonic ideas may be rooted in scales such as Shope major, in which the final triads could be built either downward (Shope harmony) or upward (Aeolian). If the opening fifths of both final triads are combined, they produce a quintal-quartal vertical.[11]

Kalimanku Denku

Kalimanku Denku (God Mother Denku) is recognized as one of the most well-known choral obrabotki of Krasimir Kyurkchiiski (CD, Track 34). Hristova describes the first stage performance of Kalimanku Denku in 1971 as a turning point in the history of the choral obrabotki genre. Prior to this performance, according to Hristova, folk choirs and their repertoire were not "considered seriously by the [Western] Europe-oriented Bulgarian music society" (2007: 55). Written particularly for the female choir at the Bulgarian National Radio, Kalimanku Denku became one of the symbols of modern Bulgarian choral traditions.

The arrangement is based on a free-rhythm folk song from the region of Strandzha, Southeastern Bulgaria.[12] According to Todorov, Kyurkchiiski does not develop an "authentic song," but rather creates his own version of the song as sung by Yanka Rupkina, the soloist on the recording (1978: 152–6). Hristova, the current conductor of Le Mystère des Voix Bulgares, expresses a different opinion. According to her, "in Kalimanku Denku, the regional ornamentation of the Strandzha song is completely preserved by the authentic singer, Yanka Rupkina. In Kyurkchiiski's texture, one may feel balance, a unity of professional and folk thinking, freedom, and improvisation" (2007: 83–4).

---

[11]   For example, if the final note (or tonic) is B, a triad built upward would produce the open fifth B-F♯. A triad built downward from the same note would have an open fifth of E-B (V for Shope major). The two open fifths combined create the quintal-quartal vertical of B-E-F♯-B. The same harmonic phenomenon (suggesting more than one possible tonic) was observed in the introduction of Kopanitsa as performed by the Harmanliiskata Troika (Chapter 5, Example 5.18) and in the introduction of Papazov's Second Otkrivane (Chapter 6, Example 6.30).

[12]   See Map 4.5 in Chapter 4.

The Kalimanku Denku obrabotka has a homophonic texture presented by a soloist and three accompanying voices, but only expands to a five-voice texture in several cadences. Kalimanku Denku is qualitatively different from previously discussed obrabotki in that it features chromatic relationships between keys, smooth chromatic voice-leading, and a greater use of seventh chords. The smooth voice-leading observed in this obrabotka does not relate to traditional Bulgarian polyphony. I suggest that the composer has aimed for a song effect captured in the Bulgarian metaphor *pesenta se lee*, which directly translates as "the song pours like water." In my view, the composer aimed for a similar effect in his obrabotka, where descending chromatic voice-leading gradually brings higher textures to the lower register, final cadences, and tonic.

The original Strandzha song is in E minor polymode with a variable 2nd scale degree (Aeolian/Phrygian). As observed in multiple analyses, the most characteristic tonal juxtaposition for this particular minor polymode is relative major-main minor key. According to this formula, one would expect Kyurkchiiski to harmonize significant sections of the song in the relative key, G major.

The form of the obrabotka is binary (**AB**) plus Coda, where **B** has the dual role of contrasting section and restatement of the opening material. The form is hardly perceivable by ear due to the non-metric nature of the obrabotka. However, a detailed look at the original song, as sung by the soloist in section **A** (Example 7.23), greatly assists in the formal analysis.

Each verse of the original song has three subsections, marked **a**, **b**, and **c**, which are based on antecedent-consequent phrasing. Sections **b** and **c** are very similar and have near-identical consequent phrases.

The second section of the obrabotka, **B**, is based on the second verse of the original song. In order to achieve contrast, Kyurkchiiski transposes the first subsection of the second verse, **a**, to the major dominant key, B major (III of G♯ minor), followed by progressions in the new contrasting key of G♯ minor. In the following subsection, **b**, Kyurkchiiski prepares and reaches the culmination of the piece, which is followed by restatements of significant portions of the **b** and **c** subsections of **A** in the main key of E minor. The Coda contains lyrics from the third verse of the song, but it is melodically independent, with the exception of a final restatement of the beginning of the original song at the very end of the obrabotka.

Following the harmonic standards of tonal plans for Phrygian/Aeolian minor polymode, Kyurkchiiski initiates the **a** subsection of **A** in the relative major key area (Example 7.24).

Example 7.23   Kalimanku Denku, first verse of the original song

Example 7.24   Kalimanku Denku, subsection **a** of **A** (antecedent phrase)

Rather than maintaining G as a tonal center for the entire antecedent phrase (typical of 1980s–1990s village and wedding styles), Kyurkchiiski initiates a progression that leads to the tonic of the main key, E minor. Immediately after the G major opening vertical, he moves to a iii chord (B minor) followed by a tonicization of ii (in V^6_5/ii, G♯ is spelled as an A♭). The expectation of an arrival at a ii chord is obscured by an inserted pitch, D4, which can be reinterpreted as a $\hat{7}$-$\hat{1}$ drone in the middle voices (shown with an arrow in the example) inserted in a plagal cadence in E minor. E minor is perceived as an arrival on the tonic due to an inserted scale degree $\hat{1}$ pedal in the lowest voice that is sustained for the rest of the phrase. The pedal harmony on top is a delayed reference to the drone tradition that, in earlier obrabotki, is placed at the very beginning of the obrabotka. The pedal harmony in the present context also has a conclusive effect, as it is based on a standard minor plagal cadence of IV-iv-(i). The expected i at the end of the cadence (Example 7.24) is evaded and postponed to the beginning of the consequent phrase (Example 7.25).

Example 7.25   Kalimanku Denku, subsection **a** of **A** (consequent phrase)

The technique of evaded resolutions is typical for Kyurkchiiski's style, and suggests the use of nineteenth-century Wagnerian techniques adapted to Bulgarian polymodes. The consequent phrase of **a** includes a tonicization of III followed by an inconclusive-sounding cadence of descending parallel 6th chords, III₆-II₆-i₆. The II₆ chord acknowledges the Phrygian descent ($\hat{3}$-$\hat{2}$-$\hat{1}$) in the solo, but, as already pointed out, a II-i Phrygian cadence is atypical for Bulgarian harmony.

Section **b** follows the same basic framework (III-i) with evaded cadences (Example 7.26).

Example 7.26   Kalimanku Denku, subsection **b** of **A**

The antecedent phrase of **b** contains a fuller cadence tonicizing the relative major of the type V/V-V-I. The F♯ minor vertical (labeled as ii in parentheses) that follows V/V is a retrogression used as a harmonic embellishment in a cadence. The antecedent phrase is prolonged after the end of the solo with IV-VI⁶₄, which once again functions as an evaded cadence spinning out the harmonic motion.

The consequent phrase of **b** has III as the first vertical, but in order to avoid harmonic repetition, Kyurkchiiski applies quintal-quartal chords. The end of **b** is harmonized as a pedal with atypical chords on top (V/iv and iv with an added

7th scale degree). Kyurkchiiski provides a tonic triad at the end of the phrase immediately followed by a dominant chord, thereby avoiding the perception of a conclusion. The dominant chord suggests the final chord of a harmonization in Shope major, but it can also be interpreted as part of a plagal extension in E minor.

After applying evasive cadences in **a** and **b**, section **c**, which is the last section of the first verse, is expected to conclude with one of the standard cadences for the Aeolian/Phrygian polymode listed in Chapter 4. The analysis (Example 7.27) shows that Kyurkchiiski not only concludes with a standard iv-i plagal cadence, but also harmonizes the greater portion of section **c** as a tonic prolongation, which references established harmonic conventions and the drone tradition.

Example 7.27   Kalimanku Denku, subsection **c** of **A**

The **B** section of the song (second verse) introduces a contrasting key, G♯ minor. The modulation to a distant key is gradual and quite atypical of Bulgarian music. For the **a** subsection of **B**, Kyurkchiiski has chosen once again the standard relative major-home key juxtaposition. The relative major, B, is stated by the very first vertical sonorities. Kyurkchiiski does not prepare the arrival of the new key with a cadence, since B major is the V of E minor (harmonic). Despite the fact that there is no raised 7th scale degree in the E polymode of the previous section, the new tonic-dominant relationship does not sound abrupt (Example 7.28).

Example 7.28   *Kalimanku Denku*, subsection **a** of **B**

The chordal vocabulary seen in Example 7.28 is similar to that at the beginning of **A,** but it also involves new sonorities and clusters resulting from the transferal of the melody to the lowest voice. The applied dynamic contrasts (*sub. pp*) and the textural contrast (four soloists) have a dual purpose: first, they blur the similarity between the chordal progressions of the opening sections of **A** and **B**; and second, they prepare the arrival of the culmination in the antecedent phrase of subsection **b** (Example 7.29).

Example 7.29   Kalimanku Denku, subsection **b** of **B** (antecedent phrase)

The first element of the culmination is a register transfer of the solo from the fourth voice to the soloist on top of the texture. The dynamic at this point is increased to *mf*. A second element is an ascent of the choir with a *crescendo*. A third element is the registral transfer of the melody back to the third voice, combined with *forte* dynamic. A fourth and final element is a cluster with a minor second on top (marked in the example with a dotted box). From the viewpoint of harmony, the inverted B major 7th is the dominant of the main key (E minor), making possible (in Western classical music terms) a smooth modulation. Rather than resolving the dominant to tonic, the composer applies a chromatic common-tone modulation. This surprise modulation to Em via V$^4_2$/III is accomplished by sustaining B in soprano, with the additional help of a common tone F♯ in middle voices.

After this climax, Kyurkchiiski applies *sub. p* and continues the section in E minor polymode with an exact textural and chordal repetition of the same section in **A**. The rest of section **B** has the same harmonization as **A**, only with a slower harmonic rhythm.

The obrabotka ends with a Coda that, melodically speaking, is not based on the original song. The Coda contains new melodic motives, harmonic elements, and a series of passing chromatic tones. As seen in Example 7.30, all of these elements are supported by a tonic pedal leading to the last chord of the song, a $i_{7\flat}$ sounded in a *ppp* dynamic.

Example 7.30   Kalimanku Denku, Coda

Codas of this type are characteristic of obrabotki of the 1970s and 1980s. Although in the 1950s–1960s the concluding measures tend to be primarily triadic or involve extended tertian verticals, a tendency toward "mysterious" conclusions in the 1970s–1980s gradually emerged. Kyurkchiiski's final chord can be interpreted as a blend of the two common tonal areas for E minor polymodes, G major (III) and E minor, where the G major triad has been modified to an augmented triad. The perception of G augmented overpowers E minor due to the greater number of singers singing the root of the chord, scale degree $\hat{3}$. On the other hand, E as a pedal has already built expectations for an arrival on E as a minor tonic. Kyurkchiiski's final textual statement is a *ppp* echo of the beginning of the song.

Several of Kalimanku Denku's features typify obrabotki from the 1970s and 1980s. These features include evasive cadences, pedal tonic prolongations, masking repetition through register transfers, use of clusters at culmination, modulations to distant keys, the overall preservation of the original song form, and a "mysterious" Coda.

As a harmonization, Kalimanku Denku tested the limits of the singers' abilities in Bulgarian choirs. As already stated, this choral obrabotka has been successfully recorded only once; this recording is included on the attached CD, Track 34.

Kalimanku Denku is a highly praised obrabotka due to its balance between traditional and modern sounds. The prestigious status of this obrabotka in both past and present choral repertoires provoked me to experiment with a Western reductive analytical approach, one that has not yet been applied to Bulgarian modal music. My reductive analysis is based on Schenkerian principles modified to fit the modal context of the Kalimanku Denku obrabotka. Similar to a standard Schenkerian approach, I considered chordal hierarchies within the Aeolian/ Phrygian polymode, examined the structural significance of cadences, and searched for a hidden background structure or a Phrygian *Urlinie* (a 3-, 5-, or 8-line fundamental descent). Example 7.31 shows my reductive analysis of the first section of the obrabotka, **A**, or the first verse of the original song.

Example 7.31   Kalimanku Denku, reductive analysis

Despite the modal context and lack of Western authentic cadences, my reductive graph shows remarkable parallels between the structure of Kalimanku Denku and pieces written by Western classical composers. At a deeper level of structure, the **A** section includes two complete 5-lines ($\hat{5}$-$\hat{4}$-$\hat{3}$-$\hat{2}$-$\hat{1}$). The first 5-line prolongs scale degree $\hat{5}$ for more than half of section **A** (subsection **a** and the antecedent phrase of **b**), a phenomenon quite typical for Western classical compositions. The first melodic descent to scale degree $\hat{1}$, which occurs at the end of subsection **a**, is not supported by a strong cadence. Therefore, the descending line cannot be considered structurally significant; rather, it is a descent to an inner voice (scale degree $\hat{1}$) that supports further prolongation of scale degree $\hat{5}$ in the Urlinie. The second descending line, at the end of the antecedent phrase of subsection **b**, descends to the subtonic $\hat{7}$, the root of V/III, which assists for one of the multiple tonicizations of the relative major, G. The final descent of the first Urlinie, at the end of the consequent phrase of subsection **b**, is marked by a conclusive cadence in E minor supported by expected cadential harmonic gestures for an Aeolian/Phrygian polymode.

If compared to the first, the second Urlinie ($\hat{5}$-$\hat{4}$-$\hat{3}$-$\hat{2}$-$\hat{1}$), found at the background level of subsection **c**, moves at a much quicker pace, summarizing all previously introduced ideas: a prolongation of scale degree $\hat{5}$; multiple tonicizations of the relative major; and a standard plagal final cadence.

The bass line of the reductive analysis highlights a harmonic juxtaposition between the relative major and main minor keys. Moreover, the fundamental bass line seen in the graph is in complete agreement with one of the Bulgarian movable drone types, $\hat{3}$-$\hat{1}$, which is typically associated with Aeolian/Phrygian polymodes.

The application of reductive analysis to Kalimanku Denku, along with other pieces not included in this book, led me to surprising conclusions regarding Bulgarian harmony. At deeper structural levels, harmonized Bulgarian music has not traveled far beyond the drone types discussed in Chapter 3. As previously stated, Bulgarian harmony stemmed from several types of drone-based traditional polyphony. I find it remarkable that a modern Western analytical tool could bring a complex Bulgarian harmonic texture such as the one of Kalimanku Denku back to its source—a melody over a drone.

Prochul Se Strahila

Prochul Se Strahila (Word Spread about Strahil) is another choral obrabotka by Krasimir Kyurkchiiski that I have selected as an example of innovative harmony in makam Hicaz. The recording (CD, Track 35) was made by the Cosmic Voices choir.[13]

Prochul Se Strahila obrabotka is based on a free-rhythm folk song from the region of Thrace.[14] The text praises Strahil, a guerilla leader who lived during the seventeenth century and fought against the Turks in the period of Ottoman political domination (fourteenth through nineteenth centuries). Kyurkchiiski shortened the traditional ballad to one verse, leaving aside the long story line that is typically told in traditional ballads. In her book *Izkustvoto na Folklornite Kamerni Vokalni Ansambli* (The Art of Folk Chamber Vocal Ensembles), designed as a manual for conductors of folk choirs, Dora Hristova uses Prochul Se Strahila as an example of a song in non-legato style that presents major difficulties for singers and conductors (2004: 72).

The obrabotka, in C Hicaz, preserves the melody and structure of the original song. Rather than exploring contrasting key changes, Kyurkchiiski plays with established listener's expectations about standard harmonizations in makam Hicaz. According to conventions established in Chapter 4, the most likely tonicization in Hicaz is that of the subdominant (IV or iv). Expected cadences are vii-I (standard) and v$^{\sharp}_7$-I (modern). In the analysis that follows, a standard (basic)

---

[13]   Cosmic Voices is a vocal formation founded in 1994 by the producer Emil Minev, who sought to repeat the success of Le Mystère des Voix Bulgares.

[14]   Refer to Map 4.3 in Chapter 4.

harmonization in each example has been provided to illustrate how Kyurkchiiski's chord progressions deviate from the established harmonic standards.

Each verse of the original song has seven phrases (Example 7.32).

Example 7.32   Prochul Se Strahila, original song

In the obrabotka, Kyurkchiiski has preserved the phrase structure, adding only a Coda. The first two phrases have the overall plan of starting from IV and cadencing in the main key, C Hicaz. In the standard harmonization (abbreviated "SH"), I have outlined the likely placement of basic chords, and indicated with vertical arrows the places where the standard harmonization matches the chordal language chosen by Kyurkchiiski.

The first chord matches the expected beginning of the song from the subdominant for C Hicaz, which, in the Roman numeral analysis, is represented as I in F major (Example 7.33a). Immediately after, however, Kyurkchiiski inserts iii (similar to the first chord connection in Kalimanku Denku) followed by a Hicaz-type tonicization of VI for F major (vii/VI-VI$_5^6$).

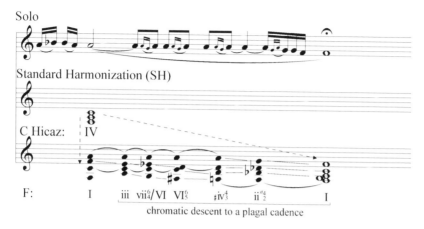

Example 7.33a   Prochul Se Strahila, phrase 1

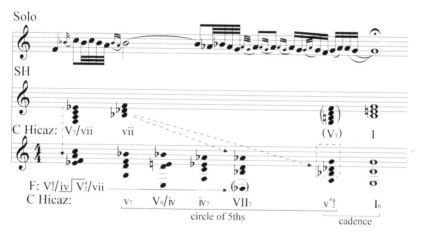

Example 7.33b   Prochul Se Strahila, phrase 2

After the tonicization, the progression is interrupted, and Kyurkchiiski inserts a ♯iv⁴₃, which is difficult to differentiate functionally in F or in C Hicaz, and can be explained only as a passing chord over a tonic pedal. The ii°⁴₃ chord that follows is part of a plagal cadence leading to the tonic (F major). This excerpt can be summarized as "IV-moving away-returning." If a Schenkerian graph of this excerpt were to be constructed, it would show that on a deeper structural level, F major is the chord prolonged for its entirety, which fully matches the basic harmonization.

The second phrase (Example 7.33b) has the basic harmonization of B♭m-C, which is a standard cadence (vii-I) in C Hicaz. A 1990s wedding-style harmonic

embellishment of the above progression would include the insertion of G7 before
C. As a result, the cadence would be perceived not as conclusive for C Hicaz,
but as part of a tonicization leading back to F (beginning of phrase 3), which
postpones the main cadence in C Hicaz with two extra lines (end of line 4). In
such a harmonic context, the chords G7 and C function as V₇/V-V of IV in C
Hicaz. Another explanation for the placement of G7 is that the segment could be
considered as being in F Shope major. In this view, F7-B♭-G7-C is interpreted as
V/iv-iv-V/V-V, a standard progression for Shope major. This interpretation suggests
that in later obrabotki, composers extend their harmonic thinking beyond avoiding
standard progressions to mode reinterpretation and modal borrowing.

In Kyurkchiiski's obrabotka, the expected B♭ minor (Example 7.33b)
is delayed by three chords in a fifth relationship (Gm7-C9-Fm7). At the end
of the excerpt, Kyurkchiiski chooses not to apply G7 (V in C Hicaz, or V/V
as part of a tonicization of iv). Rather, he applies the modern dominant for
Hicaz, $v_\circ^s$ in inversion. Besides being modern, this chord also satisfies listeners'
expectations, as it contains the vii chord as a vertical sonority (boxed in Example
7.33b). If the G is added, the vertical becomes v_2^{s4}, infusing a hint of the G7-C
standard progression.

The next phrase (Example 7.34) employs a standard harmonization procedure
of tonicizing iv, moving to the second predominant, II, and ending on a dominant
in C Hicaz, vii (or v_7^s). Instead of iv, Kyurkchiiski uses II, which makes the first
two verticals perceivable as a Western deceptive cadence (Example 7.34).

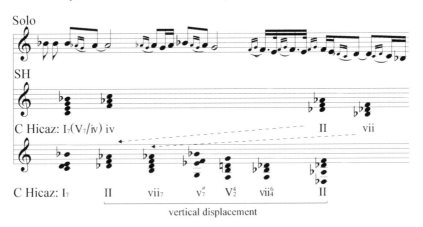

Example 7.34   Prochul Se Strahila, phrase 3

In the middle of the excerpt, the chords are the two dominants for Hicaz
(whose resolution is evaded) followed by a progression that leads to II. From
a standard harmonic perspective, the dominants in the middle—particularly the
V_2^4—are placed inappropriately.

Phrase four is especially interesting to analyze, since it involves a Western major-minor dominant (V₇) in Hicaz which, unless applied as V₇/V/iv, is commonly used as a "musical joke" by wedding musicians at Hicaz cadences (Example 7.35).

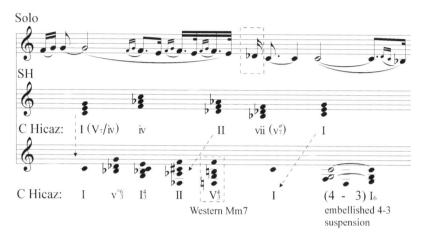

Example 7.35   Prochul Se Strahila, phrase 4

The expected progression for this excerpt suggests a standard Hicaz progression involving a full Hicaz cadence of the type (I)-iv-II-vii (v♯₇)-I. Kyurkchiiski places I and II in their expected positions. The minor subdominant, iv, is omitted, but the Hicaz dominant is replaced with a Western major-minor 7th chord in second inversion. The V₃⁴ is sustained for only one eighth note in order to prevent a conflict with the D♭, part of the 3̂-2̂-1̂ descent in the melody. The vertical presentation of the tonic in the last measure of the excerpt involves a 4̂-3̂ embellished suspension in the lowest voice, which is typical for Western choral music, but never before (or after Prochul Se Strahila) used in harmonizations within makam Hicaz. This is not the only reference to Western choral music in this obrabotka based on a scale with Middle Eastern origins.

The next segment (phrase 5) has the basic harmonization of V/iv-iv-I-iv-II-vii. Kyurkchiiski prolongs the first tonicization of iv longer than anticipated in the standard harmonization by inserting vii₇-V₃⁴/iv-iv, which is equivalent to a iv-V-i tonicization of iv, therefore avoiding the iv-I-iv in the standard harmonization (Example 7.36).

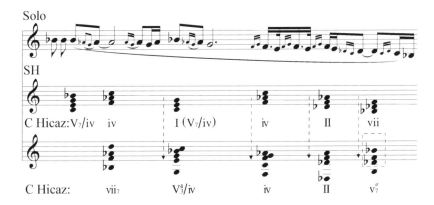

Example 7.36   Prochul Se Strahila, phrase 5

The rest of the analysis demonstrates a complete correspondence with the basic progression, where only the dominant chord is substituted with the more contemporary Hicaz dominant, v_7^a.

Example 7.37 is phrase 6 of the original song. It contains the next line of text, which, according to the standard harmonization, should move from the tonic to II.

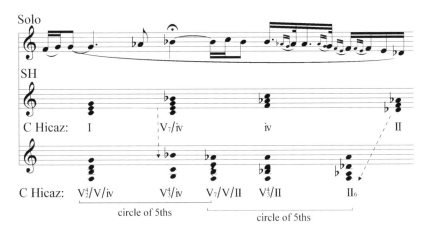

Example 7.37   Prochul Se Strahila, phrase 6

Kyurkchiiski prepares the arrival of C (tonic) with a Western V_2^4, once again demonstrating his large-scale thinking by reinterpreting the tonic resolution as V/iv. The last segment of Example 7.37 should contain iv and II as primary chords. Instead, Kyurkchiiski inserts several chords in middle voices, which, although sounding dissonant to the main key, are actually V/V-V of the following chord, II.

The next phrase is significantly shorter than the previous ones, and, as the final line of the original verse, should include the strongest cadence. Standard harmonization (Example 7.38) suggests ♭V-vii (v⁷)-I. The first chord, characteristic for Hicaz and used by Kyurkchiiski, is generally avoided in obrabotki due to its "implied" Turkish sonority.[15] Once again challenging rules and established models, Kyurkchiiski includes ♭V in its full sonority. He slightly alters the vertical, and therefore achieves the sound of a Western augmented sixth chord. From the perspective of jazz harmony, ♭V₇ can also be viewed as a tritone substitution of the tonic. Since tritone substitutions in jazz are generally applied to dominant chords, ♭V recalls the discussion of "Hicaz or harmonic minor ending on a half cadence."

Kyurkchiiski's final cadence, which concludes the last phrase of the original song, does not match expectations. Rather, the composer restates the 4̂-3̂ Western choral suspension (Example 7.38).

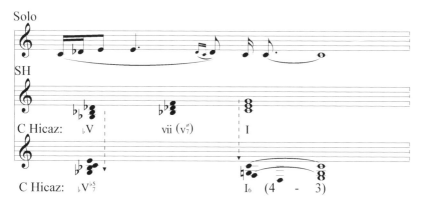

Example 7.38   Prochul Se Strahila, phrase 7

After Kyurkchiiski completes the harmonization of the original song (first verse), he includes five measures of cadential extension followed by a Coda. The cadential extension summarizes some of the chordal vocabulary used so far, and once again introduces ♭V followed by the 4̂-3̂ embellished suspension. The Coda brings back the beginning of the song (F major) and, following 1970s–1980s obrabotki standards, introduces a "mysterious" chord (Example 7.39).

Example 7.39   Prochul Se Strahila, Coda

---

[15]   See Chapter 4 and the discussion of "exotic" chords for Hicaz.

The first three chords of the Coda are a tonic prolongation. This is followed by a stepwise ascent approaching the "mysterious" vertical. In this particular Coda, the "mysterious" chord is ♭vi (F♭ is spelled as E), which is foreign to both F major and the main key, C Hicaz. This ♭vi chord is followed by a plagal descent to I (F major).

In summary, through his Coda, Kyurkchiiski makes the entire original song sound like an extended dominant pedal (C Hicaz) that finally resolves to tonic in Western terminology. However, one question remains: was Kyurkchiiski thinking in Hicaz or in F harmonic minor ending in the parallel key?

Avant-Garde Trends in Choral Obrabotki

By the mid-1970s, Kyurkchiiski had already incorporated in his works a mature system of diatonic harmonization combined with quintal-quartal harmony, whole-tone based verticals, and dissonant clusters. One of the few remaining areas of exploration for obrabotki composers and arrangers was the extended use of dissonance and twentieth-century compositional techniques, which would not be considered "too Western" or "too modern" by the censorship. Avant-garde obrabotki mark the beginning of a compositional trend that can be characterized by the "emancipation" of dissonance and a conscious departure from standardized harmonizations.

The beginning of the avant-garde obrabotki period can be traced back to the mid-1970s, and, more specifically, to Kyurkchiiski's obrabotka *Zableyalo Mi Agŭntse* (A Lamb Was Bleating), the first piece analyzed in this section. The existing literature does not provide any information about the first public performance of Zableyalo Mi Agŭntse. However, according to Hristova, by the mid-1970s, Zableyalo Mi Agŭntse entered the repertoire of several female choirs (2007: 69). In the second obrabotka analyzed in this section, *More Zazheni Se Gyuro* (Hey, Gyuro Is Getting Married), Kyurkchiiski juxtaposes traditional diaphony and whole-tone based verticals and clusters.

Zableyalo Mi Agŭntse

In Zableyalo Mi Agŭntse, Kyurkchiiski takes the exploration of dissonance a step further than any of his predecessors. This obrabotka is based on three verses of an original song, a popular free-rhythm folk song from Thrace. As in Prochul Se Strahila, the song is shortened, so the story line remains incomplete.

The recording of the obrabotka is taken from an album of Le Mystère des Voix Bulgares (CD, Track 36). From the very beginning, Kyurkchiiski states his preferences for dissonances over standard harmonizations. The first verse is preceded by an introduction that creates intonation difficulties for even the most experienced professional singers of the Mystère des Voix Bulgares choir. The original song is in Aeolian mode, and the first verse of the obrabotka is in Aeolian on F♯.

As seen in the analysis shown in Example 7.40a and Example 7.40b, the first verse rarely matches the standard harmonization of the song. In fact, Kyurkchiiski attempts, to the best of his abilities, to avoid standard harmonizations. One of the tools he employs is to think of the song as being in Shope major on E ending with a half-cadence (with B major as the final vertical built downwards), as seen in m. 11. A Shope major reinterpretation of Aeolian allows the composer to avoid the standard placement of the tonic as well.

The second verse (Example 7.41a and Example 7.41b) starts in m. 16, and in m. 22 Kyurkchiiski once again substitutes the tonic with the V of E Shope major (B major). At the end of the second verse, Kyurkchiiski fulfills the listener's expectations for the first time in the piece by using a completely standard Aeolian progression (tonicization of the relative major, followed by a plagal cadence in the main key of the type IV-iv-i).

This can be considered an area of stability preceding the entrance of a contrasting third verse, which introduces a new key (E minor) and modulates to G♯ minor in m. 32 (Example 7.42a and Example 7.42b).

The final Coda (Example 7.43) is built on the opening motive of the original song, and brings back the main key of F♯ minor. After exploring all possible dissonances (seconds, tritones, sevenths, fourths, and clusters), Kyurkchiiski inserts a final reference to something that is "forbidden" in Western common practice: audible parallel fifths in the lowest voices (m. 37).

Table 7.1 summarizes all compositional processes in Zableyalo Mi Agŭntse.

Table 7.1   Summary of compositional processes in Zableyalo Mi Agŭntse

Form	Techniques	Key
Introduction, mm. 1–5	1. Exploration of dissonance (M2)	Atonal
A (first verse), mm. 6–15	1. Avoidance of standard progressions	F#m
	2. The tonic triad in m. 11 is substituted with a HC typical for Shope major	
	3. Expected chords are provided in 12–15	
A' (second verse), mm. 16–25	1. Six-voice texture and 9th chords	F#m
	2. Substitutions of secondary dominants	
	3. Measures 19–25 are similar to mm. 9–15	
A'' (third verse), mm. 26–34	1. Solo is transferred to low voice	Em and G#m
	2. Verticalized plagal cadences	
	3. Delayed or anticipated chords	
	4. Modulation (m. 31)	
Coda, mm. 35–38	1. Initial motive	F#
	2. Exploration of dissonance	
	3. Parallel fifths and voice crossing	

Example 7.40a   Zableyalo Mi Agǔntse, first verse, mm. 1–9

Example 7.40b   Zableyalo Mi Agŭntse, first verse, mm. 10–15

Example 7.41a   Zableyalo Mi Agŭntse, second verse, Mm. 16–21

Example 7.41b   Zableyalo Mi Agŭntse, second verse, mm. 22–28

Example 7.42a   Zableyalo Mi Agŭntse, third verse, mm. 29–33

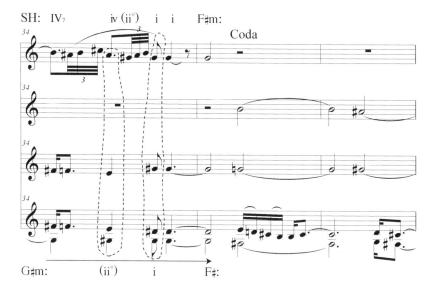

Example 7.42b   Zableyalo Mi Agŭntse, third verse, mm. 34–36

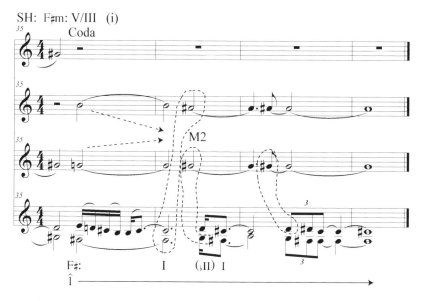

Example 7.43   Zableyalo Mi Agŭntse, Coda

I find it necessary not only to address the differences between Zableyalo Mi Agŭntse and previously discussed works by Kyurkchiiski, but also to highlight some common harmonic procedures. Despite the dissonant introduction and dissonant second verse, Zableyalo Mi Agŭntse features the same type of smooth voice-leading previously observed in Kalimanku Denku and Prochul Se Strahila. Another similarity emerges from Kyurkchiiski's register transfers of the solo to the lowest voice, which was also observed in the third verse of Zableyalo Mi Agŭntse as well as in the **B** section of Kalimanku Denku. A closer look at the chord progressions even reveals identical descending harmonic progressions, such as a recurring V_3^4/ III-III$_6$-ii$_6$-i$_6$ in both Zableyalo Mi Agŭntse and Kalimanku Denku. If Kyurkchiiski had not incorporated Shope cadences at the end of his V_3^4/ III-III$_6$-ii$_6$-i$_6$ progressions in Zableyalo Mi Agŭntse, the phrase endings of both obrabotki would have been completely identical.

Zableyalo Mi Agŭntse set a new standard for the development of harmony in choral obrabotki in the late 1970s and early 1980s. At that time, most composers and arrangers were aware of the unwritten rules of harmonization, but they also began to carefully violate them while exploring new ways of harmonizing Bulgarian music.

More Zazheni Se Gyuro

More Zazheni Se Gyuro, a choral arrangement by Krasimir Kyurkchiiski, is the first obrabotka I analyze that involves whole-tone based verticals (CD, Track 37). This obrabotka is in four sections (**A**, **B**, **C**, and **D**); sections **A** and **C** are monophonic (or diaphonic), whereas sections **B** and **D**, which are identical, are harmonized. The sections of More Zazheni Se Gyuro obrabotka that include harmony have a palindromic structure of gradual textural expansion followed by gradual textural contraction. At the center of these palindromes, Kyurkchiiski uses whole-tone based sonorities.

The main mode of the obrabotka is G Aeolian, with the third section transposed to D Aeolian (v). Example 7.44 illustrates the first section of More Zazheni Se Gyuro, which contains a 10-measure monophonic phrase followed by a nine-measure phrase with an added drone on scale degree $\hat{1}$.

Example 7.44   More Zazheni Se Gyuro, mm. 1–20

In m. 20, the drone descends to scale degree $\hat{7}$ and implies that the end of the verse should not be perceived as closure. Section **B** of the song contains the same melodic material harmonized with an intricate chordal vocabulary (Example 7.45).

Example 7.45   More Zazheni Se Gyuro, mm. 21–30

Most of the harmonic verticals include multiple major seconds that blur the perception of harmonic function. A pitch-class set analysis[16] reveals that most of the verticals, which are hard to differentiate functionally, are subsets of 6–35 (the whole-tone scale set) or supersets of 5–35 (a subset of the whole-tone scale).[17]

Certain verticals, although whole-tone based, can be perceived as functional despite the stacks of seconds. If some added seconds are removed ("normalized"), the basic progressions are i-VI-iv-VI and VI-v-i for the first and second sections, respectively. Descending and ascending bass lines also play a role in the creation of a palindromic effect.

I consider the harmony of the entire verse to be a whole-tone scale from G (the tonic). The whole-tone based verticals are interchanged with more functionally determinable ones and combined with the original song in the top voice and a drone on scale degree $\hat{1}$ (in the second voice). Despite their effect and vertical complexity, the whole-tone clusters leave the basic melody more exposed, and do not interfere with the expected cadences and tonal resolutions. Furthermore, the tonality and basic melody are enhanced by the balance between the voices. Ultimately, harmonization augments, and even exaggerates the "forceful" quality of close-interval singing against a very clear melody, all of which signifies "authentic" Bulgarian music. Although simple from the viewpoint of modern music analysis, this obrabotka is significant for the present study in that it opened new perspectives for developing the genre of choral obrabotki.

Choral Obrabotki and the Post-Socialist Transition

After four decades of state support, composers of choral obrabotki faced the post-socialist transition. A primary characteristic of this period of change in social, economic, political, and cultural spheres was a rejection of previously established cultural values. Many types of folk-based music genres (village, ensemble, and choral) suffered a massive audience withdrawal due to their association with the socialist regime. In spite of the global success of Le Mystère des Voix Bulgares, it became harder in the 1990s for composers, conductors, and performers to attract audiences. The economic crisis in the country, along with unpredictable hyperinflation, affected composers and their endeavors to further develop Bulgarian music.

---

[16]   Pitch-class set analysis is a method for comparing the pitch-class contents of pieces of atonal music to each other and making explicit structural properties of such pieces. The fundamental unit of pitch-class set analysis is the pitch-class set, an unordered set of pitches disregarding octave, enharmonic spelling, repetitions, rhythmic values, etc. For more information, refer to Forte (1973) and Straus (1990).

[17]   The pitch-class sets that are whole-tone based are marked with dotted boxes in the example above.

According to Hristova, in 1991, Le Mystère des Voix Bulgares choir also split into two vocal formations bearing the same name. The simultaneous existence of two Le Mystère des Voix Bulgares choirs confused producers and tour organizers in Western Europe and the United States. In December of 1994, the conflict was resolved in a trial in Germany, and the second choir was forced to change its name to the Bulgarian Female Choir "Angelite" (Angels) (2007: 133–4).

The mid-1990s mark a change of generations in the Mystère des Voix Bulgares choir, as well as in the newly formed Cosmic Voices and Angels choirs. The young singers, though professionally trained, lacked the motivation of the older singers recruited by Kutev and Kyurkchiiski. Choral conductors adapted the repertoire to the current aesthetic preferences of Bulgarian and Western audiences, which was often limited to obrabotki from the "golden period." As a result, many avant-garde choral obrabotki written in the 1980s and 1990s were never recorded or performed.

This chapter concludes my examination of choral obrabotki and Bulgarian harmonized repertoires. Further study of choral obrabotki could focus on innovations introduced by the composers Ivan Spasov and Georgi Andreev, both of whom set the trends for the genre in the late 1980s and the 1990s. Further study could also examine the hundreds of instrumental obrabotki created between the 1950s and 1990s, which, due to the large format of orchestral scores, could not be included in this book on Bulgarian harmony.

Chapter 8
Conclusion

This study demonstrates that analysis of functional harmony with Roman numerals is a valid method for examining harmonized Bulgarian repertoires, so long as we alter some of our Western harmonic expectations to embrace modal influence in the musical language. For example, the chordal vocabulary in Phrygian parallels chordal vocabulary in Western harmonic minor. Contemporary Bulgarian musicians prefer vii-i as final cadences in Phrygian as opposed to v°-i due to the fact that vii is a minor triad. Diminished chords in final cadences are also avoided in Western tonal music. Similarly, the chordal functions and progressions in Hicaz parallel those in major as used in Western tonal music. Regardless of the differences in chord qualities, II and iv function as predominants in Hicaz, whereas v°and VII function as dominants.[1]

Harmony in Bulgarian music stemmed from traditional polyphony (melody and drone); the steady drone predetermined later harmonic preferences for plagal cadences and ambiguous dominant functions. The variable drone $\hat{1}$-$\hat{7}$-$\hat{1}$ predetermined preferences for VII-I as final cadences (makam Hicaz, Mixolydian, and Phrygian). The drones $\hat{4}$-$\hat{1}$ and $\hat{3}$-$\hat{1}$ predetermined areas of modulation that became evident even in harmonically complex choral obrabotki. The harmony in Kalimanku Denku and Zableyalo Mi Agŭntse, based on a III-i tonal juxtaposition, is an expanded version of the $\hat{3}$-$\hat{1}$ type of variable drone. The drone a fifth below the finalis predetermined the unique harmonizations in Shope major and Shope polymodes, which conclude with half cadences. The same drone type gave birth to experiments with quintal-quartal harmony. All of the examples above suggest the existence of a strong connection between traditional Bulgarian polyphony and contemporary harmonized repertoire.

Through analysis, it becomes clear that current methods of determining mode based on the final descent, for example $\hat{3}$-$\hat{2}$-$\hat{1}$ (finalis), do not accurately describe the scalar activity in harmonized repertoire. In Bulgarian music, scale degrees $\hat{2}$, $\hat{3}$, $\hat{5}$, and $\hat{7}$ are equally valid "candidates" for finalis. Analysis of harmonized repertoire also demonstrates that certain makams (Huzzam, Hicazkar, and Suzinak) and modes (Lydian and Locrian) are not currently in use. As the frequency with which certain scales and modes appear in the repertoire declines, complex polymodes surface in their place. Variable scale degrees are not secondary

---

[1]   The only progression in Hicaz that does not parallel common Western progressions in major is the deceptive cadence. In Hicaz, a v°- vi is not perceived as a deceptive resolution due to chord quality.

features of mode; rather, they are significant markers for complex polymodes and innovative tonicizations.

Village music, wedding music, and choral obrabotki are three styles with a common focal point: the expansion of Bulgarian harmonic language. Despite the differences in instrumentation, educational background of performers, and state support of music, the harmonic patterns observed in the three styles are almost identical. This book demonstrates that the music from these styles represents a living, breathing, and changing musical tradition in which the styles contribute to and continue to influence one another.

Although this study focuses solely on Bulgarian harmonic practices, it also explains portions of the harmonic practices found in countries neighboring Bulgaria, which share similar scales and chordal vocabularies. For example, makam Hicaz, as found in the music of Greece, Serbia, Macedonia, and Romania, is harmonized with the same standard cadences and progressions outlined in Chapter 4 of this book. Harmonization of Phrygian songs with Ionian chord progressions (a third below the finalis) is a foundational harmonic practice for the music of neighboring Macedonia. Shope major progressions, with their characteristic final half cadences, are a harmonic approach favored by Serbian accompanists. Scales with raised scale degree $\hat{4}$, such as makam Mustear and major polymodes #1 and #2 harmonized with Western major-minor 7th chords as main dominants are highly popular in the music of Romania. The above statements do not suggest in any way that Bulgarian harmony served as a foundation for the harmonic practices of other Balkan countries. Rather, they highlight the practical application of this study, which provides a model for future analytical studies not only of Bulgarian music, but also the music of other Eastern European countries.

Further studies of Bulgarian harmony could focus on the music of wedding bands other than Ivo Papazov's Trakiya orchestra; the unique harmonic vocabulary of Petŭr Ralchev's compositions; avant-garde choral obrabotki written by composers Ivan Spasov and Georgi Andreev; and the vast, unstudied genre of instrumental obrabotki. By using this book as a foundation, these further inquiries could continue studying the expansion of harmony in Bulgarian music, examining the establishment of conventional standards, and following the musicians' searches for new horizons of harmonic exploration.

Appendix A
Compact Disc Track List

Track 1: Example of a steady drone on scale degree $\hat{1}$—"Izlel I.e. Delyo Haidutin," Valya Balkanska. *A Harvest, a Shepherd, a Bride: Village Music of Bulgaria* and *In the Shadow of the Mountain: Bulgarian Folk Music: Songs and Dances of Pirin—Macedonia*, track 7, Elektra/Asylum/Nonesuch Records 9 79195-2, 1988. Courtesy of Nonesuch Records.

Track 2: Example of a drone of a fourth below the finalis—"Snoshti Mi Doide," The Biserov Sisters. *The Biserov Sisters and Trakiiskata Troika with the Participation of Kostadin Varimezov—Bagpipe and Dimitŭr Dinev—Tambura*, track A4, Balkanton BHA 11383, 1984. Used by permission.

Track 3: Example of a $\hat{1}$-$\hat{5}$ steady drone—"Authentic Melodies from Pirin," Kalin Kirilov. *Bulgarian and Balkan Folk Music: Bulgarian Folk Music* and *A Trip Around the Balkans*, track 1, 2000.

Track 4: Example of a steady drone a fifth below the finalis—"Igrali Babi Po Mesechina," female group from Sestrimo, Southeastern Bulgaria. *Beyond the Mystery: Village Music of Bulgaria, Volume Three: Shopluk—Pirin*, track 19, BMA Productions BMA 1003, 2001. Used by permission.

Track 5: Example of a variable drone $\hat{1}$-$\hat{7}$-$\hat{1}$—"Vetar Vee," unknown performer. *A Harvest, a Shepherd, a Bride: Village Music of Bulgaria* and *In the Shadow of the Mountain: Bulgarian Folk Music: Songs and Dances of Pirin—Macedonia*, track 1, Elektra/Asylum/Nonesuch Records 9 79195-2, 1988. Used by permission.

Track 6: Example of a variable drone $\hat{3}$-$\hat{1}$ in minor—"Kostadine, Mili Sino Le Dzhanam," unknown performer. *A Harvest, a Shepherd, a Bride: Village Music of Bulgaria* and *In the Shadow of the Mountain: Bulgarian Folk Music: Songs and Dances of Pirin—Macedonia*, track 19, Elektra/Asylum/Nonesuch Records 9 79195-2, 1988. Courtesy of Nonesuch Records.

Track 7: Three-part Shope singing from the village of Vrazhdebna (1972). *Music in Bulgaria: Experiencing Music, Expressing Culture*, track 8, Timothy Rice, 2004. Used by permission.

Track 8: "Pristanala Ganka," Masha Byalmustakova. *Song of the Crooked Dance: Early Bulgarian Traditional Music, 1927–1942*, track 7, Yazoo Records 7016, 2000. Used by permission.

Track 9: "Ya Stani Milke," Bistrishkata Chetvorka. *Song of the Crooked Dance: Early Bulgarian Traditional Music, 1927–1942*, track 14, Yazoo Records 7016, 2000. Used by permission.

Track 10: "Plevensko Horo," Grupata na Tsvyatko Blagoev. *Song of the Crooked Dance: Early Bulgarian Traditional Music, 1927–1942*, track 20, Yazoo Records 7016, 2000. Used by permission.

Track 11: "Selska Svatba," Demir Cholakov. *Song of the Crooked Dance: Early Bulgarian Traditional Music, 1927–1942*, track 1, Yazoo Records 7016, 2000. Used by permission.

Track 12: "Pravo Horo," Boris Karlov. *Boris Karlov: Legend of the Bulgarian Accordion*, track 23 (CD 2), BMA Productions BMA-1005-6, 2003. Used by permission.

Track 13: "Kopanitsa," Village orchestra from Bistritsa, Shope region. *Beyond the Mystery: Village Music of Bulgaria, Volume Three: Shopluk—Pirin*, track 1, BMA Productions, BMA 1003, 2001. Used by permission.

Track 14: "Pazardzhishka Kopanitsa," Trakiiskata Troika. *The Biserov Sisters and Trakiiskata Troika with the Participation of Kostadin Varimezov—Bagpipe and Dimitŭr Dinev—Tambura*, track B2, Balkanton BHA 11383, 1984. Used by permission.

Track 15: "Krivo Horo," Trakiiskata Troika. *The Biserov Sisters and Trakiiskata Troika with the Participation of Kostadin Varimezov—Bagpipe and Dimitŭr Dinev—Tambura*, track B4, Balkanton BHA 11383, 1984. Used by permission.

Track 16: "Mominska Rŭchenitsa," Harmanliiskata Troika. Bulgarian National Radio Archive, 1981. Used by permission.

Track 17: "Kopanitsa," Harmanliiskata Troika. Bulgarian National Radio Archive, 1981. Used by permission.

Track 18: "Vodeno Horo," Grupa Maistori. *Grupa Maistori: Bulgarian Traditional Music*, track 6, Bebelekov Music House n.d., [2003]. Used by permission.

Track 19: Wedding-style improvisation in $\frac{8}{8}$, Ivo Papazov and Trakiya Orchestra. Kalin Kirilov's Private Collection, [ca. 1984].

Track 20: "First Otkrivane," Ivo Papazov and Trakiya Orchestra. Kalin Kirilov's Private Collection, [ca. 1982].

Track 21: "Ivan Milev's Otkrivane," Ivan Milev and Mladost Orchestra. Kalin Kirilov's Private Collection, [ca. 1985].

Track 22: "Clarinet and Saxophone," Ivo Papazov and Trakiya Orchestra. Kalin Kirilov's Private Collection, [ca. 1985].

Track 23: "Second Otkrivane, Precomposed Section," Ivo Papazov and Trakiya Orchestra. Kalin Kirilov's Private Collection, [ca. 1987–1989].

Track 24: "Second Otkrivane, Improvisations," Ivo Papazov and Trakiya Orchestra. Kalin Kirilov's Private Collection, [ca. 1987–1989].

Track 25: "Second Otkrivane Guitar Solo," Ivo Papazov and Trakiya Orchestra. Kalin Kirilov's Private Collection, [ca. 1987–1989].

Track 26: "Rŭchenitsa Accompaniment," Ivo Papazov and Trakiya Orchestra. Kalin Kirilov's Private Collection, [ca. 1988–1989].

Track 27: "Megameter Accompaniment," Ivo Papazov and Trakiya Orchestra. Kalin Kirilov's Private Collection, [ca. 1988–89].

Track 28: "Hitŭr Petŭr," Ivo Papazov and Trakiya Orchestra. Kalin Kirilov's Private Collection, 1989.

Track 29: "Kopanitsa," Ivo Papazov and Trakiya Orchestra. *Orpheus Ascending*, track 5, Hannibal Records, London/New Brunswick, NJ HNCD 1346, 1989. Used by permission.

Track 30: "Polegnala e Todora," Le Mystère des Voix Bulgares—Bulgarian State Radio and Television Female Vocal Choir. *Music of Bulgaria: Ensemble of the Bulgarian Republic*, track 2, Elektra/Asylum/Nonesuch Records 9 72011-1, 1989. Courtesy of Nonesuch Records.

Track 31 "Ergen Deda," Le Mystère des Voix Bulgares—Bulgarian State Radio and Television Female Vocal Choir. *Le Mystère des Voix Bulgares, Volume One*, track 8, Elektra/Asylum/Nonesuch Records 9 79165-1, 1987. Courtesy of Nonesuch Records.

Track 32: "Aida Tsŭfti Ruzho," Folk Choir at the Pirin Ensemble, *Pirin with the Songs of Kiril Stefanov*, track A6, Balkanton BHA 11978/79, 1987. Courtesy of Nonesuch Records.

Track 33: "Pilentse Pee Govori," Le Mystère des Voix Bulgares—Bulgarian State Radio and Television Female Vocal Choir. *Le Mystère des Voix Bulgares, Volume One*, track 1, Elektra/Asylum/Nonesuch Records 9 79165-1, 1987. Courtesy of Nonesuch Records.

Track 34: "Kalimanku Denku," Le Mystère des Voix Bulgares—Bulgarian State Radio and Television Female Vocal Choir. *Le Mystère des Voix Bulgares, Volume One*, track 3, Elektra/Asylum/Nonesuch Records 9 79165-1, 1987. Courtesy of Nonesuch Records.

Track 35: "Prochul Se Strahila," Cosmic Voices Female Folk Choir. *Cosmic Voices from Bulgaria: Bulgarian Choral Folk Songs, Volume One*, track 1, KVZ Music n.d., [2006]. Used by permission.

Track 36: "Zableyalo Mi Agŭntse," Le Mystère des Voix Bulgares—Bulgarian State Radio and Television Female Vocal Choir. *Le Mystère des Voix Bulgares, Volume One*, track 9, Elektra/Asylum/Nonesuch Records 9 79165-1, 1987. Courtesy of Nonesuch Records.

Track 37: "More Zazheni Se Gyuro," Le Mystère des Voix Bulgares—Bulgarian State Radio and Television Female Vocal Choir. *Le Mystère des Voix Bulgares, Volume Two*, track 4, Elektra/Asylum/Nonesuch Records 79201-4, 1988. Courtesy of Nonesuch Records.

Appendix B
Biographies of Bulgarian Composers[1]

KUTEV, Filip (1903–1982). Among Bulgarian composers, Filip Kutev is perhaps the most recognized name worldwide. He was one of the most respected and important Bulgarian musical figures. In 1929 he completed his musical education under Dobri Hristov in composition and under Hans Koch in violin. In 1951 he organized the first Bulgarian State Ensemble for Folk Song and Dance and turned his attention to folk music. He led this ensemble for 32 years and wrote over 500 choral and vocal chamber arrangements for it. Those arrangements established a new tradition of Bulgarian choral music. In his arrangements, Kutev retained the style of singing with free and open voices reflecting the influence of a living folk heritage. Some of these songs, such as Polegnala e Todora, Dragana i Slavei, and others, are considered monuments to the tradition he established.

KYURKCHIISKI, Krasimir (1936–2011). Krasimir Kyurkchiiski is one of Bulgaria's mainstream composers. He was composition student of Pancho Vladigerov at the State Academy of Music in Sofia. Later he continued his musical studies at the Moscow Conservatory with Dimitri Shostakovich. He is a prolific composer and has written in all genres: ballets, cantatas, instrumental concertos, and symphonic works. In terms of musical style, Kyurkchiiski adheres to tradition. He follows in the footsteps of his teacher's legacy by eschewing modernist devices, employing folk modality, diaphony, and asymmetrical rhythms in lush orchestrations. He is best known as the principal conductor of the Filip Kutev State Folklore Ensemble, for which he has received international acclaim. Kyurkchiiski has produced countless folk song arrangements which have been performed by the ensemble. His work in this genre has had a strong influence on his symphonic writing, including the choice of themes and orchestral forces.

LYONDEV, Petŭr (1936). Petŭr Lyondev is one of the most active figures on the Bulgarian folk music stage. In 1954 he entered the State Academy of Music in Sofia in the violin class of Elena Geneva, and also studied composition with Parashkev Hadzhiev and Bentsion Eliezer. In 1962 he began work as a researcher of folk music at the Institute of Musicology of the Bulgarian Academy of Sciences.

---

[1]   All of the above biographies were compiled and modified by this writer to fit the purpose and terminology of this book. Biographic information is based on material from the official website of the Union of the Bulgarian Composers (http://www.ubc-bg.com) and Anna Levy, ed., *Voices of the Plain: Monuments of Bulgarian Choral Music*. Volumes 1 and 2 (refer to a complete citation in the Bibliography).

He has been active as a lecturer and transcriber of Bulgarian village folk music. He is the author of several important folk music studies. Lyondev's compositional life began in 1975 when he published a number of works for children's and folk choirs that became very popular throughout Bulgaria. He is the recipient of several awards for more than 400 folk song arrangements, some of which appear in the series *Le Mystère des Voix Bulgares*.

STEFANOV, Kiril (1933). Kiril Stefanov is among the most important figures of Bulgarian choral art. In 1956 he completed his studies at the State Academy of Music in Sofia with a degree in choral conducting. The same year, he was appointed Musical Director of the Pirin State Ensemble for Music and Dance in Blagoevgrad. As the director of the Pirin Ensemble, he created a unique approach to the performance of folk music by introducing it as a form of musical theater. The concept proved highly innovative, adding an element of drama to the performances, and became popular with other folk ensembles. In addition to his work as a choral conductor Stefanov is active as a teacher. At present he is a professor of choral conducting at the Neofit Rilski Southwestern University in Blagoevgrad. Stefanov has been the recipient of numerous awards for his recordings and publications, among which are a Gold Record from Nashville, Tennessee (1982) and a Gold Record from Balkanton (1983).

Appendix C

Pronunciation Guide to the Sounds in the Bulgarian Alphabet[2]

a	a—f<u>a</u>ther
b	b—<u>b</u>one
v	v—<u>v</u>illage
g	g—<u>g</u>o
d	d—<u>d</u>o
e	e—s<u>e</u>t
zh	zh—plea<u>s</u>ure
z	z—<u>z</u>oo
i	i—m<u>e</u>
k	k—<u>k</u>ill
l	l—<u>l</u>ove
m	m—<u>m</u>oney
n	n—<u>n</u>o
o	o—<u>au</u>ral
p	p—<u>p</u>ut
r	r—<u>r</u>oom
s	s—<u>s</u>ea
t	t—<u>t</u>ea
u	u—d<u>o</u>
f	f—<u>fi</u>ne
h	h—<u>h</u>orse
ts	ts—pi<u>zz</u>a
sh	sh—<u>sh</u>op
ŭ	u—p<u>u</u>zzle
yu	u—<u>you</u>
ya	ya—<u>Ya</u>hoo
dzh	dzh—<u>j</u>ello
sht	sht—ma<u>shed</u>

[2] The pronunciation guide above was adapted from Anna Levy's *Voices of the Plain: Monuments of Bulgarian Choral Music*. Volume 3 (2005).

Appendix D
Glossary of Bulgarian Terms

Avtorski [áftorski]: Author's obrabotki characterized by an enhanced role of the arranger.

Chetvorka [tʃetfórka]: Quartet.

Direktsiya Muzika [diréktsija múzika]: A government agency controlling music activities.

Dobrudzha [dóbrudʒa]: Region in Northeastern Bulgaria.

Dvoyanka [dvojánka]: Double-pipe flute with one of the pipes producing a steady drone.

Dvuredki [dvurédki]: Button accordions with two rows of buttons.

Elenino Horo [elénino horó]: Elena's dance notated in $\frac{14}{16}$.

Gaida [gájda]: Traditional goat-skin bagpipe.

Glasove [glasové]: Voices.

Grupa [grúpa]: Group or band.

Gŭdulka [gʌdúlka]: A bowed string instrument held vertically.

Hicaz [hidʒás]: Microtonal or non-microtonal makam.

Hicazkar [hidʒáskjár]: Microtonal or non-microtonal makam.

Horo [horó]: An open-circle or line dance formed by dancers holding hands.

Hudozhestvena Samodeinost [hudóʒestfena samodéjnost]: Amateur art.

Huzzam [huzam]: Microtonal or non-microtonal makam.

Karcigar [kardʒagár]: Microtonal or non-microtonal makam.

Kategoriya [kategórija]: Category or performing level of a wedding orchestra.

Kaval [kavál]: An end-blown flute similar to the Turkish kaval and the Arabic *ney*.

Kolektivi [kolektívi]: Collectives for folk music.

Kolyano [koljáno]*:* Parallel or contracting period.

Kopanitsa [kópanitsa]: A dance tune in $\frac{11}{8}$ (2+2+3+2+2).

Krivo Horo [krívo horó]: Crooked dance.

Makam [makám]: Scale of Middle Eastern origin.

Mustear [mjusteár]: Microtonal or non-microtonal makam.

Narodna Muzika [naródna múzika]: Folk music, "people's music."

Narodni Pesni [naródni pésni]: Folk songs.

Obrabotki [obrabótki]: Choral arrangements. *Obrabotka* [obrabótka] is singular.

Otkrivane [otkrívane]: Opening piece for a wedding orchestra.

Palatki [palátki]: Tents temporarily erected on streets for weddings and other celebrations.

Pirin [pírin]: Pirin mountain range and region in Southeastern Bulgaria.

Pravo Horo [právo horó]: "Straight Dance," Bulgarian dance in a duple meter.

Razdrobyavane [razdrobjávane]: Subdivision, breaking down into smaller pieces.

Rhodopes [Rodópi]: Rhodope mountain range and region in Southern Bulgaria.

Rŭchenitsa [rʌtʃenítsa]: One of the most common Bulgarian dances in $\frac{7}{8}$.

Selska Svatba [sélska svádba]: Village wedding.

Shope [ʃóp]: A region in Western Bulgaria.

Shopska harmoniya [ʃópska harmónija]: Shope harmony.

Strandzha [strándʒa]: A region in Southeastern Bulgaria.

Sultani Yegah [sultaní jegjáh]: Microtonal or non-microtonal makam.

Suzinak [suzinák]: Microtonal or non-microtonal makam.

Tambura [tamburá]: Long-necked plucked lute.

Tarambuka [tarambúka]: An hourglass-shaped hand-drum.

Temi [témi]: Motivically related periods (themes) exploring a common idea.

Trakiiska [trakíjska], *Trakiiskata* [trakíjskata]: Thracian, the Thracian.

Trakiiski [trakíjski]: Thracian (plural).

Trakiya [trákija]: The region of Thrace and also the name of Papazov's wedding band.

Troika [trójka]: Trio.

Tŭpan [tʌpan]: A large cylindrical drum worn over the shoulder.

Vodeno Horo [vódeno horó]: A line dance in a metric pattern of $\frac{6}{8}$.

Yovino Horo [jóvino horó]: Yova's dance, based on a combined metric group $\frac{7}{8}+\frac{7}{8}+\frac{11}{8}$.

Bibliography and Discography

Bibliography

Abrashev, Bozhidar. *Obrabotka i Orkestratsia na Bŭlgarskata Narodna Muzika* [Arrangement and Orchestration of Bulgarian Folk Music]. Volume 1. Sofia: Muzika, 1990.

———. *Obrabotka i Orkestratsia na Bŭlgarskata Narodna Muzika* [Arrangement and Orchestration of Bulgarian Folk Music]. Volume 2. Sofia: Muzika, 1995.

Arabov, Plamen. *Harmoniya s Aranzhirane za Hor* [Harmony with Arrangement for Choir]. Sofia: Muzika, 1992.

Bárdos, Lajos. "Die *Volksmusikalischen Tonleitern bei Liszt.*" *Franz Liszt: Beiträge von Ungarischen Autoren*, ed. Klára Hamburger (1978): 168–96. Budapest: Corvina.

Bartók, Béla. *Essays*, ed. Benjamin Suchoff. New York: St. Martin's Press, 1976.

Bendix, Regina. *In Search of Authenticity: The Formation of Folklore Studies*. Madison: University of Wisconsin Press, 1997.

Buchanan, Donna. *The Bulgarian Folk Orchestra: Cultural Performance, Symbol, and the Construction of National Identity in Socialist Bulgaria*. PhD diss., University of Texas, Austin, 1991.

———. "Metaphors of Power, Metaphors of Truth: The Politics of Music Professionalism in Bulgarian Folk Orchestras." *Ethnomusicology* 39 (1995): 381–416.

———. "Wedding Musicians, Political Transition, and National Consciousness in Bulgaria." *Retuning Culture: Musical Changes in Central and Eastern Europe*, ed. Mark Slobin (1996): 200–230. Durham, NC: Duke University Press.

———. "Review Essay: Bulgaria's Magical Mystère Tour: Postmodernism, World Music Marketing, and Political Change in Eastern Europe." *Ethnomusicology* 41/1 (1997): 131–57.

———. *Performing Democracy: Bulgarian Music and Musicians in Transition*. Chicago: University of Chicago Press, 2006.

Dzhudzhev, Stoyan. *Teoriya na Bŭlgarskata Narodna Muzika* [Theory of Bulgarian Folk Music]. 4 vols. Sofia: Nauka i Izkustvo, 1954–1961.

———. *Bŭlgarskata Narodna Muzika* [Bulgarian Folk Music]. Volume 1. Sofia: Nauka i Izkustvo, 1970.

———. *Bŭlgarskata Narodna Muzika* [Bulgarian Folk Music]. Volume 2. Sofia: Muzika, 1975.

Forsyth, Martha. *Listen, Daughter, and Remember Well.* Sofia: St. Kliment Ohridski University Press, 1996.

Forte, Allen. *The Structure of Atonal Music.* New Haven: Yale University Press, 1973.

Gelbart, Matthew. *The Invention of "Folk Music" and "Art Music": Emerging Categories from Ossian to Wagner.* New York: Cambridge University Press, 2007.

Hristova, Dora. *Izkustvoto na Folklornite Kamerni Vokalni Ansambli* [The Art of Folk Chamber Vocal Ensembles]. Sofia: Art Coop, 2004.

———. *Misteriata na Bŭlgarskite Glasove: Fenomen i Vokalen Ansambŭl* [Mystery of the Bulgarian Voices: Phenomenon and Vocal Ensemble]. Sofia: Bul-Koreni, 2007.

Karastoyanov, Asen. *Melodichni i Harmonichni Osnovi na Bŭlgarskata Narodna Pesen* [Melodic and Harmonic Foundations of Bulgarian Folk Song]. Sofia: Bŭlgarska Academia na Naukite, 1950.

Kaufman, Nikolai. "Dvuglasnoto Narodno Peene v Bŭlgaria" [Folk Singing in Two Parts in Bulgaria]. *Spisanie na Bŭlgarskata Akademiya na Naukite* 4 (1958): 45–58.

———. "Triglasnite Narodni Pesni ot Kostursko" [Three-Part Folksongs from the Kostrusko Region]. *Izvestiya na Instituta za Muzika* 6 (1958): 65–158.

———. *Bŭlgarskata Mnogoglasna Narodna Pesen* [Bulgarian Polyphonic Folk Songs]. Sofia: Nauka i Izkustvo, 1968.

———. *Bŭlgarska Narodna Muzika* [Bulgarian Folk Music]. Sofia: Muzika, 1977.

———, and Todor Todorov. *Narodni Pesni ot Yugozapadna Bŭlgaria: Pirinski Krai* [Folk Songs from Southwestern Bulgaria: Pirin Region]. Sofia: Bulgarian Academy of Science, 1967.

Kirilov, Kalin. "Musical Ethnography of the Bulgarian Vlachs from Northwestern Bulgaria," MA thesis, University of Oregon, 2003.

———. "Revival of Bulgarian Folk Music during Socialism and the Post-Socialist Transition: Music and Cultural Identity." *MUSICultures* 37 (2011): 109–24.

Kutev, Filip. *Repertoaren Sbornik* [Repertoire Collection]. Sofia: Muzika, 1981.

Kuteva, Elena. "Ladovo-Harmonichni i Kompozitsionno-Strukturni Osobenosti na Pesnite 'Na Visoko' i Kombiniranite Chetiriglasni Pesni" [Scale-Harmonical and Compositional-Structural Specifics of the Songs "Na Visoko" and the Combined Four-Part Songs]. *Bŭlgarasko Muzikoznanie* 3 (1976): 30–67.

Kyurkchiiski, Krasimir. *Horovi Pesni* [Choir Songs]. Sofia: Dobrev, 2001.

Larson, Steve. "Musical Forces and Melodic Expectations: Comparing Computer Models and Experimental Results." *Music Perception* 21 (2004): 457–98.

Lausevic, Mirjana. *Balkan Fascination: Creating an Alternative Music Culture in America.* New York: Oxford University Press, 2006.

Levy, Anna. ed. *Voices of the Plain: Monuments of Bulgarian Choral Music.* Volumes 1 and 2. Burnaby, BC: Vox Bulgarica, Music Publishers, 2000.

————. *Voices of the Plain: Monuments of Bulgarian Choral Music*. Volume 3. Burnaby, BC: Vox Bulgarica, Music Publishers, 2005.

Litova-Nikolova, Lidia. *Bŭlgarska Narodna Muzika* [Bulgarian Folk Music]. Sofia: Muzika, 1982.

Manuel, Peter. "Modal Harmony in Andalusian, Eastern European, and Turkish Syncretic Musics." *Yearbook for Traditional Music* 21 (1989): 70–94.

Motsev, Alexander. *Ornamenti v Bŭlgarskata Narodna Muzika* [Ornaments in Bulgarian Folk Music]. Sofia: Bulgarian Academy of Science, 1961.

Radulescu, Speranta. "Traditional Musics and Ethnomusicology under Political Pressure: The Romanian Case," *Anthropology Today* 13/6 (1997): 8–12.

Rice, Timothy. *Polyphony in Bulgarian Folk Music*. PhD diss., University of Washington, Seattle, 1977.

————. *May it Fill Your Soul: Experiencing Bulgarian Music*. Chicago: University of Chicago Press, 1994.

————. *Music in Bulgaria: Experiencing Music, Expressing Culture*. New York: Oxford University Press, 2004.

Signell, Karl. *Makam: Modal Practice in Turkish Art Music*. Seattle: Asian Music, 1977.

Silverman, Carol. "The Politics of Folklore in Bulgaria." *Anthropological Quarterly* 56 (1983): 55–61.

————. "Reconstructing Folklore: Media and Cultural Policy in Eastern Europe." *Communication* 11 (1989): 141–60.

————. "Music and Marginality: Roma (Gypsies) of Bulgaria and Macedonia." *Retuning Culture: Musical Changes in Central and Eastern Europe*, ed. Mark Slobin (1996): 231–53. Durham, NC: Duke University Press.

————. "'Move Over Madonna': Gender, Representation, and the 'Mystery' of Bulgarian Voices." *Over the Wall/After the Fall: Post-Communist Cultures through an East-West Gaze*, ed. Sibelan Forrester, Magdalena Zaborowska, and Elena Gapova (2004): 212–37. Bloomington: Indiana University Press.

————. *Romani Routes: Cultural Politics and Balkan Music in Diaspora*. New York: Oxford University Press, 2012.

Straus, Joseph. *Introduction to Post-Tonal Theory*. Englewood Cliffs, NJ: Prentice Hall, 1990.

Todorov, Todor. *Sŭvremenost i Narodna Pesen* [Present Time and Folk Song]. Sofia: Muzika, 1978.

Discography

A Harvest, a Shepherd, a Bride: Village Music of Bulgaria and *In the Shadow of the Mountain: Bulgarian Folk Music: Songs and Dances of Pirin—Macedonia*, Elektra/Asylum/Nonesuch Records 9 79195-2, 1988.

Beyond the Mystery: Village Music of Bulgaria, Volume One: Rhodopes—Thrace, BMA Productions, BMA 1001, 1999.

Beyond the Mystery: Village Music of Bulgaria, Volume Two: Severnjashko—Dobruja, BMA Productions, BMA 1002, 2000.

Beyond the Mystery: Village Music of Bulgaria, Volume Three: Shopluk—Pirin, BMA Productions, BMA 1003, 2001.

Boris Karlov: Legend of the Bulgarian Accordion, BMA Productions, BMA-1005-6, 2003.

Bulgarian and Balkan Folk Music: Bulgarian Folk Music and *A Trip Around the Balkans*, LGS Music, 2000.

Cosmic Voices from Bulgaria: Bulgarian Choral Folk Songs, Volume One, KVZ Music n.d., [2006].

Grupa Maistori: Bulgarian Traditional Music, Bebelekov Music House n.d., [2003]. Kalin Kirilov, Private Collection.

Le Mystère des Voix Bulgares, *Volume One*, Elektra/Asylum/Nonesuch Records 9 79165-1, 1987.

Le Mystère des Voix Bulgares, *Volume Two*, Elektra/Asylum/Nonesuch Records 79201-4, 1988.

Le Mystère des Voix Bulgares, *Volume Three*, Fontana/Polygram 846 626-4, 1990.

Music of Bulgaria: Ensemble of the Bulgarian Republic, Elektra/Asylum/Nonesuch Records 9 72011-1, 1989.

Orpheus Ascending, Hannibal Records, London, UK/New Brunswick, NJ HNCD 1346, 1989.

Pirin with the Songs of Kiril Stefanov, Balkanton BHA 11978/79, 1987.

Song of the Crooked Dance: Early Bulgarian Traditional Music, 1927–1942, Yazoo Records 7016, 2000.

The Biserov Sisters and Trakiiskata Troika with the Participation of Kostadin Varimezov—Bagpipe and Dimitŭr Dinev—Tambura, Balkanton BHA 11383, 1984.

Index